DISCRIMINATION, EQUALITY AND HEALTH CARE RATIONING

Bristol Studies in Law and Social Justice

Series Editors: **Alan Bogg**, University of Bristol, UK and **Virginia Mantouvalou**, University College London, UK

This series explores the role of law in securing social justice in society and the economy. The focus is on 'social justice' as a normative ideal, and the law as a critical tool in influencing (for good or for ill) the social structures that shape people's lives.

Also available in the series:

- *Access to Social Justice* by Katie Boyle, Diana Camps, Kirstie English, Jo Ferrie, Aidan Flegg and Gaurav Mukherjee
- *Labour Law and the Person* by Lisa Rodgers
- *Low-Paid EU Migrant Workers* by Catherine Barnard, Fiona Costello and Sarah Fraser Butlin
- *Climate Litigation and Justice in Africa* edited by Kim Bouwer, Uzuazo Etemire, Tracy-Lynn Field and Ademola Oluborode Jegede
- *Class and Social Background Discrimination in the Modern Workplace* by Angelo Capuano
- *Beyond the Virus* edited by Sabrina Germain and Adrienne Yong

International Advisory Board

Find out more at:

https://bristoluniversitypress.co.uk/ristol-studies-in-law-and-social-justice

DISCRIMINATION, EQUALITY AND HEALTH CARE RATIONING

Rachel Horton

BRISTOL UNIVERSITY PRESS

First published in Great Britain in 2025 by

Bristol University Press
University of Bristol
1–9 Old Park Hill
Bristol
BS2 8BB
UK
t: +44 (0)117 374 6645
e: bup-info@bristol.ac.uk

Details of international sales and distribution partners are available at bristoluniversitypress.co.uk

British Library Cataloguing in Publication Data
A catalogue record for this book is available from the British Library

ISBN 978-1-5292-3194-6 hardcover
ISBN 978-1-5292-3196-0 ePub
ISBN 978-1-5292-3197-7 ePdf

Cover design: Blu inc
Front cover image: 123rf/battle182royal
Bristol University Press uses environmentally responsible print partners.
Printed and bound in Great Britain by CPI Group (UK) Ltd, Croydon, CR0 4YY

Bristol University Press' authorised representative in the European Union is:
Easy Access System Europe, Mustamäe tee 50, 10621 Tallinn, Estonia,
Email: gpsr.requests@easproject.com

FSC
www.fsc.org
MIX
Paper | Supporting responsible forestry
FSC® C013604

Contents

Series Editors' Preface

Bristol Studies in Law and Social Justice explores the role of law in securing social justice in society and the economy. The focus is on 'social justice' as a normative ideal, and the law as a critical tool in influencing (for good or for ill) the social structures that shape people's lives. This international series is designed to be inclusive of a wide range of methodologies and disciplinary approaches. Contributions examine these issues from multiple legal perspectives, including constitutional law, discrimination law, human rights, contract law, criminal law, migration law, labour law, social welfare law, property law, international and supranational law. The series has broad jurisdictional coverage, including single-country, comparative, international and regional legal orders, and encourages a critical and interdisciplinary approach to legal analysis.

Acknowledgements

I am very grateful to the team at Bristol University Press and in particular to Helen Davis and Grace Carroll for their enthusiasm and patience.

I have also had great help in developing my ideas from my colleagues at the University of Reading and in particular Grace James, Therese Callus and especially Chris Newdick who once knocked on my door to ask me if I knew anything about the Equality Act and is to blame for this project. I would also like to pay tribute to Malcolm Sargeant, who is no longer with us, but who supervised and encouraged my PhD research on age discrimination in health care.

And I would not have been able to complete this book without the amazing support from my family – my parents, Moya and Deryck, Anna, Naomi and, above all, Graham.

Introduction

'Anyone can use it – men, women and children. There are no age limits and no fees to pay.'[1] So promised an advertisement for the new National Health Service (NHS) in 1948. The first principle of the NHS Constitution today likewise states that 'the NHS provides a comprehensive service, available to all'.[2] Yet while our personal characteristics such as sex and age are only rarely used explicitly to ration care, concerns exist about whether the way health services are commissioned unfairly disadvantages particular groups protected by equality law: whether, for example, the way the effectiveness of new medicines and treatments is assessed disadvantages older patients or those with disabilities; or whether eligibility criteria for fertility treatment unfairly disadvantage older women or same-sex couples; or whether young people are particularly disadvantaged by a lack of provision of adequate mental health services. Problems of discrimination and equality have recently been brought into sharp focus during the COVID-19 pandemic where the unequal impact, not only of the virus but of the public health responses to it on different groups, has been well documented, and concerns were raised about whether guidance on the use of 'do not resuscitate' orders, or guidance for deciding who should be given intensive care beds if there were not enough to meet demand, unfairly disadvantaged older patients and those with disabilities.

These difficulties arise, in large part, because there are not enough resources for the NHS to fund every intervention or treatment that patients may want or need. Since the creation of the NHS a combination of factors, including demographic changes, increase in patient expectations and continuous, rapid advances in medical technology have meant demand for health care has grown relentlessly. The amount of overall funding the NHS should receive is, of course, a political choice

[1] Department of Health for Scotland (1948) *Your New National Health Service.*

[2] Department of Health and Social Care (2012) *NHS Constitution for England (updated 2023)*, available at: https://www.gov.uk/government/publications/the-nhs-constitution-for-england (accessed December 2024).

and will be the most important factor in determining what treatment it is able to provide. Yet health related spending is predicted to continue to outstrip economic growth[3] and there is widespread consensus that it is no longer likely to be possible for a publicly funded system to meet every health care need that may arise. The growing gulf between demand and what can be funded, made worse by the COVID-19 pandemic, means that the question is not whether we ration health care, but what health care we choose to provide.

The problem of how to distribute these limited resources fairly is one which gives rise to profound disagreement. When we are deciding how to allocate scarce resources for health care, should we, for example, adopt a prioritarian strategy to improve the health of the worst off first, or a cost-effectiveness strategy to buy as much 'health' as we can with the funds we have available, or some form of egalitarian strategy which aims to give everyone access to equal health outcomes or access to an equal share of health care? There is a wealth of literature devoted to this debate and there is no space to do justice to it here.[4] In the UK policy context, as we will see, cost-effectiveness – purchasing as much health improvement in the population as possible with the resources available – forms at least the starting point of many decisions about what medical interventions to fund, and for whom. This is essentially a utilitarian approach, where the health care system seeks to maximize the amount of 'health' that can be purchased without necessarily caring how that health is then distributed among the wider population. In its unmodified form, cost-effectiveness strategies may be satisfied equally where the health purchased goes to those most in need or to those who are already relatively healthy. As a result, they can produce troubling results for those with egalitarian or prioritarian values. A key ethical question for policy makers is therefore whether, and under what circumstances, cost-effectiveness should be replaced or refined in order to meet these other moral concerns.

The debate on rationing in the theoretical literature has, in recent decades, tended to shift focus from the question of *which* principles should underpin resource allocation, to the question of *how* decisions about which principles to use should be made. This is because, as Daniels claims, priority-setting dilemmas 'all rest on value judgments about which reasonable people may disagree' and because 'general principles of justice do not resolve many of

---

3 International Monetary Fund (2015) *Now is the Time: Fiscal Policies for Sustainable Growth*, Washington DC: IMF.

4 For an excellent overview see C. Newdick (2005) *Who Should We Treat? Rights Rationing and Resources in the NHS*, Oxford: Oxford University Press; see also N. Daniels (2008) *Just Health: Meeting Health Needs Fairly*, Cambridge: Cambridge University Press.

these controversies'.[5] Instead, he argues, in the absence of any consensus, now or probably in future, on the substantive principles we should choose to make decisions about health care resource allocation, we should instead focus on finding a fair process to make those decisions. This focus on procedural fairness is, as we will see in Chapter 4, one very much reflected also in the approach of the public law framework in holding decision makers to account.

The purpose of this book is to explore the role of equality law in addressing inequalities in access to health care and in health. In doing so it has two key aims. The first is to identify the key constraints – both substantive and procedural – equality law places on health care commissioners and policy makers and the circumstances in which it may permit or require cost-effectiveness strategies to be modified to take into account the needs of, or disadvantages faced by, the different groups the law protects. Under what circumstances, for example, can, or must, health care commissioners fund treatment for an individual or group where a failure to do so may create or exacerbate disadvantage and health inequality related to their 'protected characteristics' such as race, sex or disability? Second, and related, is to consider the extent to which equality law can contribute to tackling health inequalities and addressing patterns of health disadvantage that relate to our protected characteristics. Discrimination in health care – and indeed in all walks of life, including education, housing and employment – is, as we will see, an important determinant of poorer health and a cause of health inequalities. Addressing it is a key dimension of social justice. The book will consider the potential of equality law to assist in doing so.

The book brings together literature and law on health inequalities, access to health care and equality law. To date, there has only been limited research on the intersections of these disciplines and on the implications of equality law for resource allocation in health care (in part, no doubt, because of limited case law to date in this area). Bringing together these areas of inquiry, it is hoped, will generate useful insights for those engaged in health law and health care research and policy, and will help to identify gaps in our current understanding and areas for future research. A report in 2019 on the role of law in addressing health inequalities noted this is still an area in which law remains 'underutilised and poorly understood'.[6] It is hoped that this book can begin to address this gap in respect of the contribution of equality law. Health care is also an important context for equality lawyers

[5] Daniels (n 4); see also useful discussion in D. Wang and B. Rumbold (2019) 'Priority Setting, Judicial Review and Procedural Justice' in A. Phillips, T. de Campos and J. Herring (eds) *Philosophical Foundations of Medical Law*, Oxford: Oxford University Press 185–196.

[6] L. Gostin, J. Monahan, J. Kaldor, M. DeBartolo, E. Friedman, K. Gottschalk et al (2019) 'The Legal Determinants of Health: Harnessing the Power of Law for Global Health and Sustainable Development', *The Lancet* 393: 1857–1910.

to reflect on the potential and limitations of equality law more generally, giving rise, as it does, to difficult questions about prioritization and the scope of positive action, the challenges and opportunities of intersectional approaches, and the relationship between protected characteristics and socio-economic disadvantage.

Rationing is of course not the only way in which issues of equality and discrimination may arise in the NHS. Problems of capacity and consent, abortion and assisted death, and harassment and neglect all engage equality law, as do the barriers – such as transport, language or caring responsibilities – which may prevent those with protected characteristics from being able to access the services the NHS funds. However, the focus of the book is on the issues which arise when choices need to be made about who to treat and which medical interventions (whether screening, prevention or treatment) will be funded or prioritized in the face of limited resources. It should also be noted that this book cannot attempt to deal with the problems of social care in any depth, although funding and management of social care has an enormous impact on both the NHS and on the health and wellbeing of those who need it.

The rest of this introductory chapter will now outline the relevant institutional and legal framework to provide some background and context for the discussion that follows – first the ways in which decisions are made within the NHS and by whom and then the key provisions of public and equality law relevant to resource allocation in health care. We will return to these provisions and consider them in more detail throughout the book.

Institutions and decision makers

The NHS is made up of a complex network of hundreds of organizations. The NHS budget is set by the government but decisions about how the budget is spent are largely delegated to a network of commissioning bodies under the oversight of NHS England.[7] Priority setting takes place at many levels. Forty-two Integrated Care Boards (ICBs), each with their own budgets, have responsibility for commissioning primary and secondary care services for their areas and for protecting and improving the health of their local populations. In doing so, they are under a statutory obligation to break even in each financial year.[8] ICBs were established by the Health and Social Care Act 2022, as part of wider Integrated Care Systems – partnerships that bring together local authorities, health authorities and the third sector in order to foster joined up commissioning with the aim of improving

[7] On 13 March 2025 the government announced its intention to abolish NHS England and to bring its functions within the Department of Health and Social Care. At the time of writing, further details are not yet available.

[8] National Health Service Act 2006, s 223GC.

health and care services, including by reducing heath inequalities.[9] Before ICBs came into being, local health care commissioning was primarily the responsibility of Clinical Commissioning Groups, and before that of Primary Care Trusts – these predecessor organizations are referred to frequently in the case law discussed in the book. In addition to ICBs, a number of other organizations retain responsibility for specialist areas of commissioning. These include NHS England, which retains responsibility for commissioning national screening programmes and a number of other services; and NHS Blood and Transplant which sets and reviews criteria for allocating organs for transplant.

The National Institute for Health and Care Excellence (NICE) is a non-departmental public body, accountable to parliament, with statutory responsibility for setting guidance and standards for commissioners and providers of health and social care. It was created in 1999 with a view to, among other things, ending the 'postcode lottery' in health care, where access to treatment varied significantly depending on where you lived, through the creation of national standards. One of its key responsibilities is evaluating the evidence for the cost-effectiveness of new and existing drugs, technologies and interventions, and producing guidance and recommendations as to whether or not these should be funded by the NHS. NICE does not itself make rationing decisions – and it does not have a commissioning budget. In most cases the NICE guidance is not mandatory and ICBs may lawfully depart from it under certain circumstances.[10] The exception to this is its Technology Appraisal Guidance because ICBs and other commissioning bodies are required by statute to fund medicine and treatment recommended this way.[11] In drawing up its guidance, NICE evaluates the evidence of the cost-effectiveness of a drug or other intervention and then reaches a decision on whether or not to recommend that treatment be funded by the NHS. It has developed a detailed methodology for doing so, which is explained in detail in Chapter 2. Generally speaking, where the cost-effectiveness of a particular treatment falls below the threshold set by NICE, it will be recommended for funding. Where it does not, it will normally not be, although NICE will consider whether or not there may be other reasons to recommend it.[12]

---

9 Department of Health and Social Care (11 February 2022) *Health and Social Care Integration: Joining Up Care for People, Places and Population*, available at: https://www.gov.uk/government/publications/health-and-social-care-integration-joining-up-care-for-people-places-and-populations (accessed December 2024).

10 See *R (on the application of Rose) v Thanet CCG* [2014] EWHC 1182.

11 Health and Social Care Act 2012.

12 This assessment process is explained in detail in Chapter 2.

Arguably, decisions by clinicians as to what treatments to suggest and support for their individual patients may also amount to a form of rationing, albeit one much harder to identify. In the everyday exercise of their common law duty of care, clinicians will be required to determine what treatment, if any, is clinically appropriate for an individual patient and whether (where a patient lacks capacity to consent for themselves) treatment is in the patient's best interests. In addition, triage policies in a secondary care settings – surgical waiting lists, for example, or decisions about whether to admit patients to intensive care – will usually delegate decision making to clinicians who will need to prioritize patients on the basis of need or of clinical benefit. While clinicians will therefore sometimes have a role as gatekeepers to NHS resources, rationing by clinicians, as Harrison notes, is often covert and 'renders the process of rationing as if it were politically invisible, by fragmenting it across space and time into individualised and private transactions between doctors and patients'.[13] The potential for discrimination to arise in this context is considered in Chapter 2 and again in Chapter 7 (in the context of intensive care).

The legal framework

Public law

It would be wrong to claim that there is a legally enforceable 'right to health care' in the UK. While the National Health Service Act 2006 imposes a duty on the Secretary of State for Health to 'continue the promotion … of a comprehensive health service'[14] it is clear that this does not give individual patients a legal right to demand any particular form of health care. In *R v Secretary of State for Social Services ex parte Hinks* the Court made clear that the scope of this obligation is rather to provide services only 'to such an extent as he considers necessary to meet all reasonable requirements such as can be provided within the resources available'.[15] Nor does the Human Rights Act 1998 (incorporating the rights under the European Convention on Human Rights [ECHR]) provide a right to treatment in all but the most exceptional circumstances.[16] Where claims that the state

13 S. Harrison (1998) 'The Politics of Evidence Based Medicine in the United Kingdom', *Policy and Politics* 26: 15–31.

14 National Health Service Act 2006, s 1.

15 *R v Secretary of State for Social Services, ex p Hincks* [1980] 1 BMLR 93, 95.

16 Where the patient is in detention, for example, or where lack of health care might leave the patient in such intense physical or mental suffering that it meets the (extremely high) threshold of inhuman treatment under Article 3. See, for example *Price v United Kingdom* [2001] ECHR 458 but compare *R (on the application of Watts) v Bedford Primary Care Trust* [2003] EWHC 2228 (Admin).

has an obligation to fund a particular form of health care have been bought under the relevant Articles – including Article 2 (the right to life), Article 3 (protection from torture or inhuman or degrading treatment) and Article 8 (the right to private life) – these have generally failed on the basis that states (and in a domestic context, governments) are afforded a wide 'margin of appreciation' where the issues involve an assessment of priorities in the context of the allocation of limited resources.[17] While there is no right to require the state to fund any particular form of health care, decisions by the NHS about what health care to fund are subject to judicial review and must be made in a way that is not illegal, irrational or unreasonable, or in a way that involves procedural impropriety.[18]

Equality law

Public bodies exercising public functions and providing services – as will be the case for commissioning bodies in the UK including ICBs, NHS England and NICE – have obligations under both the Equality Act 2010 (the Equality Act) and the Human Rights Act 1998, which incorporates the ECHR. These are both introduced in what follows.

The aims and principles underpinning the body of laws that are referred to as 'equality' and 'anti-discrimination' law are a matter of dispute both in respect of the concept of equality that the law should aim to achieve and the nature of the harms that the law should aim to prevent. Is it sufficient, for example, that the law should require equal treatment of individuals where there are no relevant differences between them or should the law go further and seek to secure equality of access to important goods, or – further still – equality of outcomes (and if so which ones)? Is discrimination harmful because it undermines dignity through stigma and stereotyping or because it results in unfair exclusion from important goods and institutions? It has long been agreed by most legal theorists that there is not a single normative underpinning to the law but several. Sandra Fredman has proposed a four-dimensional framework for understanding what is required by the right to substantive equality, arguing that equality law should 'be responsive to those who are disadvantaged, demeaned, excluded or ignored'.[19] The four dimensions are, accordingly, to redress disadvantage; to address stigma, stereotyping, prejudice and violence; to enhance voice and participation; and to accommodate difference and achieve structural change. According

[17] See, for example, *Sentges v Netherlands* [2004] 7 CCL Rep 400.

[18] *R v North and East Devon Health Authority ex parte Coughlan* [2000] 3 All ER 850.

[19] S. Fredman (2016) 'Substantive Equality Revisited', *International Journal of Constitutional Law* 14: 712–738.

to this framework, decision makers need to be alert to a range of harms that discriminatory policy may give rise to – not just a lack of access to a particular treatment or medical intervention but the stigma and exclusion that may also result.

The Equality Act, passed in the last days of the 1997–2010 Labour government, was primarily an attempt to bring together and make coherent the various different legislative instruments that preceded it, including the Sex Discrimination Act 1975, the Race Relations Act 1976 and the Disability Discrimination Act 1995. From these beginnings the body of law known as discrimination law has evolved piecemeal over the decades in response to a number of factors – including compliance with developing EU law, judicial decisions on the scope and meaning of legislative provisions, and effective research and campaigning by different interest groups – and has seen different protected characteristics added to the scope of its protection as well as the extension of protection from origins in labour law to cover a broad range of areas of life, including education, and goods and services, including public services. The Equality Act now creates a framework that provides broadly similar protection across different characteristics and areas of life, although with a long list of tailored provisions and exceptions for specific circumstances. The key protections relevant to the book are outlined in the next section and are then expanded in greater detail when relevant in the individual chapters.

The protected characteristics

In relation to the provision of services and public functions, discrimination is prohibited in relation to the following characteristics: sex, pregnancy, race (which includes colour, nationality, and ethnic or national origin), disability, sexual orientation, religion or belief, gender reassignment and age (but only in respect of those 18 or over). Disability is defined as having 'a mental or physical impairment' which 'has a substantial and long-term adverse effect on … ability to carry out normal day to day activities'.[20] An individual has the protected characteristic of gender reassignment if that person is 'proposing to undergo, is undergoing or has undergone a process (or part of a process) for the purpose of reassigning the person's sex by changing physiological or other attributed of sex'.[21] At the time of writing there is no provision in the Equality Act which explicitly prohibits discrimination because of more than one characteristic or because of a combination of characteristics, making it difficult to challenge discrimination and disadvantage relating to

[20] Equality Act 2010, s 6(1).
[21] Ibid, s 7(1).

multiple characteristics. Article 14, which would prohibit discrimination 'because of a combination of two relevant protected characteristics' is not currently in force.[22]

What links the characteristics protected under the Equality Act is the subject of some debate,[23] but the rationale is generally understood to include a combination of both immutability (the characteristics are ones we cannot ourselves choose to change or – in the case of religion and belief – can only change at fundamental cost to our identity) and historic and ongoing disadvantage. The protected groups (or at least subsets of them) have, at some time, experienced disadvantage and exclusion from important goods and institutions as a result of stigma and a history of structural and institutional discrimination. The relationships between the protected characteristics and experience of health related disadvantage and inequality are explored in Chapter 1.

Discrimination

The Act prohibits different forms of discrimination, of which three are particularly relevant in the context of this book – direct discrimination, indirect discrimination and the failure to make reasonable adjustments. The prohibition of direct discrimination captures the principle that likes should be treated alike – the Act provides that 'A person (A) discriminates against another (B) if, because of a protected characteristic, A treats B less favourably than A treats or would treat others'.[24] The protected characteristic has to be the *reason* for the less favourable treatment and a causal link must be established.[25] If the characteristic is the reason for the treatment, it does not matter why this is the case. It is clear that the treatment does not have to be intentional (or even conscious) and that motive is irrelevant.[26] There is, generally, no opportunity to legally justify direct discrimination, with a few important exceptions.

First, age discrimination is treated differently from discrimination on other grounds and treatment that would otherwise amount to direct age discrimination can be justified where it is 'a proportionate means to achieve

---

22 Ibid, s 14. At the time of writing the government have signalled their intention to bring this into effect in due course: Labour Party (2024) *Labour Party Manifesto 2024: Our Plan to Change Britain*.

23 For a useful summary see, for example, S. Fredman (2023) *Discrimination Law (3rd Edition)*, Oxford: Oxford University Press; T. Khaitan (2015) *A Theory of Discrimination Law*, Oxford: Oxford University Press.

24 Equality Act 2010, s 13.

25 *R (E) v JFS Governing Body* [2009] UKSC 15.

26 *Nagarajan v London Regional Transport* [2000] 1 AC 501, HL.

a legitimate aim'.[27] Second, while the protection of the Act is normally 'symmetrical' (men and women, believers and atheists are all protected alike) the protection is asymmetrical in respect of disability. It will not amount to direct discrimination, therefore, to treat somebody *more favourably* because they have a disability.[28] Third, the Act contains a number of specific exceptions which permit treatment that would otherwise be direct discrimination in specific circumstances. For the purposes of this book, two of these will be particularly relevant; the 'single sex services' exemption which enables service providers to provide services exclusively to members of one sex where this is a proportionate means of achieving a legitimate aim and where specified conditions are met;[29] and the positive action provisions which permit decision makers to treat members of a protected group more favourably where this is proportionate and aims to address disadvantage or exclusion experienced by the members of that group or to address the different needs of that group.[30]

The prohibition on direct discrimination is only part of the story, however. Anti-discrimination law has long reflected a recognition that treating people equally is often the cause of disadvantage because often members of protected groups are different in important ways, or face barriers or challenges that others do not. Rules that are apparently neutral can create and reinforce structural injustices.[31] The Act therefore also includes a number of prohibitions and obligations which reflect the fact that disadvantage can be created or entrenched where the differences between groups sharing particular characteristics are not recognized and accommodated. These include the duty to make reasonable adjustments in the case of disability; and indirect discrimination which arises where an apparently neutral policy or practice serves to disadvantage those sharing a protected characteristic and cannot be justified.

Indirect discrimination

Indirect discrimination arises where a policy or practice which applies to everyone – or at least applies both to those who share a protected characteristic and those who do not – creates a particular disadvantage for those in the protected group and cannot be justified by showing it is

[27] Equality Act 2010, s 13(2).

[28] Ibid, s 13(3).

[29] Ibid, Schedule 3 (para 27).

[30] Ibid, s 158.

[31] See D. Hellman, 'Indirect Discrimination and the Duty to Avoid Compounding Injustice' in H. Collins and T. Khaitan (eds) *Foundations of Indirect Discrimination Law*, Oxford: Hart, pp 105–121.

a proportionate means of achieving a legitimate aim.[32] There is no need to be able to explain the *reason* a particular policy disadvantages members of a protected group – it is usually enough to show that it has this effect.[33] A decision by the NHS to not fund a particular drug may apply to everyone. But if that drug would be particularly beneficial to women, or to those over 70, then particular disadvantage will be caused to these groups by the decision and the relevant commissioning body will need to be able to justify the decision by showing that it is a proportionate means of achieving a legitimate aim. Much, in the commissioning context, will depend on the circumstances in which decisions like this can be legally justified, something explored throughout the book.

The duty to make reasonable adjustments

In relation to disability, the Equality Act provides where there is a policy, criterion or practice which puts disabled persons at a substantial disadvantage in comparison with persons who are not disabled, service providers are obliged to take such steps as are reasonable to avoid the disadvantage.[34] Failure to do so amounts to unlawful discrimination. The duty is an anticipatory one, meaning that, in a commissioning context, policy makers will be required to consider in advance whether there are likely to be any barriers to accessing a particular form of treatment for those with disabilities and whether any reasonable steps can be taken to eliminate or mitigate the disadvantage. The application of the duty in the commissioning context is considered in more detail in Chapter 3.

The Public Sector Equality Duty

Finally, the Public Sector Equality Duty is a positive obligation which requires public policy and decision makers to take into account the need to eliminate unlawful discrimination and to promote equality.[35] It is, as we will see, essentially a procedural duty rather than one which requires any particular outcome to be achieved; having taken into account the impact of a policy on the groups protected under the Equality Act, decision makers are free to ignore it (provided, of course, that the decision does not otherwise amount to unlawful discrimination). But, as will be argued throughout this book, the duty has the potential to play an important role in addressing health

[32] Equality Act 2010, s 19.
[33] *Essop v Home Office* [2017] UKSC 27.
[34] Equality Act 2010, s 20 and 21.
[35] Ibid, s 149.

inequalities and in ensuring that the needs of vulnerable groups, which may otherwise be overlooked, are taken into account.

Article 14 of the European Convention on Human Rights

Article 14 of the ECHR binds the decisions of public authorities under the Human Rights Act 1998. It provides that '[t]he enjoyment of the rights and freedoms set forth in [the] Convention shall be secured without discrimination on any ground such as sex, race, colour, language, religion, political or other opinion, national or social origin, association with a national minority, property, birth or other status'. It differs from the Equality Act in a number of important ways.

First, in some respects Article 14 offers a broader protection than does the Equality Act because it does not limit the characteristics it protects. The list of protected characteristics is not fixed and there is scope to add to those in the list. The European Court of Human Rights (ECtHR) has done so on numerous occasions and the characteristics protected under Article 14 now include disability, sexual orientation, gender identity and age, among many others. Importantly, the open nature of the list makes it more likely that Article 14 is able to offer protection from intersectional discrimination than the Equality Act.[36]

Second, Article 14 is not a free-standing prohibition of discrimination but will only apply if there has been discrimination in the exercise of one or more of the other Convention rights. There is no need for a claimant to establish a breach of the other right in order to succeed in a claim under Article 14, but they will be required to establish that the relevant circumstances at least fall within the 'ambit' of another right. In relation to challenges to allocation of health care resources the most likely Convention rights to be relevant are Article 2 (the right to life), Article 3 (the right to freedom from torture) and, perhaps most importantly, Article 8 (the right to respect for private and family life). Generally, as noted earlier, claims that states are under a positive obligation to provide health care in relation to any of these rights (other than in unusual or extreme circumstances) have met with little success. But this does not mean that challenges under Article 14 will be similarly unsuccessful. Even where the state is under no positive obligation to provide health care, if it chooses to do so, it must not do so in a way that is discriminatory.

---

[36] For discussion of this point see C. O'Cinneide (2020) 'The Potential and Pitfalls of Intersectionality in the Context of Social Rights Adjudication' in S. Atrey and P. Dunne (eds) *Intersectionality and Human Rights Law*, Oxford: Hart, pp 59–82.

Finally, Article 14 does not define discrimination nor distinguish between its different forms. In this respect it is 'relatively non-technical' and 'avoids some of the legalism that has affected domestic discrimination law'.[37] The Court has recognized that both direct discrimination and (more recently) indirect discrimination[38] can be unlawful. All forms of discrimination can in theory be justified – direct as well as indirect – and the test of justification the courts apply is generally one of proportionality. The approach of the courts to justification is considered in some detail in Chapter 4. In addition to direct and indirect discrimination, the ECtHR has also recognized that failure, without justification, to treat people differently when their situations are different will be a breach of Article 14.[39] States (and public bodies in the UK) may therefore be required to amend policy, or to make exceptions, where individuals would be otherwise disadvantaged in these circumstances. This obligation is discussed in Chapter 3.

The structure of the book

The rest of this book is in two parts. The first part will explore the relationship between anti-discrimination law and the broader institutional and policy challenges of priority setting. Chapter 1 considers the relationship between health inequalities and protected characteristics and assesses the potential of equality law to tackle them. Chapters 2 and 3 then look at commissioning, and other forms of priority setting, in detail. Chapter 2 examines the way NICE and ICBs calculate and use cost-effectiveness as a basis for resource allocation decisions and the potential for direct or indirect discrimination to arise here. It also considers the ways discrimination may result from decision making by clinicians or because of gaps in health research. Chapter 3 then looks at the circumstances under which commissioners are permitted or required to take positive action to make exceptions for groups or individuals who may otherwise be disadvantaged by decisions about what to fund. Finally, Chapter 4 examines the role of the courts in reviewing resource allocation decisions involving potential discrimination and the impact of this approach on the ability of equality law to require decision makers to identify and act on disadvantage and inequality related to protected characteristics. The second part of the book then explores some of the issues we have identified as they arise in three different contexts: public health, including the public health response to COVID-19 (Chapter 5), access to fertility treatment (Chapter 6) and intensive care (Chapter 7). These examples have

[37] *Burnip v Birmingham City Council* [2012] EWCA Civ 629.

[38] *DH v Czech Republic* [2007] 11 WLUK 289.

[39] *Thlimmenos v Greece* [2001] 31 EHRR 15.

been chosen because they give us an opportunity to look at resourcing decisions in three very different decision-making environments and ones where concerns about discrimination and equality have been the subject of recent public debate. The book ends with a short conclusion which brings together some of the main themes.

1

Health Inequalities

Introduction

Much of the research on health inequalities has focused – rightly – on the relationship between health and socio-economic status. The statistics are stark. Life expectancy at birth for men living in the most deprived areas of England is 9.7 years lower than those living in the least deprived (and for women it is 7.9 years). Women in the most deprived areas of the UK can expect to live 19.3 fewer years in good health than those in the least deprived (and for men it is 18.6 years).[1] Understanding and tackling these inequalities is imperative. In the words of Frank Dobson, Secretary of State for Health in the 1997 Labour government, 'inequality in health is the worst inequality of all. There is no more serious inequality than knowing that you'll die sooner because you are badly off'.[2]

Alongside research on socio-economic causes (and effects) of health inequality, there has been increasing recent interest in understanding health inequalities that relate to groups sharing personal characteristics and the part discrimination may play in causing or perpetuating these – both as a determinant of poor health in the first place and as an explanation for uneven access to health care to tackle it. Problems of discrimination and inequality were bought into sharp focus during the COVID-19 pandemic where the unequal impact of the virus and of public health responses to it

[1] Office for National Statistics (25 April 2022) *Health State Life Expectancies by National Deprivation Deciles, England: 2018 to 2020*, available at: https://www.ons.gov.uk/peoplepopulationandcommunity/healthandsocialcare/healthinequalities/bulletins/healthstatelifeexpectanciesbyindexofmultipledeprivationimd/2018to2020 (accessed December 2024).

[2] Local Government Chronicle (12 August 1997) 'Govt Takes Action to Reduce Health Inequalities', available at: https://www.lgcplus.com/archive/govt-takes-action-to-reduce-health-inequalities-12-08-1997/ (accessed December 2024).

on different groups – in particular in relation to gender, ethnicity, disability and age – has now been well documented.[3]

This chapter aims to unpick the complex relationships between personal characteristics, discrimination, socio-economic inequality and patterns of health inequality in the UK and to consider the role and potential of anti-discrimination law in addressing health inequalities. It will note that equality law – and especially proactive duties such as the Public Sector Equality Duty (PSED) – has a potentially important role to play both in tackling the determinants of ill health and in shaping policy responses to it. However, this potential is currently limited in a number of key respects. In particular, existing law is ill equipped to address problems of intersectionality and problems of socio-economic inequality (which itself intersects with protected characteristics in complex ways).

What are health inequalities?

Defining equality in any context is notoriously troublesome and defining health equality is no exception. First, there are difficulties in deciding what it is we want to measure and compare. We might, for example, choose to look at life expectancy or we might focus on years of 'healthy' life. We might look at particular conditions and compare how well or poorly different groups fare in relation to diabetes or mental health or cancer. Or we might choose to focus on equality in access to health care resources. The expression 'health inequalities' is used in different ways in the literature. The World Health Organization defines health inequalities as simply 'differences in health status or in the distribution of health determinants between different population groups'.[4] In discussing unfair health inequalities – the subset of health inequalities that arise as a result of circumstances that are avoidable and unfair, such as the social conditions in which we grow, live and work, or the distribution of health resources – it prefers the expression health inequity.[5] Other definitions of health inequality build in the notion of inequity. The UK government, for example, has defined health inequalities as '*avoidable* differences in health outcomes between groups or populations – such as differences in how long we live, or the age at which we get preventable diseases or health conditions'

[3] See, for example, C. Bambra, J. Lynch and K. Smith (2021) *The Unequal Pandemic: COVID-19 and Health Inequalities*, Bristol: Bristol University Press.

[4] World Health Organization (2018) *Health Inequities and Their Causes*, World Health Organization, available at: https://www.who.int/news-room/facts-in-pictures/detail/health-inequities-and-their-causes (accessed February 2025).

[5] Ibid.

(my emphasis).[6] And along similar lines the National Institute for Health and Care Excellence (NICE) defines health inequalities as 'differences in health across the population, and between different groups in society, that are systematic, unfair and avoidable'.[7] These definitions suggest that health inequalities both can and should be diminished or eliminated by appropriate policy choices. It is in this sense that the expression will be used in this chapter.

What those policy choices should be is, inevitably, a matter of some contention and will depend on our understanding of the causes of avoidable health inequalities and in particular on the degree to which ill health is understood to arise as a result of environmental factors and structural inequalities in wider society. In 2010 an independent review of health inequalities commissioned by the Secretary of State for Health and chaired by Professor Sir Michael Marmot (the Marmot Review) was clear that health inequalities result from social and economic inequalities – the lower your social position, the worse your health.[8] It found the gradient between the deprivation of a neighbourhood, and both the life expectancy and healthy life expectancy of those within it, to be 'remarkable', and concluded that tackling health inequalities must therefore involve action on all of the 'social determinants of health' – non-medical causes of ill health including education, housing, employment and the wider social and physical environment.[9] Ten years on, and just before the COVID-19 pandemic took hold, a review of progress made since the Marmot Review had concluded that far from improving, health inequalities were increasing and health deteriorating for those in the most deprived areas, largely as a result of austerity based cuts to public spending.[10] The COVID-19 pandemic itself then served to shine a spotlight on and exacerbate these already worsening health inequalities.

---

6 Office for Health Improvement and Disparities (11 October 2022) *Health Disparities and Health Inequalities: Applying All Our Health*, available at: https://www.gov.uk/government/publications/health-disparities-and-health-inequalities-applying-all-our-health/health-disparities-and-health-inequalities-applying-all-our-health (accessed December 2024).

7 National Institute for Health and Care Excellence (nd) *NICE and Health Inequalities*, available at: https://www.nice.org.uk/about/what-we-do/nice-and-health-inequalities (accessed December 2024).

8 M. Marmot (February 2010) *Fair Society, Healthy Lives: The Marmot Review: Strategic Review of Health Inequalities in England Post-2010*, available at: https://www.parliament.uk/globalassets/documents/fair-society-healthy-lives-full-report.pdf (accessed December 2024).

9 Ibid at 2.6.

10 M. Marmot J. Allen, T. Boyce, P. Goldblatt and J. Morrison (2020) *Health Equity in England: The Marmot Review 10 Years On*, Institute of Health Equity, available at: the-marmot-review-10-years-on-full-report.pdf (accessed December 2024).

As Kamunge observes, 'the inequalities stemming from COVID-19 [were] not an aberration but the norm made worse'.[11]

Recently more attention has also been paid to role of discrimination in producing or accelerating health inequalities, both directly and by mediating our access to key social determinants of health – including education, employment and housing – as well as to health care. Research has also begun to draw attention to the role of law in facilitating or challenging the structures that give rise to health inequalities – the legal determinants of health.[12] There has, however, so far been little explicit consideration of the role of equality and anti-discrimination law in addressing the causes of ill health or unequal access to health care. It is to the role of discrimination, and of the law which purports to tackle it, that this chapter will now turn.

Health inequalities and protected characteristics

Tracking the relationship between health inequalities and protected characteristics is not straightforward. The causes of health inequalities involve a complex web of interactions – social, economic, behavioural, biological and environmental – and all of these elements may in turn be governed, at least to some extent, by our personal characteristics and the groups to which we belong. An illustration of these interactions is provided in the recent inquiry by the Women and Equalities Committee of the House of Commons into Black Maternal Health. Black women are four times more likely to die in childbirth than White women, with significant disparities also present for Asian women and women of mixed ethnicity but the Committee noted that:

> [T]he reasons for ethnic disparities in mortality are not fully understood. Across aggregated ethnic groups, women are dying from the same causes, but Black and Asian women are dying more frequently. We heard that there were many possible reasons for the disparity in the frequency of deaths, including pre-existing conditions and co-morbidities; socio-economic factors including deprivation; and factors

[11] B. Kamunge (2021) *Which Inequalities Should We Focus On in Evaluating Health Policy Before, During, and Following COVID-19?*, UK Pandemic Ethics Accelerator, available at: www.ukpandemicethics.org (accessed December 2024).

[12] See, for example, J. Coggon (2020) 'Legal, Moral and Political Determinants within the Social Determinants of Health: Approaching Transdisciplinary Challenges through Interdisciplinary Reflection', *Public Law Ethics* 13(1): 41–47; L. Gostin, J. Monahan, J. Kaldor, M. DeBartolo, E. Friedman, K. Gottschalk et al (2019) 'The Legal Determinants of Health: Harnessing the Power of Law for Global Health and Sustainable Development', *The Lancet* 393: 1857–1910; M. Thomson (2022) 'Legal Determinants of Health', *Medical Law Review* 30(4): 610–634.

> impacting on the care that women received, including ignorance, bias, microaggressions and racism.[13]

A second layer of complexity is added when the intersections between different protected characteristics, and between protected characteristics and socio-economic status, are considered – particularly because, as Hill notes, in relation to intersectionality, data is often not collected in a way that makes it easy to explore how different aspects of identity affect the health of individuals.[14]

The COVID-19 pandemic has proved to be a case study for many of the ways in which these different aspects of the relationship between protected characteristics, socio-economic disadvantage and health outcomes can interact.[15] While the nature and impacts of the disease are still being understood, it is clear that the risk factors that predicted who would do worse or better during the pandemic were a complex mix of biological, socio-economic and behavioural. There were some biological explanations for who did worse – those who were older (because of comorbidity or frailty) and those with particular disabilities (like Type 2 diabetes, some forms of which also tend to be more prevalent among minority ethnic communities).[16] Women, particularly in middle age, appear much more susceptible to Long COVID.[17] But differences relating to living and working conditions were also important. At higher risk of transmission included those living in crowded and/or multigenerational households, who were more likely to belong to particular ethnic minority groups;[18] and those in frontline or care work, mainly comprised of women and those from ethnic minorities.[19]

---

13 Women and Equalities Committee (19 April 2023) *Black Maternal Health: Third Report of Session 2022–2023*, House of Commons, HC 94, at p 7.

14 S. Hill (2015) 'Axes of Inequalities and Intersectionality' in K. Smith, C. Bambra and S. Hill (eds), *Health Inequalities: Critical Perspectives*, Oxford: Oxford University Press, pp 95–108.

15 For an excellent overview of the uneven impacts of COVID-19 see Bambra et al (n 3).

16 L.M. Goff (2019) 'Ethnicity and Type 2 Diabetes in the UK', *Diabetic Medicine* 36(8): 927–938. E. Barron, C. Bakhai, P. Kar, A. Weaver, D. Bradley, H. Ismail et al (2020) 'Associations of Type 1 and Type 2 Diabetes with COVID-19-Related Mortality in England: A Whole Population Study', *The Lancet Diabetes & Endocrinology* 8(10): 813–822.

17 R.A. Evans, H.J.C. McAuley, E.M. Harrison, A. Shikotra, A. Singapuri, M. Sereno et al (2021) 'Physical, Cognitive, and Mental Health Impacts of COVID-19 after Hospitalisation (PHOSP-COVID): A UK Multicentre, Prospective Cohort Study', *Lancet Respiratory Medicine* 9(11): 1275–1287.

18 Office for National Statistics (2020) *Why Have Black and South Asian People Been Hit Hardest by COVID-19?* ONS, available at: https://www.ons.gov.uk/peoplepopulationandcommunity/healthandsocialcare/conditionsanddiseases/articles/whyhaveblackandsouthasianpeoplebeenhithardestbycovid19/2020-12-14 (accessed December 2024).

19 Office for National Statistics (2020) *Which Occupations Have the Highest Potential Exposure to the Coronavirus (COVID-19)*, ONS, available at: https://www.ons.gov.uk/releases/whichoccupationshavethehighestpotentialexposuretothecoronaviruscovid19 (accessed December 2024).

There were also differences in risks and outcomes because of decisions made by policy makers in response to the pandemic and because of the attention or lack of attention policy makers paid to certain groups. A lack of attention to the needs and particular vulnerabilities of those with learning disabilities, for example, resulted in a lack of planning and failure to prioritize this group, leading to much poorer outcomes;[20] and the risks for pregnant women were increased by the confused and inconsistent approach to vaccination.[21] Importantly, many of these disadvantages were intersectional.[22] The public health response to COVID-19 is discussed in more detail in Chapter 5. With this complexity in mind, the following discussion identifies four important relationships between protected characteristics and poor health: biological, cultural/behavioural, socio-economic and discrimination.

Biological explanations

In some instances, differences in health status between different protected groups arise at least partly as a result of biological differences between them – some diseases or health conditions affect only, or mainly, those with particular protected characteristics. However, biological explanations are generally challenged in the literature as being overly simplistic because they ignore the relevance of social and organizational factors both in giving rise to the ill health and in determining the response to it. Social context and policy can influence health choices for both men and women.[23] The relationships can be difficult to untangle because, as Hill notes in relation to sex, 'health differences between women and men cannot be attributed proportionally to the biological or the social. Rather, the two elements interact in their impacts on health'.[24] Social context is therefore needed to understand gendered health outcomes, even when linked to our biological starting point. The same is true of other characteristics including disability.

---

20 N. Scherer, P. Wiseman, N. Watson, R. Brunner, J. Cullingworth, S. Hameed et al (2023) '"Do They Ever Think About People Like Us?": The Experiences of People with Learning Disabilities in England and Scotland during the COVID-19 Pandemic', *Critical Social Policy* 43(3): 423–447.

21 M. Limb (2023) 'COVID-19: Confusion around Vaccination in Pregnancy Likely to Have Contributed to the Deaths of 27 Women in the UK', *British Medical Journal* 383: 2388.

22 B. Kamunge (2021) *Intersectional Approaches to Tackling Pandemic Inequalities*, UK Pandemic Ethics Accelerator, available at: https://ukpandemicethics.org/wp-content/uploads/2021/12/Intersectionality-Framework.pdf (accessed December 2024).

23 C.E. Bird and P.P. Rieker (2008) *Gender and Health: The Effects of Constrained Choices and Social Policies*, Cambridge: Cambridge University Press.

24 Hill (n 14) p 99.

While many forms of ill health will lead to disability, it is important to have in mind that disability is normally understood to result from the interaction between mental and physical impairment and social structures or processes.[25] The disabling effect of some forms of impairment or ill health can be removed or minimized by adapting those social structures or processes. It is also important to be careful in conceptualizing the relationship between disability and health inequality and not to do so in a way that assumes all disabled health states are undesirable and of lower value than non-disabled health states. This issue is discussed in more detail in Chapter 2.

The case of sickle cell disease is a good example of this complex interaction between biological and social factors. Sickle cell is a blood disorder that disproportionately affects those from Black African and Caribbean populations who are at higher risk for the gene mutation that gives rise to the disease.[26] Untreated it can give rise to painful episodes, infection and anaemia; but with access to good care it need not give rise to inequality in health related quality of life.[27] An investigation by an All Party Parliamentary Group in 2021 found that individuals with sickle cell often receive sub-standard treatment for a number of reasons. These include a lack of recognition and understanding of the disease by practitioners as a result of a lack of training. Disturbingly, there was also evidence that those presenting with symptoms of sickle cell were being denied opioid pain relief because some staff make racist assumptions that Black patients are simply seeking drugs.[28]

A final useful example of the complex relationship between biological and other explanations is age. Health inequalities between age groups may arise as a result of biological differences that make younger or older patients more susceptible to disease. But, of course, my health state at any given chronological age will be a product, not just of genetics and 'natural' ageing, but of the health related advantages and disadvantages – social, economic and so on – that I have encountered through my life course.[29] And 'healthy

[25] For a useful summary of the issues see J. McLaughlin (2022) 'Disability' in L. Monaghan and J. Gabe (eds) *Key Concepts in Medical Sociology (3rd Edition)*, London: SAGE, pp 147–152.

[26] National Institute for Health and Care Excellence (2021) *How Common is Sickle Cell Disease?* NICE, available at: https://cks.nice.org.uk/topics/sickle-cell-disease/background-information/prevalence/ (accessed December 2024).

[27] J. Jabbal (2023) *Access to Care: Reducing Health Inequalities for People Living with Sickle Cell Disorder*, The King's Fund, available at: https://www.kingsfund.org.uk/insight-and-analysis/blogs/reducing-health-inequalities-sickle-cell-disorder (accessed December 2024).

[28] All Party Parliamentary Group for Sickle Cell and Thalassaemia (SCTAPPG) (15 November 2021) *No One's Listening: A Report*, SCTAPPG, available at: https://www.sicklecellsociety.org/no-ones-listening/ (accessed December 2024).

[29] J. Grimley Evans (2003) 'Age Discrimination: Implications of the Ageing Process' in S. Fredman and S. Spencer (eds) *Age as an Equality Issue*, Oxford: Hart, pp 11–20.

ageing' will also reflect the availability of high quality health and social care and other support structures and interventions. Research on 'frailty' increasingly rejects the notion that it is a natural and inevitable part of the biological ageing process and should instead be seen as something which can often be slowed and reduced through appropriate intervention.[30]

Behavioural/cultural explanations

Individual behaviour – and in particular what we eat and whether we exercise, smoke, drink or use drugs – has an important impact on health outcomes. The extent to which individuals can be held responsible for lifestyle choices that impact negatively on health – and the appropriate public health response to lifestyle illness – remains a subject of much contention.[31] However it is generally accepted that our healthy or unhealthy behaviours are shaped to some degree by wider determinants of health – the 'causes of the causes' – including the social, environmental, cultural and economic circumstances in which we find ourselves.[32] More recently, attention has also turned to understanding the 'commercial determinants of health' – activities by the private sector including the production, marketing and pricing of food, alcohol and tobacco which impact public health.[33]

Mapping behavioural contributions to poor health onto personal characteristics is, unsurprisingly, another complex task. Take smoking, for example, one of the leading risk factors for preventable ill health and mortality in the UK.[34] Smoking prevalence shows a 'complex distribution against multiple axes of identity' with patterns of smoking behaviour showing strong relationships with characteristics including socio-economic disadvantage, ethnicity and gender.[35] Office for National Statistics data shows that, in 2021, the proportion of people who smoke in the most deprived

---

30 For a helpful overview of the issues see E. Gordon and R. Hubbard (2022) 'Frailty: Understanding the Difference Between Age and Ageing', *Age and Ageing* 51(8): 1–6.

31 C. Newdick (2017) 'Health Equality, Social Justice and the Poverty of Autonomy', *Health Economics, Policy and Law* 12(4): 411–433.

32 Department of Health and Social Care (nd) *Wider Determinants of Health*, available at: https://fingertips.phe.org.uk/profile/wider-determinants (accessed December 2024); Marmot et al (n 10).

33 N. Maani, M. Petticrew and S. Galea (eds) (2020) *The Commercial Determinants of Health*, Oxford: Oxford University Press.

34 N. Steel, J.A. Ford, J.N. Newton, A.C.J. Davis, T. Vos, M. Naghavi et al (2018) 'Changes in Health in the Countries of the UK and 150 English Local Authority Areas 1990–2016: A Systematic Analysis for the Global Burden of Disease Study 2016', *The Lancet* 392: 1647–1661.

35 Hill (n 14) p 100.

areas of England and Wales was more than three times higher than in the least deprived areas.[36] For both men and women, the highest smoking prevalence was seen in the mixed ethnic group; but when gender and ethnicity are considered together significant differences become apparent between sexes, particularly in Asian (13.9 per cent in men and 2.9 per cent in women), Chinese (12.6 per cent in men and 4.0 per cent in women) and Black (12.9 per cent in men and 6.9 per cent in women) groups.[37] While ethnic differences in smoking behaviour map onto socio-economic disadvantage, other factors, such as cultural norms and failure to engage ethnic minority groups with public health messaging and support, may also play a part.[38] And while men smoke more than women across all ethnicities, women are more susceptible to chronic diseases caused by smoking.[39] Understanding the causes and consequences of smoking – and other behaviours that impact on health – therefore requires intersectional understanding and approach. As Hill argues, focusing on one aspect of social identity gives an incomplete picture and undermines attempts to tackle health inequalities connected to lifestyle choices.[40]

Socio-economic explanations

It is unsurprising that there is a clear and persistent relationship between socio-economic disadvantage and poorer health outcomes. It is also unsurprising that there is considerable overlap and intersection between many of the groups protected by anti-discrimination legislation and socio-economic disadvantage. One of the purposes of the anti-discrimination and equality law is to address the exclusion and marginalization of members of protected groups from sources of material security – and in particular the

36 Office for National Statistics (2023) *Deprivation and the Impact on Smoking Prevalence, England and Wales 2017–21*, ONS, available at: https://www.ons.gov.uk/peoplepopulationandcommunity/healthandsocialcare/drugusealcoholandsmoking/bulletins/deprivationandtheimpactonsmokingprevalenceenglandandwales/2017to2021 (accessed December 2024).

37 Office for National Statistics (2020) *Adult Smoking Habits in the UK: 2019*, ONS, available at: https://www.ons.gov.uk/peoplepopulationandcommunity/healthandsocialcare/healthandlifeexpectancies/bulletins/adultsmokinghabitsingreatbritain/2023 (accessed December 2024).

38 S. Karlsen, D. Millward and A. Sandford (2012) 'Investigating Ethnic Differences in Current Cigarette Smoking Over Time Using the Health Surveys for England', *European Journal of Public Health* 22(2): 254–256.

39 S. Peters, R. Huxley and M. Woodward (2014) 'Do Smoking Habits Differ Between Women and Men in Contemporary Western Populations? Evidence from Half a Million People in the UK Biobank Study', *BMJ Open* 4(12): e005663.

40 Hill (n 14).

labour market – and the consequent socio-economic disadvantages to which this gives rise.[41] Race, sex and disability are particularly associated with an increased risk of poverty. The gender pay gap, together with the demands of care and particular vulnerability to cuts in welfare, leaves women in single-income households – and particularly pensioners and single mothers – at higher risk of income poverty; members of minority Black and ethnic groups (and some groups in particular) are far more likely to be in insecure and low paid work or to be unemployed; and there is very strong correlation between disability and poverty which is likely to indicate both cause and effect. Almost half of working age adults in poverty have someone who is disabled in their households.[42] Importantly, evidence suggests that intersectionality is highly significant – the more protected characteristics a person has, the more risk of poverty they bear.[43]

The most striking statistics on health inequalities are often illustrated geographically. Females born in the 10 per cent most deprived areas can expect to live for 51.9 years in good health and 26.4 years in poorer health; females born in the 10 per cent least deprived areas can expect to live eight years longer in total with 70.7 years in good health and 15.6 in poorer health.[44] Again there is a strong correlation between protected characteristics – particularly ethnicity – and areas of deprivation:

> People from all ethnic minority groups except the Indian, Chinese, White Irish and White Other groups were more likely than White British people to live in the most overall deprived 10% of neighbourhoods in England; people from the Pakistani and Bangladeshi ethnic groups were over 3 times as likely as White British people to live in the most income-deprived 10% of neighbourhoods.[45]

---

[41] See, for example, S. Fredman (2022) *Discrimination Law (3rd Edition)*, Oxford: Oxford University Press.

[42] S. Davies and D. Collings (2021) *The Inequality of Poverty*, University of Bristol, available at: https://www.bristol.ac.uk/media-library/sites/geography/pfrc/The-Inequality-of-Poverty-Full-Report.pdf; Equality and Human Rights Commission (2017) *Being Disabled in Britain: A Journey Less Equal*, EHRC, available at: https://www.equalityhumanrights.com/our-work/our-research/being-disabled-britain-journey-less-equal (accessed December 2024).

[43] Davies and Collings (n 42).

[44] Office for National Statistics (2022) *Health State Life Expectancies by National Deprivation Deciles, England: 2018 to 2020*, available at: https://www.ons.gov.uk/peoplepopulationandcommunity/healthandsocialcare/healthinequalities/bulletins/healthstatelifeexpectanciesbyindexofmultipledeprivationimd/2018to2020 (accessed December 2024).

[45] Ministry of Housing, Communities and Local Government (2019) *English Indices of Deprivation 2019*, available at: https://www.gov.uk/government/statistics/english-indices-of-deprivation-2019 (accessed December 2024).

Discrimination

Increasingly, research suggests that there is a direct link between individual experience of discrimination and inequality and ill health because of the biological consequences of those experiences. Evidence shows that the chronic stress which can be caused by experiences of discrimination and social inequality acts on a number of different biological pathways – including developmental, immune, hormonal and vascular – resulting in damage to health.[46] Racial intolerance, incivility and anti-immigrant sentiment are shown to impact directly on the health of targeted groups;[47] and there is evidence of poorer mental health among individuals discriminated against because of sexual orientation or gender reassignment.[48] Damage to health may also be caused by behaviour which is a direct response to experience of discrimination because discrimination or fear of discrimination can act as a barrier to healthy lifestyle choices (such as exercise) or lead to people engaging in unhealthy behaviour (such as alcohol consumption) as a coping mechanism.[49] Aside from these direct consequences, discrimination in all its forms – individual, institutional and structural – can serve to exclude protected groups from access to the means to improve their socio-economic circumstances in relation to employment, education, housing and other essential services, all key social determinants of health. Redressing and eliminating this exclusion is a central rationale of anti-discrimination and equality law.[50] And evidence shows that, separate from and additional to the health consequences of material deprivation, perceived inequality itself has direct consequences for mental and physical health.

Unequal access to health care may compound avoidable differences in ill health and create new ones. Potential discrimination in access to health care may can arise through deliberate rationing choices – for example, a decision not to prioritize funding for an intervention that only or mainly benefits one group or a decision not to take into account protected characteristics

---

46 N. Krieger (2000) 'Discrimination and Health Inequities' in L. Berkman, I. Kawachi and M. Glymour (eds) *Social Epidemiology*, Oxford: Oxford University Press, pp 63–125; A. Karpin and K. O'Connell (2022) 'The Challenge of Bioinequality: Addressing the Health Impact of Unequal Treatment Through Law', *Medical Law Review* 30(4): 635–657; S. Jackson, R. Hackett and R. Steptoe (2019) 'Associations Between Age Discrimination and Health and Wellbeing: Cross-sectional and Prospective Analysis of the English Longitudinal Study of Ageing', *The Lancet* 4: 200–208; Hill (n 14).

47 D. Williams and S. Mohammed (2009) 'Discrimination and Racial Disparities in Health: Evidence and Needed Research', *Journal of Behavioural Medicine* 32(1): 20–47.

48 W.B. Bostwick (2014) 'Discrimination and Mental Health among Lesbian, Gay, and Bisexual Adults in the United States', *American Journal of Orthopsychiatry* 84(1): 35–45.

49 Jackson et al (n 46); Hill (n 14).

50 S. Moreau (2020) *Faces of Inequality: A Theory of Wrongful Discrimination*, Oxford: Oxford University Press; Fredman (n 41).

when making decisions about whether or not to fund treatment for an individual. It may also arise because of a lack of research into conditions which predominantly effect a particular group or because a group has tended to be excluded from clinical trials, resulting in an understandable reluctance on the part of clinicians or commissioners to prescribe and fund the relevant intervention.[51] The potential for discrimination to arise in these circumstances – and the legal framework governing such choices – is the subject of this book. It is important to note that discrimination can also arise in the context of access to funded health care because of the way in which services are provided by institutions or clinicians. This may arise because of racist or ageist or sexist attitudes among providers or because the way in which services are designed and delivered creates barriers for particular groups. The National Health Service (NHS) Race Observatory, for example, has recently reported on the barriers to access to mental health services faced by ethnic minorities,[52] including for Gypsy, Roma and Traveller communities.[53] Likewise, recent research has highlighted an array of barriers faced by Muslim women in accessing health care across a range of specialisms.[54] These forms of discrimination are largely beyond the scope of this book but will be equally fundamental in the context of addressing health inequalities and are of course often themselves related to a lack of resources.

What is the role of equality law?

There has been growing attention to the role of law in perpetuating or redressing health inequalities. A 2019 report on the 'legal determinants of health' drew attention to the fact that law is currently 'underutilised and poorly understood' both as a cause of health inequalities – in the ways it fails to tackle the systemic social injustices that produce poor health – and, in particular, as a mechanism to tackle inequalities through the creation and

---

[51] J.A. Michaels (2021) 'Potential for Epistemic Injustice in Evidence Based Healthcare Policy and Guidance', *Journal of Medical Ethics* 47: 417–422.

[52] National Collaborating Centre for Mental Health (2023) *Ethnic Inequalities in Improving Access to Psychological Therapies (IAPT): Full Report*, London: National Collaborating Centre for Mental Health, available at: https://www.nhsrho.org/wp-content/uploads/2023/10/Ethnic-Inequalities-in-Improving-Access-to-Psychological-Therapies-IAPT.Full-report.pdf (accessed December 2024).

[53] NHS Race & Health Observatory (2023) *Inequalities in Mental Health Care for Gypsy, Roma, and Traveller Communities*, NHS Race & Health Observatory, available at: https://www.nhsrho.org/wp-content/uploads/2023/05/Inequalities-in-mental-health-care-for-Gypsy-Roma-and-Traveller-communities.pdf (accessed December 2024).

[54] See, for example, S. Dogra (ed) (2023) *British Muslims, Ethnicity and Health Inequalities*, Edinburgh: Edinburgh University Press.

regulation of effective health institutions.[55] Others have subsequently called for a widening of this enquiry to engage more explicitly with the law's role in addressing the wider social determinants of health[56] and to understand 'law' as broadly as possible in this context and as 'part of a broader array of mechanisms that represent sociopolitical power and its exercise'.[57]

It is one of the aims of this book to contribute to the project of exploring law's potential, in a UK context, through an assessment of the role of equality and discrimination law. Its key focus is on the provision of *health care* – both the ways in which this legal framework prohibits decisions that will cause or reinforce disadvantage, related to protected characteristics, and the ways in which it serves as a framework within which policy makers can (or must) address health inequalities, including through positive action. But equality and discrimination law also regulates areas of life which will have a direct bearing on the wider causes of ill health. There is an obvious link between discrimination and access to the 'social determinants' of health. It is clear that uneven access to sources of material security, often mediated by discrimination, may result in health inequalities. The successes and failures of anti-discrimination law more generally – in employment, education and housing, and beyond – as well as the broader human rights framework will therefore have a direct impact on health inequalities. Indeed two of the recommendations of the Marmot Review are of particular relevance when considering the role equality law can play in closing the gaps. The first is 'to enable everyone to maximise their capabilities and have control over their lives'. Absence of discrimination is fundamental to this goal. The second is 'to create fair employment and good work for all'. While equality and discrimination law can be only part of the puzzle here – access to good work demands law which provides adequate scope of protection and a minimum floor of workplace rights for all – robust enforcement of existing anti-discrimination law has the potential to improve access to good work for all groups. Women, disabled people, ethnic minorities and young workers are often disproportionately likely to be in insecure work.[58]

In many cases the Equality Act or Article 14 of the European Convention on Human Rights (ECHR) will offer a potential remedy for individuals discriminated against or disadvantaged in all of these contexts – work, housing, education and access to health care – but individual enforcement is difficult and challenging. This is both because of general barriers to access

55 Gostin et al (n 12).

56 Thomson (n 12).

57 Coggon (n 12).

58 R. Florisson (2022) *The UK Insecure Work Index: Two Decades of Insecurity*, Work Foundation, available at: https://www.lancaster.ac.uk/work-foundation/publications/the-uk-insecure-work-index (accessed December 2024).

to justice – including difficulties in accessing funded or free legal advice and representation – and because of the well-known difficulties of proving discrimination.[59] The difficulties claimants face in proving discrimination in all walks of life have been acknowledged by the courts and has resulted in changes to the law to shift the burden of proof to the defendant once a case of prima facie discrimination is made out.[60] In a health care context, however, to compound the usual difficulties in proving discrimination, it is plausible that the nature of medical expertise, and the complex health economic and clinical data on which resourcing decisions are made, means that patients and their carers (and indeed their lawyers) may not be well placed to access or assess the evidence in order to determine whether a decision to refuse treatment can be challenged in this way. Further research on this would be helpful. Certainly, there are only a few reported cases and research in the European Union suggested that legal advisors, when faced with instances of potential discrimination in health care (on any ground), are more likely to recommend pursuing a claim in medical negligence than one founded on anti-discrimination rights.[61] Reasons for this include the difficulties in proving discrimination (in particular in relation to finding an appropriate comparator) as well as the perception that judicial deference, evident in public law challenges to measures which implicate resource allocation, will mean that defendants will find it easy to justify discrimination by invoking resource constraints.[62] The issue of judicial deference is discussed in Chapter 4.

An individual enforcement model is also limited in its ability to effect the structural changes needed to make real progress on health inequalities.[63] To some extent this is potentially addressed by the role of the Equality and Human Rights Commission (EHRC), a statutory body which has a range of powers to assist in enforcement of equality and human rights law, including the power to produce statutory codes of practice and other guidance, to institute or intervene in legal proceedings, to conduct inquiries

---

[59] Women and Equalities Committee (2019) *Enforcing the Equality Act: Law and the Role of the Equality and Human Rights Commission (Tenth Report of Session 2017–19)* (HC 1470, 30 July 2019), available at: https://publications.parliament.uk/pa/cm201719/cmselect/cmwomeq/1470/1470.pdf (accessed December 2024).

[60] Equality Act 2010, s 136.

[61] European Union Agency for Fundamental Rights (2013) *Inequalities and Multiple Discrimination in Access to and Quality of Healthcare*, Luxembourg: Publications Office of the European Union.

[62] Ibid. Other reasons given included low non-pecuniary damages in discrimination law, especially when compared to awards for medical negligence, and difficulties presented by the 'comparator requirement' in EU anti-discrimination law.

[63] Women and Equalities Committee (n 59).

and investigations, and to issue notices requiring steps to be taken to address discriminatory policies and practices.[64] However, the EHRC lacks resources to engage in anything approaching comprehensive enforcement of equality law and instead must focus resources on a number of strategic priorities,[65] and its approach in doing so has been subject to some criticism as 'timid and … tethered to the individual complaints model'.[66]

The Public Sector Equality Duty

Another alternative to individual enforcement with the potential to achieve structural change is the Public Sector Equality Duty (PSED). The PSED was introduced under the Equality Act and replaced the Gender, Race and Disability duties that existed under the predecessor legislation. Section 149 of the Equality Act now provides that, in the exercise of their functions, public authorities must have 'due regard' to the need to eliminate unlawful discrimination, advance equality of opportunity between those who share a characteristic and those who do not, and to foster good relations between the various groups protected under the Act. Public authorities, for the purposes of the duty, include those responsible for the commissioning and provision of health care. Section 149(3) gives more detail as to what is required of public bodies in relation to advancing opportunity, providing that it involves having due regard, in particular, to the need to remove or minimize disadvantages suffered by persons who share a relevant protected characteristic that are connected to that characteristic; to take steps to meet the needs of persons who share a relevant protected characteristic that are different from the needs of persons who do not share it; and to encourage persons who share a relevant protected characteristic to participate in public life or in any other activity in which participation by such persons is disproportionately low.

The general duty is supplemented by specific duties and the duty operates slightly differently in England and in relation to devolved authorities in Scotland and Wales. In England and non-devolved authorities in Scotland and Wales these include an obligation to publish equality objectives every four years; and to publish information to demonstrate compliance with the duty. There is no obligation to conduct equality impact assessments, nor to develop action plans. By contrast, devolved authorities in Scotland and Wales are under additional obligations including to conduct and

---

64 Equality Act 2006, s 20–32.

65 EHRC (2022) *Strategic Plan 2022–2025*, available at: https://www.equalityhumanrights.com/about-us/our-strategy/strategic-plan-2022-2025 (accessed December 2024).

66 Fredman (n 41) p 461; see also Women and Equalities Committee (n 59).

publish equality impact assessments when reviewing policy or practices or developing new ones.[67]

The purpose and potential of the duty is to shift the onus on tackling discrimination and inequality from individual to organization and from reactive to proactive. As explained by Dame Vera Baird at the committee stage of the Equality Bill, the duty shifts responsibility from 'combating discrimination and disadvantage after it had happened – a passive model of waiting for discrimination to occur and then tackling it – to putting the onus firmly on public authorities to consider how to prevent and protect against the discrimination in the first place'.[68] The potential of the PSED in tackling inequalities lies also in its scope – the duty requires authorities to consider going further than compliance with their obligations to avoid unlawful discrimination and to consider measures to advance equality. The Equality Act prohibits the adoption of policies which give rise to direct or to unjustified indirect discrimination and the PSED is a tool to help policy makers identify when this is likely to be the case. But the PSED requires authorities to go further and to consider whether and when policies that have disparate impact but are legally justified should be modified to avoid that impact; and when to engage in lawful positive action so as to reduce or eliminate inequalities between groups that do not arise as a result of unlawful discrimination.

The PSED requires of public authorities only that they pay 'due regard' to avoiding discrimination and advancing equality, not that they achieve it. This aspect of the duty has been argued to undermine the potential of the duty to effect real change.[69] The House of Lords Committee on the Equality Act and Disability, for example, argued that it meant a public authority could 'make no progress towards the aims of the general duty and yet be judged compliant with it'.[70] It seems particularly odd, perhaps, that there is only a duty to have due regard to the need to eliminate unlawful discrimination – something which runs counter to the idea that the duty is in some way a solution to the difficulties faced by individual litigants in enforcing their rights.[71] Proposals were made to strengthen the duty – for example, by requiring authorities to at least take proportionate or reasonable steps towards achieving the goals set out in the legislation – but these suggestions were rejected. In the absence of a specific duty, in England at

---

67 Equality Act 2010 (Statutory Duties) (Wales) Regulations 2011, SI 2011/1064; Equality Act 2010 (Specific Duties) (Scotland) Regulations 2012, SI 2012/162.

68 Solicitor General, Vera Baird, Equality Bill Debate, HC Deb, 30 June 2009, col 545.

69 S. Fredman (2011) 'The Public Sector Equality Duty', *Industrial Law Journal* 40(4): 405–427.

70 House of Lords Equality Act 2010 and Disability Committee, *Equality Act 2010: The Impact on Disabled People*, 24 March 2016, HL Paper 117 of session 2015–16, p 99.

71 S. Fredman (2014) 'Addressing Disparate Impact: Indirect Discrimination and the Public Sector Equality Duty', *Industrial Law Journal* 43(3): 349–363; and see discussion in Chapter 3.

least, to even develop an action plan to achieve the goals, there is reason to be concerned that authorities who are not already minded to foreground equality in their policy making are unlikely to feel under any pressure to change approach in response to the duty.[72]

Nevertheless, working within these limitations, the courts have generally (though not consistently) taken a reasonably robust approach to interpreting the demands of the duty.[73] In *Bracking* it was emphasized that '[t]he 2010 Act imposes a heavy burden upon public authorities in discharging the PSED and in ensuring that there is evidence available, if necessary, to demonstrate that discharge',[74] and in *Hotak* the Supreme Court summarized the obligations, derived from previous case law, to exercise the duty 'in substance, with rigour and with an open mind' and with 'a proper and conscientious focus on the statutory criteria'.[75] The intensity with which the courts scrutinize the performance of the duty is discussed further in Chapter 4. While the courts have made clear that, specific duties aside, the PSED is one of substance rather than form,[76] and have discouraged a 'checklist' approach to compliance with the duty, they have established a number of requirements which authorities will normally need to meet in order to fulfil the obligation to have due regard. Two points are perhaps particularly interesting in the current context. The first is that the PSED includes a duty of inquiry. It is clear that the exercise of the PSED requires authorities to proactively investigate the potential adverse impact, or risk of impact, of a policy or measure on groups sharing a protected characteristic and the ways in which that risk may be mitigated or removed, before the policy is adopted.[77] Where there is no or insufficient evidence of impact on protected groups then authorities are under a duty to 'take reasonable steps to make enquiries about what may not yet be known to a public authority about the potential impact of a proposed decision or policy', although the extent of this duty 'is dependent on the context and does not require the impossible'.[78] Health care commissioners may therefore not rely simply on the data presented to them but must take reasonable steps to discover data which will illuminate relevant inequalities and the potential disparate impact of policy decisions under review.

A second point on the scope of the duty is evident from *R (Runnymede Trust and Good Law Project) v SoS for Health and Social Care and the Prime*

---

[72] See comprehensive discussion in Fredman (n 41).

[73] Ibid.

[74] *R (Bracking) v Secretary of State for Work and Pensions* [2013] EWCA Civ 1345 at 59.

[75] *Hotak v Southwark LBC* [2015] UKSC 30 at 75.

[76] *R (Baker) v Secretary of State for Communities and Local Government* [2008] EWCA Civ 141.

[77] *R (Bracking)* (n 74).

[78] *R (Bridges) v Chief Constable of South Wales* [2020] EWCA Civ 1058 at 181.

Minister,[79] which concerned a successful claim that there had been a lack of compliance with the PSED in the appointment of a number of key decision makers critical to the government's response to the COVID-19 pandemic. The Court found that insufficient evidence had been provided by the defendants to confirm what actions were undertaken to comply with this duty. In this respect the department's use of a recruitment firm with a track record on diversity was not accepted as sufficient to discharge the duty because '[t]hat goes only so far, which is nowhere near far enough'.[80] While the duty does not oblige authorities to ensure diversity in appointments, it is at least clear therefore that the importance of diversity should be properly considered in deciding on a process for public appointments. Ensuring, as far as possible, a diverse range of perspectives among policy makers may be key to ensuring that disadvantage and disparate impact affecting particular groups is not inadvertently overlooked.

The duty therefore offers some potential in relation to addressing health inequalities, something to which we will return throughout the book. However, it was evident in the brief survey of the relationships between health inequalities and protected characteristics, earlier, that many of the relationships between protected characteristics and poor outcomes are intersectional – disadvantage is found both at the intersection of multiple protected characteristics and at the intersection of protected characteristics and socio-economic disadvantage. Tackling health inequalities will therefore require focus on these dimensions of inequality. At present, however, the PSED does not clearly require policy makers to pay attention to intersectional disadvantage or to the overlap between status and socio-economic inequality.

Intersectionality

An approach to the PSED which simply takes a characteristic by characteristic approach is likely to miss pockets of significant disadvantage. For example, a commissioning body exercising the PSED when considering whether or not to fund a particular intervention and looking at data on the effectiveness of that drug disaggregated by gender or by race only, may miss the significant benefit that intervention may make to Black women in particular.

There is no clear legal requirement, at the moment, for intersectional discrimination and inequalities to be addressed by public authorities in the exercise of the PSED, although of course they are able to choose to do so. Insofar as the first limb of the duty requires public authorities to have due

[79] *R (Runnymede Trust and Good Law Project) v SoS for Health and Social Care and the Prime Minister* [2022] EWHC 298 (Admin).

[80] Ibid at 116.

regard to the need to eliminate unlawful discrimination, it is important to note that there is no clear prohibition on multiple discrimination under the Equality Act. Section 14 of the Act, which would prohibit direct discrimination because of 'a combination of two relevant protected characteristics' is not currently in force.[81] The utility of this provision is a matter of debate – both because it is limited to only two characteristics and because it is at least arguable that it is already possible to bring claims of multiple discrimination under the existing 'single axis' provisions of the Act, supported to a limited extent by some of the case law.[82] Nonetheless it is unlikely that a lack of clear prohibition on intersectional discrimination is helpful when it comes to focusing the attention of public authorities on the need to consider disadvantage at the intersection of two or more characteristics when exercising the PSED. The ECHR's technical guidance on PSED (updated in 2021) does remind decision makers of the diversity of experience within any particular group and draws their attention to the fact that people have multiple characteristics.[83] There is no clear direction to consider intersectional disadvantage in the exercise of the duty however. The Equality Commission in Northern Ireland, in its guidance on the equivalent duty in Northern Ireland,[84] goes slightly further, noting that when deciding what data should be collected in the exercise of the duty public authorities should consider whether they 'will need to address multiple identity issues'.

The courts have not addressed the question directly although it is clear that, in discharging the duty, authorities may be required to focus their regard on a particular subset of a group sharing a characteristic rather than simply on the group as a whole. In *Bracking*, a case concerning the decision of the Secretary of State to close the Independent Living Fund, which provided financial support for those with disabilities, the claimant argued successfully that it had not been sufficient, in discharge of the PSED, for the Secretary of State to consider the impact on disabled people as a whole. Rather the Court held that the duty required the respondent to demonstrate that 'a focussed regard was had to the potentially very grave impact upon individuals

[81] The Labour Party had indicated in their election manifesto that they may bring the Section into force: Labour Party (2024) *Labour Party Manifesto 2024: Our Plan to Change Britain*, available at: https://labour.org.uk/updates/stories/labour-manifesto-2024-sign-up/ (accessed December 2024).

[82] See, for example, J. Hand (2011) 'Combined Discrimination – Section 14 of the Equality Act 2010: A Partial and Redundant Provision?', *Public Law* July: 482–490.

[83] Equality and Human Rights Commission (2014) *Technical Guidance on the Public Sector Equality Duty: England*, EHRC, updated 2023, at para 2.16; *Technical Guidance on the Public Sector Equality Duty: Scotland*, EHRC, updated 2023, at para 2.36; and *Technical Guidance on the Public Sector Equality Duty: Wales*, EHRC, updated 2023, at para 2.21.

[84] Northern Ireland Act 1998, s 73.

in this group of disabled persons, within the context of a consideration of the statutory requirements for disabled people as a whole'.[85] This suggests that there is at least room to argue that an authority has failed in its discharge of the PSED where it has not had due regard to the potentially more serious impact of a measure on subgroups of those with protected characteristics. This, in turn, may require an intersectional approach. In the case of *Bracking*, however, there was clear evidence that the policy would effect this particular subgroup. Had there not been, it is not clear that the duty, in its current form, would have required the Secretary of State to seek it out.

Commissioners do sometimes reference the need to address intersectionality in addressing health inequalities. NHS England and NHS Improvement, for example, in their statement of equality objectives and information, make reference to 'the wider priority of reducing avoidable health inequalities using an intersectional lens where data permits'.[86] Nonetheless, there is a risk that without a consistent and systematic approach to the issue, commissioners will take only a 'characteristic by characteristic' basis to the implementation of the PSED and that areas of disadvantage arising at the intersection of two or more characteristics will be overlooked. Frustration has certainly been expressed that a failure to get to grips with intersectionality was evident in policy responses to COVID-19.[87]

Operationalizing an explicit duty to consider intersectional discrimination and inequality in the context of health policy would be no easy task and much more work is needed to find ways to make intersectional approaches to the PSED feasible and effective.[88] Perhaps chief among the challenges is in relation to gathering and managing what will sometimes be highly complex data. On the one hand, commissioners are under a positive duty of inquiry. As we have seen, this includes a duty to proactively seek out evidence of impact on protected groups if this is not already available. On the other hand, commissioners are often reliant on the data gathered through research conducted elsewhere, including through clinical trials which are typically carried out by private pharmaceutical companies not themselves subject

[85] *R (Bracking)* (n 74) 61.

[86] NHS England and NHS Improvement (19 May 2022) *Equality Objectives and Information as at 31 March 2022*, NHS England and NHS Improvement, available at: https://www.england.nhs.uk/wp-content/uploads/2022/05/B1587-nhsei-equality-objectives-and-information-31-march-2022.pdf (accessed December 2024).

[87] I. Qureshi, M. Gogoi, A. Al-Oraibi, F. Wobi, D. Pan, C. Martin et al (2022) 'Intersectionality and Developing Evidence Based Policy', *The Lancet* 399(10322): 355–356.

[88] O. Hankivsky D. Grace, G. Hunting, M. Giesbrecht, A. Fridkin, S. Rudrum et al (2014) 'An Intersectionality-based Policy Analysis Framework: Critical Reflections on a Methodology for Advancing Equity', *International Journal for Equity in Health* 13: 119; Kamunge (n 11).

to the PSED (although the Research Ethics Committees that approve and regulate the trials may be). While there is some recognition for the need for an intersectional approach among research funders,[89] research suggests that intersectional approaches are not typically used in either the design of interventional health research or its evaluation, leaving crucial gaps in the data available for analysis by those seeking to adopt commissioning strategies to reduce health inequalities.[90] Recognition of these difficulties, among others, led to a review of equality evidence data in Scotland and a commitment by the Scottish government to work with data providers to improve the intersectionality of data held on relevant systems.[91] Any change to the legal framework would need to come with considerable guidance and support for public authorities and careful thought to the tools that they will need in order to seek out and respond to intersectional health related inequalities in a meaningful way.

Socio-economic disadvantage

As is evident from the foregoing discussion, socio-economic disadvantage is also fundamental to understanding the causes and persistence of health inequalities. It is, alone, a key determinant of health but it also overlaps with status to generate complex patterns of inequality that demand attention and response from policy makers. This was nowhere more evident than in the COVID-19 pandemic.

The Equality Act does not, currently, deal directly with discrimination and inequality caused by socio-economic status. Socio-economic status is not a protected characteristic under the Equality Act, although some argue that it should be.[92] This means that the Act provides no legal mechanism to directly address stigma and hostility directed at individuals at socio-economic disadvantage, with the consequent impact on health to which this gives rise.[93] Nor does it provide means for an individual, disadvantaged by policy

[89] National Institute for Health and Care Research (2022) *Equality, Diversity and Inclusion Strategy 2022–2027*, NIHR, available at: https://www.nihr.ac.uk/about-us/who-we-are/research-inclusion/strategy-2022-27 (accessed December 2024).

[90] A. Rojas-Garcia, D. Holman, L. Tinner, S. Ejegi-Memeh, Y. Ben-Shlomo and A. Laverty (2022) 'Use of Intersectionality Theories in Interventional Health Research in High-income Countries: A Systematic Scoping Review', *The Lancet* 400(1): S58.

[91] The Scottish Government (March 2023) *Scotland's Equality Evidence Strategy 2023–2025*, available at: https://www.gov.scot/publications/scotlands-equality-evidence-strategy-2023-2025/ (accessed December 2024).

[92] A. Benn (2021) *Arguments to Include Class: The Big Gap in Discrimination Law: Class and the Equality Act 2010*, Oxford Human Rights Hub.

[93] M. Douglas (2016) 'Beyond "Health": Why Don't We Tackle the Cause of Health Inequalities?' in K. Smith, C. Bambra and S. Hill (eds) *Health Inequalities: Critical Perspectives*, Oxford: Oxford University Press, pp 109–123.

as a result of socio-economic disadvantage, to bring a claim of indirect discrimination under the Act.

Not in force in England at the time of writing, Section 1 of the Equality Act does provide that relevant public authorities, when making strategic decisions about how to exercise their functions, must have 'due regard to the desirability of exercising them in a way that is designed to reduce the inequalities of outcome which result from socio-economic disadvantage'. It is in force in both Scotland (since 2018) and Wales (since 2021) and the new Labour government (of 2024) have signalled their intention to bring it into force in due course.[94] Like the PSED, it does not impose any obligation as to outcome or any constraint on the substance of policy, but it does require authorities to seek to understand the likely impact of decisions and to 'ensure that the need to address entrenched inequalities is considered in a systematic way'.[95] In this respect it has potential to direct the attention of health care commissioners, and others engaged in making policy relevant to health, to the relationship between material inequalities and health inequalities and to the impact of their decisions on both.

In the absence of direct duties in relation to socio-economic inequality, the PSED has been used, with mixed success, as a mechanism to challenge policy and decisions which exacerbate socio-economic disadvantage where – as is often the case – that disadvantage intersects with other status such as race, sex or disability.[96] Thus, for example, a series of challenges to the 'bedroom tax' – a government policy to reduce housing benefit payable to those living in social housing who had rooms deemed to be 'spare' – were made on the basis that the decision maker had failed to pay due regard to the disadvantageous impact on those with disabilities and their carers and on women who were victims of domestic violence.[97] Such challenges have been met with mixed success, largely as a result of the relative ease with which decision makers can demonstrate they have complied with the duty, but these claims at least demonstrate the potential of the PSED to tackle these forms of intersectional disadvantage. Of course the PSED is of little help where overlaps between socio-economic disadvantage and status are not easily demonstrated.

---

[94] The Equality Act 2010 (Commencement No. 13) (Scotland) Order 2017, SI 2017/403; The Equality Act 2010 (Authorities subject to a duty regarding Socio-economic Inequalities) (Wales) Regulations 2021, SI 2021/295; Labour Party (n 81).

[95] Government Equalities Office (2010) *The Equality Bill: Duty to Reduce Socio-Economic Inequalities: A Guide*, London: Government Equalities Office, p 4.

[96] S. Fredman (2011) 'The Potential and Limits of an Equal Rights Paradigm in Addressing Poverty', *Stellenbosch Law Review* 22(3): 566–590; J. Sigafoos (2016) 'Using Equality Legislation as a Sword', *International Journal of Discrimination and the Law* 16(2–3): 66–82.

[97] *R (Carmichael) v Secretary of State for Work and Pensions* [2016] UKSC 58.

Use of equality law to tackle socio-economic disadvantage also extends to Article 14 of the ECHR, which is drafted in such a way that socio-economic status and indeed intersectional discrimination may be included within its protective scope. O'Cinneide notes that there are examples of both the European Court of Human Rights (ECtHR) and national courts reading Article 14 in such a way as to give recognition to the vulnerability that arises at the intersections of poverty and status inequality.[98] In *JD*, for example, one of the bedroom tax cases referred to earlier, the ECtHR held that the state owed particular obligations to address the disadvantage caused to the claimant because of her status as a victim of domestic violence taken together with her dependence on welfare support.[99] Nonetheless, according to O'Cinneide, both these developments in the case law and the grasp of the courts on intersectionality remain limited. In any event, Article 14 does not impose on public authorities proactive duties such as the PSED. Even if it can serve as a remedy in respect of individual claimants, therefore, it is unlikely to direct policy makers to pay systematic attention to this dimension of policy making.

The potential of the existing legal framework to address socio-economic inequality – and the health inequality to which it gives rise – is therefore limited and patchy and is contingent upon the ability to demonstrate clear overlap with disadvantage arising from status. Addressing socio-economic equality through creative reliance on measures designed primarily to address status inequality risks, in the words of O'Cinneide, a 'lopsided growth' of intersectional social rights jurisprudence where the impact of poverty and material inequality is overshadowed by the better recognized and strategically more useful status grounds. Further, the lack of a structured legal framework to address socio-economic inequality and the intersection between socio-economic and status related disadvantage has, it is argued, resulted in a failure by policy makers properly to understand and address the relationships between poverty and other forms of disadvantage, including in relation to COVID-19.[100] As a result, law's ability to address structural injustices in relation to health and access to health care is undermined.

Some policy makers already address socio-economic inequalities – both in Scotland and Wales, where the duty is in force, and in a number of public

---

98 C. O'Cinneide (2020) 'The Potential and Pitfalls of Intersectionality in the Context of Social Rights Adjudication' in S. Atrey and P. Dunne (eds) *Intersectionality and Human Rights Law*, London: Bloomsbury, pp 59–82.

99 *JD v United Kingdom* [2019] 10 WLUK 716.

100 See S. Atrey (2019) *Intersectional Discrimination*, Oxford: Oxford University Press; S. Atrey (2023) 'A Prioritarian Account of Gender Equality', in R. Cook (ed) *Frontiers of Gender Equality: Transnational Legal Perspectives*, Pennsylvania: University of Pennsylvania Press, pp 55–67.

authorities in England on a voluntary basis.[101] NICE itself includes the need to reduce health inequalities as one of its core principles which provides that

> we think about equality in relation to the protected characteristics stated in the Equality Act 2010. We also take into account inequalities arising from socioeconomic factors and the circumstances of certain groups of people, such as looked-after children and people who are homeless. If possible, our guidance aims to reduce and not increase identified health inequalities.[102]

Arguably, however, the introduction of a statutory duty to do so has at least the potential to increase the frequency and consistency with which considerations of socio-economic inequality are embedded in decision making. It is unlikely to be a panacea. In the first place much will depend on the approach taken to implementing the duty. Given the relatively recent introduction of the duty in Scotland and Wales it is still too early to assess the impact with confidence but research by the EHRC on its implementation found mixed results. Most authorities had created structures to incorporate formal consideration of poverty and socio-economic disadvantage into the decision-making process but faced challenges in 'developing systems that avoided "box-ticking" consideration of socio-economic disadvantage'.[103] Certainly the effective implementation of the duty does and would need proper support. As with intersectionality, much of the potential of the duty to drive change will depend on the availability of rich and accessible data.

Finally, it is worth noting that an additional duty to have regard to health inequalities exists by virtue of the National Health Service Act 2006. This imposes an obligation on the Secretary of State for Health to 'have regard to the need to reduce inequalities between the people of England with respect to the benefits they can obtain from the health service'.[104] This is drafted very broadly – with scope to include both socio-economic and

---

[101] Recent research by Greater Manchester Poverty Action found that around one in seven councils had adopted a socio-economic duty voluntarily – Greater Manchester Poverty Action (2022) *Briefing on the Current Scale of the Socio-economic Duty in England*, GMPA, available at: https://www.resolvepoverty.org/wp-content/uploads/2022/06/SED-findings-briefing-FINAL-DRAFT-002.pdf (accessed December 2024).

[102] National Institute for Health and Care Excellence (nd) *Our Principles: Principle 9*, available at: https://www.nice.org.uk/about/who-we-are/our-principles (accessed December 2024).

[103] E. Smith, D. Rodriguez and J. Brawner (2021) *Evaluating the Socio-economic Duty in Scotland and Wales*, EHRC, available at: https://www.equalityhumanrights.com/our-work/our-research/evaluating-socio-economic-duty-scotland-and-wales (accessed February 2025).

[104] National Health Service Act 2006, s 1C.

intersectional perspectives on health inequalities – but there has been little opportunity for courts to explore the scope of the duty. It was considered by the Court of Appeal in a claim which involved a challenge to a decision to reduce funding for pharmacies, which, it was argued, would threaten the viability of community pharmacies.[105] The claimant argued that the decision failed properly to take into account the detrimental impact of the potential closure of community pharmacies, which tended to be clustered in areas of greater deprivation. In dismissing the claim the Court of Appeal declined to decide whether the duty to 'have regard' was weaker or otherwise significantly different from the duty to 'have due regard' under the PSED and held that the duty had been satisfied on the facts. It accepted that the Secretary of State 'had very much in mind the potential adverse impact on those in deprived areas, and concluded that they would not be substantially worse' and stressed that, provided the decision maker had proper appreciation of the potential impact – as was the case here – the duty was discharged.[106] The need to reduce inequalities was, the Court noted, only one example of the many factors that the Secretary of State needed to take into account in the discharge of his statutory functions and he was therefore to be afforded substantial discretion in deciding how to balance these.[107] It is not clear, therefore, that this provision can serve to fill the gaps in the PSED in relation to intersectionality and socio-economic disadvantage.

Conclusion

While it would be wrong to overstate the potential of the PSED – and in due course, if implemented, the Socio-Economic Duty – to transform the landscape of health inequalities, it has the potential to make a contribution by requiring decision makers to ensure that important inequalities are not overlooked. As Hepple argued, the Equality Act can been seen as simply one element in the processes of social change and cannot on its own be expected to redress pervasive structural inequalities. Through mechanisms such as the PSED, however, it at least has the potential to 'direct … power into legitimate procedures' which recognize the interests of disadvantaged groups.[108] Above all, the strength of the duty is the creation of an obligation to pay attention. Given the focus on procedure rather than outcome, it is most likely to be effective for decision makers who are willing to take

[105] *R (on the application of Pharmaceutical Services Negotiating Committee) v Secretary of State for Health* [2018] EWCA Civ 1925.

[106] Ibid at 97.

[107] Ibid at 81.

[108] B. Hepple (2014) *Equality: The Legal Framework (2nd Edition)*, Oxford: Hart, at p 228.

steps to tackle inequalities where these are apparent but who – because of a lack of information or attention or diversity of experience – are not always aware of their existence. It is a significant weakness, therefore, that the duties do not currently require attention to be paid to some of the most pressing inequalities.

2

Making Policy

Introduction

A limited budget means that the National Health Service (NHS) cannot fund all available medical interventions. When new drugs or innovations in treatment are trialled and approved, the NHS must decide whether or not to fund the treatment as well as or instead of its current offering for the same condition. Refusal to do so is often controversial – unsurprising, particularly when innovations may offer hope for patients with particularly debilitating or life limiting conditions – attracting criticism from patients, charities and drug companies alike. Even where interventions are funded, some are not available to everybody with a potential to benefit and come with threshold criteria such as age for in vitro fertilization (IVF) or body mass index for bariatric surgery. Sometimes eligible patients need to be prioritized at the point of access – for example, where there are not enough intensive care beds or organs for everyone or where there are waiting lists for hip replacements or treatment for mental health. Rationing can take several forms. While denial is the most obvious example, rationing may also include delay (such as through waiting list management or triage policies), deflection (referral to a different service or provider), deterrence (dissuading patients from seeking a particular intervention by, for example, withholding information) and dilution (provision of a service but in some reduced form).[1]

This chapter and the next explore how (some) policy decisions are made about which treatments to fund and what the access criteria for these treatments should be, and identifies the respects in which the policy-making framework is constrained or facilitated by equality law. The focus of this first

[1] S. Harrison and D. Hunter (1994) *Rationing Health Care*, London: Institute of Public Policy Research; see also R. Robertson (2016) *Six Ways in which NHS Financial Pressures Can Affect Patient Care*, The King's Fund, available at: https://www.kingsfund.org.uk/insight-and-analysis/long-reads/nhs-financial-pressures-patient-care (accessed December 2024).

chapter is on identifying the potential for unlawful discrimination, and the disadvantage and inequality this may cause or reinforce, in a number of aspects of policy making – in particular in relation to decisions made on the basis of cost-effectiveness, including where the methodology involves the use of Quality Adjusted Life Years (QALYs); the use of characteristics such as age as proxies or markers for risk or capacity to benefit in decision making; lack of inclusion in research; and variation in local provision, often referred to as the 'postcode lottery'. The next chapter then explores the circumstances under which equality law may require or permit policy makers to modify a rationing strategy based on cost-effectiveness and treat groups or individuals differently to the rest of the patient population because of the personal characteristics they share in order to be sensitive to their different needs, or to address disadvantage and inequality related to those characteristics.

Cost-effectiveness as a basis for priority setting

Much, though by no means all, priority setting in the NHS is based on cost-effectiveness – the amount of 'health' a treatment or intervention generates per pound when compared with existing – or no – treatment. In this way resources can be targeted at maximizing overall health improvement in the population by buying as much 'health improvement' as possible within the allocated budget. In producing guidance to assist commissioners in making rationing decisions, the National Institute for Health and Care Excellence (NICE) normally uses cost-effectiveness analysis at least as a starting point because 'formally assessing the cost effectiveness of an intervention, service or programme can help decision-makers ensure that maximum gain is achieved from limited resources. If resources are used for interventions or services that are not cost effective, the population as a whole gains fewer benefits'.[2] While cost-effectiveness evaluations form the basis for decision making, NICE makes it clear that final decisions as to whether or not an intervention is recommended should include a wider range of factors, noting that 'decisions about whether to recommend interventions should not be based on cost effectiveness alone' but should also take into account factors including the need to prevent discrimination and promote equity as well as to consider the appropriate 'trade-offs between efficient and equitable allocations of resources'.[3] In developing their Technology Appraisal Guidance – mandatory

[2] National Institute for Health and Care Excellence (2014) *Developing NICE Guidelines: The Manual (PMG 20)*, NICE, 7.2, available at: https://www.nice.org.uk/process/pmg20/resources/developing-nice-guidelines-the-manual-pdf-72286708700869 (accessed December 2024).

[3] Ibid at 7.8.

guidance for funding of medicines, diagnostic techniques and surgical interventions which the NHS is required by law to fund – NICE applies 'modifiers' to its cost-effectiveness analysis to take into account particular considerations that arise when the intervention under consideration is for an illness that is particularly severe, or particularly rare. These modifiers are discussed in more detail in what follows.

Within the scope of their discretion, health care commissioners, including individual Integrated Care Boards (ICBs), then have their own approaches to priority setting, usually under the auspices of a policy or ethical framework which sets out the key principles that will be used to determine which services to commission and for whom. For many commissioning decisions, the relevant NICE guidance will form the starting point for decision making but – unlike NICE – ICBs and other commissioners are required to make funding decisions within the context of an overall fixed budget and may therefore be unable to fund all recommended treatments and may need to choose between them. Cost-effectiveness is, again, central but not determinative in most cases. By way of example, some ICBs currently use a matrix under which various factors are scored for each medical intervention under consideration in order to assist in decision making – these factors include cost-effectiveness, quality of evidence, magnitude of health improvement, the degree to which the intervention is preventative and the impact of the intervention on health inequalities.[4] NHS England, which directly commissions some highly specialized and public health services, as well as overseeing the work of the ICBs, states in its own Ethical Framework that 'new treatments should be assessed for funding … according to the principles of clinical effectiveness, safety, cost-effectiveness and then prioritised in a way which supports consistent and affordable decision-making' but also notes that 'in making commissioning decisions, priority may be given to health services targeting the needs of sub-groups of the population who currently have poorer than average health outcomes (including morbidity and mortality) or poorer access to services'.[5]

If we are concerned with avoiding discrimination and reducing health inequalities, cost-effectiveness strategies will sometimes need to be modified because priority setting on the basis of cost-effectiveness alone – without

---

4 Staffordshire and Stoke on Trent Integrated Care Board (8 July 2022) *Policy on the Prioritisation of Healthcare Resources*, available at: https://staffsstoke.icb.nhs.uk/your-nhs-integrated-care-board/our-publications/governance-handbook/all-policies/commissioning/icb-policy-on-the-prioritisation-of-healthcare-resourcesmaster/?layout=file (accessed February 2025).

5 NHS Commissioning Board (2013) *Commissioning Policy: Ethical Framework for Priority Setting and Resource Allocation*, NHS Commissioning Board, available at: https://www.england.nhs.uk/wp-content/uploads/2013/04/cp-01.pdf (accessed December 2024).

consideration of other factors – may produce or reinforce inequalities, including for groups sharing protected characteristics. For example, a treatment for serious illness which is clinically effective but very expensive may not be cost-effective when compared with other treatments for less severe conditions in terms of the amount of overall 'health' the money can buy. Funding may therefore be spent on patients who are – health-wise – already better off. Likewise, a decision to fund only the cheaper of two equally effective (in the general population) drugs for a particular condition may mean that some are excluded from access (because, for example, their disability or religious beliefs mean that the cheaper drug is not accessible for them). While policy frameworks for commissioning do take into account a range of other factors, as we have seen, one key question for this chapter and the next is when commissioners could be required to modify a cost-effectiveness approach, or could choose to do so, and in what circumstances, in order to comply with the requirements of equality law.

While it is not the only relevant consideration, in determining whether a commissioning policy or decision complies with the provisions of the Equality Act or with Article 14 of the European Convention on Human Rights, the key legal question will often be whether the policy amounts to a proportionate means to achieve a legitimate aim. This is a test used to decide whether a policy is legally justified when it disadvantages those who share a protected characteristic (potential indirect discrimination) or where it uses sex or age as a barrier to accessing a particular intervention (potential direct discrimination).[6] The aim of commissioners in restricting access to a safe and otherwise clinically effective service will of course normally be to ensure that they are able to act within their budgetary constraints and to distribute resources as effectively or fairly (as determined by their ethical framework) as possible. This is, it is suggested, likely to be legitimate. For claims made under the Equality Act, we know that certainly in an employment law context, cost saving, without more, is unlikely to amount to legitimate aim – employers may not engage in discriminatory behaviour simply because it is cheaper to do so. However, courts have treated aims expressed in terms of prudent use of resources more sympathetically. Thus, while the Court of Appeal in *Woodcock*, an employment case, agreed that 'considerations based on cost alone, or on economic or financial factors alone, cannot justify treatment that is discriminatory on grounds of age',[7] subsequent cases have noted that

6 Direct age discrimination can be justified as a proportionate means of achieving a legitimate aim under Equality Act 2010, s 13. The provision of single sex services can be justified where this amounts to a proportionate means to achieve a legitimate aim and other conditions are met under Schedule 3, para 27.

7 *Woodcock v. Cumbria PCT*, [2012] EWCA Civ 330 at 55.

it is 'legitimate for an organisation to seek to break even year on year and to make decisions about the allocation of its resources'.[8] This is even more likely to be the case in relation to the provision of publicly funded services where – as will be discussed in detail in Chapter 4 – courts recognize the complex and deeply political nature of the choices that need to be made by commissioners and tend to take a deferential approach. The same applies to decisions about whether discrimination under Article 14 is justified. In *SC*, a challenge to legislation establishing a 'two child limit' for the payment of child benefit on the basis that (among other things) it amounted to indirect sex discrimination, the Supreme Court held that 'protecting the economic well-being of the country' and 'ensuring that a benefits system is fair and reasonable' were both legitimate aims.[9] Against this background, and while the question has not been addressed directly in this context so far, it is difficult to imagine courts deciding that aims of targeting scarce resources most efficiently to those most likely to benefit or achieving a cost-efficient distribution of health care resources are not legitimate.

A more difficult legal question – and perhaps a more likely basis for legal challenge to commissioning policy – is whether the means chosen to achieve the chosen distributive aims are proportionate: are they appropriate and necessary to achieve those aims and has a fair balance been struck between the adverse impact of the policy on those with protected characteristics and the likely benefits of the measure?[10] The remainder of this chapter explores this question further in the context of a number of different aspects of policy making, beginning with an aspect of the methodology used to establish cost-effectiveness which has proved particularly controversial from a discrimination perspective – the use of QALYs.

Quality Adjusted Life Years

A standard approach for determining the effectiveness of a given medical intervention, used across institutions, is the QALY. QALYs combine the health related quality of life a patient may expect to have after a medical treatment or intervention with the likely duration of that effect – often remaining life expectancy. The number of additional QALYs generated by a new drug or other intervention can then be combined with its cost to create an incremental cost-effectiveness ratio (ICER) – the cost

---

8 See, most recently, *Heskett v. Secretary of State for Justice*, [2019] UKEAT/0149/18/DA at 25.

9 *R (SC) v Secretary of State for Work and Pensions* [2021] UKSC 26.

10 See Introduction and Chapter 4 for a more detailed account of the different elements of the proportionality test.

per QALY. In this way QALYs provide a 'common currency' to allow those with responsibility for resource allocation to compare the costs and benefits of a range of interventions and new drugs and technologies and to set priorities accordingly. QALYs are used to inform decisions about resource allocation by NICE, particularly in their evaluation of new and existing health technologies, and are used more widely in research which informs commissioning decisions nationally and locally. Indeed, NICE recommends they be used in the development of clinical guidelines whenever there is suitable data to support this.[11] Generally speaking, where the ICER for a particular treatment or intervention is below £20,000, NICE will consider it cost-effective and recommend (or occasionally require) it be funded. There is no upper or lower limit above or below which NICE will never or always recommend funding but NICE guidelines make clear that their advisory bodies will be expected to provide explicit reasons for deciding not to fund an intervention where the ICER falls below £20,000, and likewise to make an increasingly strong case for deciding to fund interventions where the ICER exceeds £20,000.[12] NICE explains that its approach 'takes into account the "opportunity cost" of recommending one intervention instead of another, highlighting that there would have been other potential uses of the resource. It includes the needs of other people using services now or in the future who are not known and not represented'.[13] This reflects the simple fact that more money spent funding one intervention means less money available for another and a corresponding disadvantage caused to a, normally, unidentified group of patients.

The use of QALYs by heath care commissioners in the UK and further afield has raised concerns about discrimination, in particular in relation to age and disability. Indeed, in 1992 the State of Oregon in the United States made significant amendments to its plan to prioritize Medicaid spending using QALY-based methodology because lawyers at the US Department of Health and Human Services raised concerns that the methodology was not compliant with the Americans with Disabilities Act. The Health and Human Services Secretary wrote to the *New York Times* to say that '[o]ur principal concern is that Oregon's plan in substantial part values the life of a person with a disability less than the life of a person without a disability.

[11] National Institute for Health and Care Excellence (2014) *Developing NICE Guidelines: The Manual,* NICE, updated 29 May 2024, available at: https://www.nice.org.uk/process/pmg20 (accessed December 2024). NICE suggests where data is not available, other methods of determining cost-effectiveness such as life years gained, cases averted or more disease specific outcomes be used.

[12] Ibid at 173.

[13] Ibid.

This premise is discriminatory and inconsistent with the Americans with Disabilities Act'.[14]

The concerns about QALYs and discrimination tend to fall into three broad categories:

- a concern that measuring effectiveness using quality and duration of health improvement is inherently discriminatory on grounds of age and disability;
- a concern that the methods chosen to measure health related quality of life are themselves discriminatory on grounds of age and disability; and
- a concern that – because all health improvements are treated as equal – the methodology fails to prioritize those who are worst off (a problem with cost-effectiveness more generally).

The first concern is that using length and quality of life as measures of effectiveness is necessarily going to disadvantage those whose remaining life expectancy is shorter – because of age or life limiting conditions – as well as those whose health related quality of life is reduced through disability. Other things being equal, treating a 50-year-old will normally produce fewer QALYs than treating a 30-year-old and more than treating a 70-year-old; and a 50-year-old with a life expectancy of 55 because of a life limiting disability will generate fewer QALYs than a 50-year-old with a life expectancy of 83. Likewise, an intervention which can extend life expectancy without improving health related quality of life will generate more QALYs in those whose quality of life is better to start with than in those for whom health related quality of life is poor. This has the potential to give rise to a number of problems. If QALYs were to be used to decide which of two individual patients it is most cost-effective to treat, when there are only resources to treat one, then the answer would be to treat the patient who is younger, or who has a normal life expectancy, or whose health related quality of life will be higher post-intervention because of absence of disability. At a policy level QALYs may indicate that particular treatments are cost-effective only in patients with a minimum remaining life expectancy and therefore should be denied to older patients or those with life limiting conditions. And treatments which only or mainly benefit older patients or those with life limiting conditions may not be cost-effective to fund at all. This may amount to direct or indirect age or disability discrimination where it is not possible to legally justify the approach taken.

[14] L. Sullivan (1 September 1992) 'Oregon Health Plan Is Unfair to the Disabled', *New York Times*, available at: https://www.nytimes.com/1992/09/01/opinion/l-oregon-health-plan-is-unfair-to-the-disabled-659492.html (accessed December 2024).

Policy makers – and NICE in particular – have tended to respond to these concerns in three ways. First is to note that while all QALYs are normally regarded as equal, the weights attached to QALYs may be modified in some circumstances. In relation to Technology Appraisal Guidance (which is mandatory), NICE uses a 'severity modifier' in its calculation of the ICER. This modifier is intended to capture the idea that each additional QALY generated is likely to be more valuable for patients with severe disease than for those less severe disease. Measures of severity capture both quality and quantity of life lost to the disease. QALYs produced in the treatment of severe disease are then given greater weight in the calculation of the ICER, meaning that medicines that treat severe disease are more likely to prove cost-effective. In other words, NICE is likely to be willing pay more per QALY for a medicine if it is used to treat severe disease. The severity modifier replaces an earlier 'end of life' modifier which assigned higher value to medicines and interventions which extend life at the very end of life. The severity modifier therefore can potentially meet some of the concerns about disability discrimination as well as age by ensuring that medicines that treat life shortening and more severe conditions are more likely to be funded, even where they would not prove cost-effective on an ordinary QALY analysis.[15]

A second response to the charge that using QALYs gives rise to age and disability discrimination is that, while the use of QALYs to measure effectiveness has the *potential* to disadvantage on grounds of age or disability in the ways described earlier, this does not happen in practice. First, because NICE (and ICBs) generally operate at a 'macro' level – determining which from a range of possible treatments or interventions are most cost-effective for society, or a local population, as a whole – rather than at an individual level. Where choices must be made between individual patients this tends to happen at clinical level – triage, waiting list management, and so on – where other principles, particularly clinical need, are central.[16] In relation to age, for example, it is argued that it is NICE's normal practice to 'assume that what applies to one age group within a particular appraisal will apply inter alia to others' and to aggregate the QALYs an intervention produces across a range of ages and conditions.[17] Thus, most of NICE's recommendations

[15] National Institute for Health and Care Excellence (2022) *NICE Health Technology Evaluations: The manual*, NICE, updated 31 October 2023 at 6.2.12, available at: https://www.nice.org.uk/process/pmg36/chapter/introduction-to-health-technology-evaluation (accessed December 2024).

[16] See, for example, NHS England (2022) *Guidance for Emergency Departments: Initial Assessment*, NHS England, available at: https://www.england.nhs.uk/guidance-for-emergency-departments-initial-assessment/ (accessed December 2024) (Chapter 7 considers prioritization in intensive care during the COVID-19 pandemic).

[17] A. Stevens N. Doyle, P. Littlejohns and M. Docherty (2012) 'National Institute for Health and Clinical Excellence Appraisal and Ageism', *Journal of Medical Ethics* 31: 373–375.

do not restrict access by age – treatments are generally recommended for all ages or for none, although there are exceptions – and much of the theoretical potential for QALYs to generate discriminatory results is thereby avoided. The same is true in relation to disability. This does not eliminate the potential for discrimination altogether, however. While there are very few age stratified results among NICE's recommendations (where access to a particular intervention is recommended only for a particular age group) some do exist (one example – access to IVF – is discussed in detail in Chapter 6) and it remains the case that interventions which would primarily or only benefit the older population (rather than society as a whole) are able to produce fewer QALYs and may not be funded as a result.

Harris and others, however, have responded to this defence of its methodology by NICE by noting that the fact that the QALY methodology does not disadvantage older patients in practice is not the end of the story as far as age discrimination is concerned. The argument, he suggests, gives us

> no reasons to suppose that suggestion of unjustified discrimination on the grounds of life expectancy does not arise simply because NICE does not, in point of fact, put its money where its mouth is. To suggest that people are a low priority for health resources, are less worth helping, are less worth the concern and respect of the State as expressed through its publicly funded bodies like the NHS and indeed NICE is offensive. It is an attack on their dignity and standing in the community, and therefore prejudicial and unacceptable. That these principles have not, and according to NICE officials, probably will never be, put into practice does not mean that the public espousal of them and the ageist ideas that inform them do not amount to discrimination.[18]

A third response is that procedures are in place to mitigate against the possibility that their appraisals will give rise to unfair age or disability discrimination in these situations. Calculations of cost-effectiveness using QALYs are only a starting point and, once done, consideration is given to whether or not to fund treatment that exceeds the recommended ICER for the population or for particular groups, taking into account a wider range of considerations.[19] Chapter 3 looks in more detail at how equality law may impact on the way that decisions to do so are made. As we will see, it is not always clear how other concerns are taken into account and what trade-offs will be acceptable.

---

18 J. Harris and S. Regmi (2012) 'Ageism and Equality', *Journal of Medical Ethics* 38: 263–266; see also G. Cupit (1998) 'Justice, Age and Veneration', *Ethics* 108(4): 702–718.

19 National Institute for Health and Care Excellence (n 15); see also Stevens et al (n 17).

The second concern, or category of concerns, with the use of QALYs relates to the measurement of health related quality of life. Even if it is accepted that cost-effectiveness is an appropriate basis on which to allocate resources and that prioritizing interventions which generate the most QALYs for equivalent cost is an appropriate methodology for measuring cost-effectiveness, there remain difficulties in capturing and valuing health states, which may build in discrimination on grounds of disability and age or other protected grounds. The data on which NICE and health care commissioners rely to measure and value health states come from two main sources. The first is from patients themselves. This describes health states – patients undergoing clinical trials (and sometimes their carers) are asked to describe their health state before and after treatment. The most commonly used measure is the EQ-5D-3L – which asks patients to rate their health state on one of three levels (no problems, some problems, extreme problems) against five dimensions of health (mobility, self-care, usual activities, pain/discomfort and anxiety/depression). The next step is to ascribe values to those health states in order to translate them into QALYs by ranking them on a scale. For this stage the views of the public are sought and NICE are clear that utility values should normally be derived from public opinion.[20]

Research suggests that both patients and the public may report in ways which distort the true improvement. The public generally overestimate the impact of impairments for those who have them and as a result can significantly undervalue the health related quality of life of those living with disabilities.[21] It was this concern that was at the heart of the controversy over the Oregon plan and what eventually led to its modification. On the other hand, while patients are usually best placed to assess their own health, there is still some concern that patients assessing health states based on their own experience may not adequately reflect on the extent to which they have been able to adapt to their conditions and may therefore overestimate their health states.

Another problem is that the method may fail to capture the social causes of disability. The impact of mobility impairment on quality of life will depend very much on the extent to which the environment is designed or adapted to be inclusive. A world in which it was possible for an individual with mobility impairment to move with ease to and around workplaces and social spaces would be one in which a higher value might be ascribed to that state of health. Existing measures of health related quality of life do not

[20] National Institute for Health and Care Excellence (n 15) at 4.3.1.

[21] G. Helgesson, O. Ernstsson, M. Astrom and K. Burstrom (2020) 'Whom Should We Ask? A Systematic Literature Review of the Arguments Regarding the Most Accurate Source of Information for Valuation of Health States', *Quality of Life Research*, 29: 1465–1482.

take into account the extent to which negative experiences of the patient result from the existence of external barriers or a failure of institutions to make reasonable adjustments, as they are required to do by law. This means that the existence of structural discrimination may then result in the health state of an individual with a disability being undervalued, compounding disadvantage. A similar problem exists in relation to age. Here, the concern is that the method used to calculate health related quality of life fails to take into account the experiences and priorities of older patients. It is argued that the currently used measure of health related quality of life – the EQ-5D-3L – may, for example, overstate the importance of physical functioning and understate the importance of other indicators; in addition there is evidence that the measure is not sufficiently sensitive to factors such as changes in expectations and perceptions of health with age. This may lead to an underestimation of health related qualify of life in older people which, in turn, will impact on the number of QALYs an intervention is capable of generating in an older patient.

The extent to which this has the potential to translate to discrimination when policy decisions are made is not easily assessed. What matters in many cases is not the value ascribed to the quality of life before or after the intervention but the measure of the *improvement* in health related quality of life – and this may remain unaffected by an undervaluation of health states provided this is consistent. Of more concern would be the impact on treatment that improves length rather than quality of life because if there is an underestimation of health related quality of life in these circumstances, then the number of QALYs generated by the intervention will be reduced and the cost per QALY be higher than it should be – risking that the intervention not be funded.[22]

Thus there is considerable debate as to whether the use of QALYs in the methodology of NICE (and other commissioners) amounts to prima facie disability and/or age discrimination; and whether – where it does so – it is ethically justifiable. Whether or not it gives rise to unlawful, or at least potentially unlawful, discrimination, or is legally justifiable, has not been considered by the courts. The government's view, set out during the consultation process on the implementation of the age discrimination provisions in the Equality Act, is that fundamental changes in NICE's methodologies are unlikely to be necessary in order to comply with the legislation.[23] The choice of QALYs as a methodological tool will not in

[22] I am grateful for a useful conversation on this point with Professor Matthew Taylor, Hayden Holmes and Heather Davies at the York Health Economics Consortium.

[23] Government Equalities Office (2012) *Equality Act 2010: Banning Age Discrimination in Services, Public Function and Associations: Government Response to the Consultation on Exceptions*, London: Government Equalities Office, section 3.5.

itself amount to unlawful discrimination. Unlawful discrimination will only arise where policy generated by use of QALYs actually disadvantages a particular group (whether defined by age or disability or some other characteristic) and cannot be justified (indirect discrimination); or where such policy leads to the less favourable treatment of a patient because of a characteristic of theirs – because it has resulted in the use of age limits for access to treatment, for example – and again (at least in the case of age) cannot be justified (direct discrimination).

Where this does happen, the lawfulness of the measure in question will turn on justification. A number of issues are likely to be particularly relevant here. First, it is certainly likely that if it can be shown a decision was reached on the basis of inaccurate and discriminatory data it will not be proportionate. Second, it is likely to be relevant to an assessment of proportionality whether or not NICE, or other commissioners, have properly considered whether the policy gives rise to prima facie discrimination and, if so, whether it can be justified. This is something they are in any case obliged to do in order to comply with the Public Sector Equality Duty (PSED). In *R (Coll)* for example, the Ministry of Justice was not able to justify its policy of unequal provision of hostels to which male and female prisoners could be released on parole. There were 94 hostels across the country for men but only six for women, which meant that women were much more likely to be required to live in a hostel a long way from home and family. This amounted to prima facie sex discrimination and could not be justified as a proportionate means of achieving a legitimate aim under the separate sex services exemption of the Equality Act because the Ministry of Justice had not 'addressed the possible impacts upon women, assessed whether there is a disadvantage, how significant it is and what might be done to mitigate it'.[24] ICBs or other commissioners relying on NICE guidance should also be aware that the PSED is non-delegable and should ensure that they carry out this exercise themselves.[25]

Also relevant to the ability of commissioners to legally justify any prima facie discrimination which arises may be the opportunity of individual patients (or groups of patients) to ask for an exception to be made. Courts have not taken a consistent approach to the question of the importance of this to the assessment of proportionality. It was a relevant consideration in determining proportionality under Article 14 of the European Convention on Human Rights in *AL (Serbia)*, where the Court concluded that the government policy of using family status to determine eligibility for indefinite leave to remain was proportionate, in part because 'it permitted

[24] *R (Coll) v Secretary of State for Justice* [2017] UKSC 40 at 42.

[25] *R (Bracking) v Secretary of State for Work and Pensions* [2013] EWCA Civ 1345 at 59.

compelling claims by those falling outside the policy to be recognised and accommodated'.[26] On the other hand, in an employment context under the Equality Act, the Supreme Court held that 'where it is justified to have a general rule, then the existence of that rule will usually justify the treatment which results from it' and concluded that requiring employers to justify the application of rules to individual employees would normally negate the value of having a rule in the first place.[27] The circumstances under which equality law may permit or require commissioners to make exceptions to general policy – for individuals or groups – is considered in detail in Chapter 3.

These points aside, it is – it is suggested – likely that when engaging in any balancing exercise to determining the proportionality of a policy measure, that courts will be slow to find that the disadvantage caused to a particular group by the policy decision outweighs an overall aim of distributing resources so as to maximize health gains in the national (for NICE or NHS England) or local (for ICBs) populations. While this will of course be context dependent, courts – as we will explore in detail in Chapter 4 – tend to give considerable weight to the perspective of the authorities who are engaged in economic and social policy, particularly where this involves allocation of resources, in recognition of the difficult and often political nature of the decisions involved. In particular, while the disadvantage to the individual patient or group challenging an allocation decision may be compelling, courts are ever conscious of the opportunity cost of the decision – the divestment of resources from other unknown patients (who may themselves be even more disadvantaged, including in relation to protected characteristics) which would be required.

What of the concern advanced by Harris to the effect that, even if no distributive inequalities are produced in practice, the use of QALYs in priority setting and resources allocation conveys a message that older people and those with disabilities are less valued than others by commissioners? This is certainly something that could be considered by authorities in their exercise of the PSED, although it is an issue the case law has yet to address. Many accounts of discrimination law, as seen in the Introduction, recognize that the law has a role to play in addressing harms that are not simply distributive, including forms of stigma and stereotyping that can undermine dignity.[28] Where policy making creates a perception that some individuals are less valued because of their characteristics, even though no distributive unfairness results, commissioners should be mindful of this and

---

26 *AI (Serbia) v Secretary of State for the Home Department* [2008] UKHL 42 at 3.

27 *Seldon v Clarkson, Wright and Jakes (a Partnership)* [2010] UKSC 16 at 65 and 66.

28 S. Fredman (2016) 'Substantive Equality Revisited', *International Journal of Constitutional Law* 14: 712–738.

consider how this might be mitigated through transparency about policy making, through careful communication, and through steps to ensure that no disadvantage is created in practice.

Using characteristics as proxies

Some of our protected characteristics – perhaps most obviously our sex, age and disabilities – can be of crucial relevance to diagnosis and treatment. Sometimes they may be determinative and sometimes they may be a key factor in determining the risk or prognosis of illness. Likewise, clinical trial data will provide statistical information about the relationship of these characteristics to the effectiveness or side effects of treatment. For these reasons, policy makers will make decisions based on personal characteristics. IVF may be recommended only in a certain age group because of evidence of its effectiveness; screening for breast cancer is routinely undertaken only in women (or trans men) even though men (and trans women) get breast cancer too; breast cancer screening is also routinely done for a particular age group because of evidence that the risk is lower and the available tests less effective outside that group. These examples are considered in detail in Chapters 5 and 6.

It is clear that clinicians also use personal characteristics to make decisions about clinically appropriate treatment options for individual patients. This may arise because – as for policy makers – a characteristic is a useful proxy for the risks and harms a course of treatment may produce in an individual patient. For example, there may be a strong statistical correlation between age and risk and no reliable test for assessing biological age,[29] although others caution against overstating this likelihood. For example, Grimley Evans has argued that:

> We have grown so inured to using a patient's age as an excuse for laziness in investigating him or her properly that we have failed to build into our scientific paradigms proper identification of the true physiological determinants of outcome. … If one knows enough about the physiological condition of the patient, age should drop off the end of the predictive equation for outcome.[30]

---

[29] See, for example, Department of Health (2012) *The Impact of Patient Age on Clinical Decision Making in Oncology*, Department of Health, available at: https://www.gov.uk/government/publications/the-impact-of-patient-age-on-clinical-decision-making-in-oncology (accessed December 2024), which suggests that the lack of an objective way of assessing biological age in some contexts may lead to clinicians using chronological age as a proxy.

[30] J. Grimley Evans (2003) 'Age Discrimination: Implications of the Ageing Process' in S. Fredman and S. Spencer (eds) *Age as an Equality Issue*, Oxford: Hart, pp 11–20.

There is relatively little research on the ways in which age is used by individual clinicians but that which there is suggests that chronological age may be used as a proxy for a number of indicators including risk or capacity to benefit. Thus, for example, some clinicians participating in a study of the influence of patient age on decision making on coronary care, noted that a patient's chronological age may influence their views on whether to refer them for surgery as it served as a proxy for the risk of mortality or the development of complications.[31] Assessment of a patient on the basis of chronological age – rather than on the basis of actual frailty, comorbidity and polypharmacy – may also involve unwarranted 'ageist' assumptions, such as, for example, mistaken assumptions about the preferences or lifestyle needs of an individual patient and therefore of the 'benefit' an intervention is likely to produce. One doctor, for example, noted that 'they wouldn't want an angiogram if they were over 70', another that 'I don't think bypass surgery in an 87 year old is in their interests'.[32]

There is certainly evidence that age is used in this way. Age appears to affect preventative care, the likelihood of investigation and referral, and the type of care and treatment (if any) subsequently available, across a range of specialities. Almost ten years ago a report by the Royal College of Surgeons found that, as patient age increases, the likelihood of developing certain conditions increases but the likelihood of surgical intervention for those conditions declines. A clear example is in the case of cancer services. Most cancers are more prevalent in later life. Over half of all cancers diagnosed are in people aged 65 or over; a third of all cancers diagnosed are in those aged 75 or over.[33] Despite this age profile, however, a 2012 study by the Department of Health concluded that there is a marked decline in referral for more 'intensive' treatment – including surgical intervention – as patient age increases.[34]

The increasing likelihood of the presence of comorbidity and complex health and physiological changes in the older patient may be one explanation for the lower rate of surgical and (other more intensive) interventions for the treatment of cancer in the older age group. The more invasive the treatment, the greater the risks may be for those with more complex health states – and this may in turn affect both the willingness of the clinician to refer a patient for particular treatment and/or the wiliness of the patient to undergo the treatment. However, a number of studies which have attempted to control

---

31 C. Harries, D. Forrest, N. Harvey, A. McClelland and A. Bowling (2007) 'Which Doctors are Influenced by a Patient's Age? A Multi Method Study of Angina Treatment in General Practice, Cardiology and Gerontology', *Quality and Safety in Health Care*, 16: 23–27.

32 Ibid.

33 Department of Health (n 29).

34 Ibid.

for the presence of comorbidity and other factors in their assessment of the role of chronological age in access to services have found that the patterns of treatment could not be wholly accounted for in this way. The 2012 Department of Health study, for example, concluded that, in making decisions about access to oncology services, and in particular in determining the level of intensity of the treatment which should be provided, 'clinicians may over rely on chronological age as a proxy for other factors which are often but not necessarily associated with age, such as comorbidities or frailty'.[35] And a recent study concluded that 'clinician decisions about breast cancer treatments for older women are at least partially driven by age-based assumptions about what older women want or can cope with', rather than by evidence of actual frailty or comorbidity.[36]

Making decisions about individuals because of their sex or race or other personal characteristics rather than an assessment of their own needs and merits is of course often argued to be wrong simply because it fails to treat them as individuals, in addition to any distributive harm that may result. This is reflected in the fact that under the Equality Act 2010, direct discrimination (other than for age and in relation to some specific exceptions and positive action) cannot be justified. This means that it is generally unlawful to make decisions based on proxies or stereotypes unless their use reflects real and relevant differences between those who have the characteristic and those who do not. This is not the case only in relation to uses of stereotypes that are pernicious or untrue. Courts have also raised concerns about the use of 'statistical discrimination' where characteristics are used as proxies for other kinds of relevant information, based on available data. In *Roma Rights*,[37] for example, the House of Lords found that immigration officers at Prague airport had directly discriminated against Roma in implementing a pre-entry clearance scheme at Prague airport because they had used the fact of being Roma as a (according to the Court of Appeal, statistically very accurate) proxy for the likelihood an individual was planning to seek asylum. Lady Hale held that 'the object of the legislation is to ensure that each person is treated as an individual and not assumed to be like other members of the group'.[38] Likewise in *Test Achats*, a case at the European Court of Justice concerning the charging of cheaper premiums for women's car insurance because of statistical evidence that women were less likely to make claims than men,

[35] Ibid.

[36] D. Neal, J. Morgan, R. Kenny, T. Ormerod and M. Reed et al (2022) 'Is There Evidence of Age Bias in Breast Cancer Health Professionals' Treatment of Older Patients?', *European Journal of Surgical Oncology* 48: 2401–2407.

[37] *R (European Roma Rights Centre and Others) v Immigration Officer at Prague Airport and Another* [2004] UKHL 55 at 74.

[38] Ibid at 82.

it was held that using sex as a proxy for risk in this way was incompatible with the principle of equal treatment. Aside from situations where it could be established 'with certainty' that there are relevant differences between men and women, the Court of Justice suggested that positive action was the only way to justify sex discrimination.[39]

The position is slightly different in relation to age (where direct discrimination can be justified under the Equality Act) and sex (where the 'single sex service' exemption of the Equality Act may apply) and under Article 14 (where direct discrimination can potentially be justified in relation to all characteristics). In these cases the use of a characteristic as a proxy might be lawful where it amounts to a proportionate means to achieve a legitimate aim. In this respect, many of the points made in the discussion of the justification of QALYs and cost-effectiveness, earlier, will be equally applicable in this context. There are, however, a few additional points of relevance. First, when considering the use of age in decision making by individual clinicians in relation to individual patients, the legitimate aim is unlikely to be related (and certainly not explicitly so) to efficiency or fairness in resource allocation.[40] More likely is that doctors will be aiming to act in the best interests of the patient by not exposing them to any potentially harmful or unnecessary intervention. While the courts have accepted 'protective' aims as legitimate in an employment context, this has not been without some misgiving, and they are perhaps more vulnerable to challenge than are the other legitimate aims considered earlier in the context of policy making. In this respect it is worth remembering that in other areas of law regulating the doctor–patient relationship, such as informed consent, there has been, in recent years, a marked move away from 'medical paternalism' and towards patient autonomy; doctors may not withhold information from patients for fear of causing them distress unless in exceptional circumstances and may certainly not do so in order to prevent 'the patient from making an informed choice … which the doctor considers to be contrary to her best interests'.[41]

Second, in relation to proportionality, there are a number of additional considerations which may be important in this context. First is the possibility of an alternative to using age as a proxy, such as an alternative test or individual assessment. Given that a measure or treatment must be

---

[39] *Association Belges des Consommateurs Test-Achats ASBL v Conseil des Ministres (C-236/09)*. It should be remembered that there is a 'single sex services' exemption in the Equality Act (Schedule 3, para 27) which enables service providers to provide services exclusively to members of one sex where this is a proportionate means of achieving a legitimate aim and where specified conditions are met.

[40] Although see discussion in Chapter 7 of the allocation of intensive care beds during the COVID-19 pandemic.

[41] *Montgomery v. Lanarkshire Health Board*, [2015] UKSC 11 at 91.

'necessary' to achieving an aim in order to be proportionate, the availability of an alternative may suggest it cannot be justified. Of course the existence of an alternative will depend on the context and indeed on the way the legitimate aim is itself described. When dealing with the use of an age limit in a policy which applies to a large section of the population (such as a cut-off for funding of IVF or invitation to cancer screening) individual assessment may be unrealistic and expensive and not an appropriate mechanism to achieve a cost-effective distribution of resources. It was recognized in *Bibi*, for example, that the cost and administrative workability of an alternative test are relevant considerations.[42] Individual assessment is more likely to be realistic in relation to the use of age by individual clinicians. Chronological age may be a useful starting point, in some cases, for diagnosis or choice of treatment pathway. However, where clinicians have the opportunity to assess, in some respects at least, whether what may generally be true for patients of a particular age is in fact true for the patient in front of them, basing decisions on a failure to do so may be unlawful.

Finally, and related, the accuracy of the proxy may also be relevant. Accuracy should matter in proportionality assessment. The less accurate the proxy, the more people are likely to be on the 'wrong side' of the line and excluded from access to the benefit in question. Certainly, in an employment context, the European Court of Justice has been prepared to find disproportionate those measures using age as a cut-off where this is based on questionable or no evidence. In *Prigge*, for example, the Court was asked to consider a rule in a collective agreement requiring compulsory retirement of airline pilots at 60, where age was used as a proxy for a decline in the physical capacities needed to perform the role safely. While apparently accepting that age can sometimes stand as a proxy for physical capacity, the Court found the choice of 60 to be disproportionate in this case because there was no evidence to support it. National and international legislation permitted pilots to continue working in certain circumstances until 65, and no evidence had been provided to justify a departure from this standard.[43] We return to this issue in the context of the use of age limits in public health screening and vaccination programmes in Chapter 5.

Research

Commissioning decisions – whatever the principles used to prioritize between treatments – rest on evidence of clinical safety and effectiveness in different groups. Sometimes decisions not to fund a treatment for a

[42] *R (Bibi) v Secretary of State for the Home Department* [2013] EWCA Civ 322.

[43] *Prigge v. Deutsche Lufthansa* C 447/09, [2011] IRLR 1052.

particular group may be made because there is an absence of evidence of clinical effectiveness or safety rather than because of positive evidence that the health gains are small or that the intervention poses significant risks for that group. This may, in turn, result in what is sometimes termed 'epistemic injustice' where the fairness of a decision may be undermined by evidential failings, no matter how carefully the decision makers had attempted to adhere to principles of equality and distributive justice.[44]

It is common, for example, for older people to be excluded from clinical trials. As a result, there is a lack of evidence of the effect of many drugs (or other treatments) on the older population, resulting in understandable reluctance on the part of policy makers and clinicians to recommend or fund those interventions for this age group.[45] The reasons given for the exclusion of older people from trials include the increased likelihood of the presence of comorbidity/polypharmacy, which may complicate (and increase the cost of) a successful trial; and concerns about the ethics of involving 'vulnerable' patients in research.[46] The discriminatory impact of excluding older people from clinical trials was recognized by the government during their consultation on the extension of the prohibition of age discrimination to the NHS and they stated their intention to work with organizations responsible for the design of clinical trials to improve the rate of inclusion of older people.[47] The National Institute for Health and Care Research has also recognized the need to improve diversity and inclusion among research participants and has included this goal in its Research Inclusion Strategy 2022–2027.[48]

Concerns have also been raised about uneven data across the breadth of health care research arising from a lack of representation in the design, analysis and reporting of data.[49] In relation to pain, for example – where lived experience is particularly important to determining appropriate intervention – knowledge creation has often been based on 'majority white, middle class, Eurocentric populations' giving rise to a risk of unequal

[44] J.A. Michaels (2021) 'Potential for Epistemic Injustice in Evidence-based Healthcare Policy and Guidance', *Journal of Medical Ethics* 47: 417–422.

[45] Centre for Policy on Ageing (2009) *Ageism and Age Discrimination in Secondary Health Care in the United Kingdom*, Centre for Policy on Ageing, section 8.

[46] Ibid.

[47] Government Equalities Office (2012) *Equality Act 2010: Banning Age Discrimination in Services, Public Functions and Associations: Government Response to the Consultation on Exceptions*, London: Government Equalities Office, section 3.5.

[48] National Institute for Health and Care Research (2022) *Equality, Diversity and Inclusion Strategy 2022–2027*, available at: https://www.nihr.ac.uk/about-us/who-we-are/research-inclusion/strategy-2022-27 (accessed December 2024).

[49] Michaels (n 44).

and inappropriate approaches to pain management.[50] On similar lines, the Women's Health Strategy published by the Department of Health and Social Care in 2022 raised concerns about a 'male as default' approach to research design and scope (including underrepresentation in clinical trials, especially among some subgroups of women).[51] This has resulted in a lack of data and understanding of conditions which only or primarily affect women, such as menopause or endometriosis; and a lack of understanding of the ways in which conditions which affect everybody, may affect men and women differently, such as cardiovascular disease. These gaps in knowledge are even more significant at the intersections of different characteristics.[52]

This problem is tricky to resolve and it is not immediately clear what law's contribution could be. Reliance on available data in making policy decisions is likely to be proportionate to aims of achieving safety and cost-effectiveness (although, as we saw in the last chapter, in relation to assessing the potentially disparate impact of a policy proposal the PSED imposes a duty of inquiry on public authorities, requiring them to seek out relevant data where they do not already have access to it). A decision, for example, that a drug should not be prescribed in a particular age group, because there is no evidence of its safety and effectiveness, as a result of exclusion of that age group from clinical trials, may amount to prima facie direct discrimination but is likely to be justified as a proportionate means of achieving goals of effectiveness and safety when no less discriminatory means – in the form of alternative, more inclusive data – is available.

The institutional landscape for medical research is highly fragmented across public and private organizations and funders. Both research ethics committees, which oversee clinical trials, and public research funding bodies are likely to be subject to the PSED. Research ethics committees may have a role to play in encouraging diversity in inclusion in trials and intersectionality in data analysis but will have little role in deciding on research agendas. Research funders are perhaps best placed to encourage diversity in this respect. Some work is ongoing here – the National Institute for Health Research diversity strategy, for example, involves a commitment to ring-fence funding for projects related to gender, disability, socio-economic

50 C. MacGregorJ. Walumbe, E. Tulle, C. Seenan and D. Blane (2023) 'Intersectionality as a Theoretical Framework for Researching Health Inequities in Chronic Pain', *British Journal of Pain* 17(5): 479–490.

51 Department for Health and Social Care (2022) *Women's Health Strategy for England*, available at: https://www.gov.uk/government/publications/womens-health-strategy-for-england (accessed December 2024).

52 A. Rojas-Garcia, D. Holman, L. Tinner, S. Ejegi-Memeh, Y. Ben-Shlomo and A. Laverty (2022) 'Use of Intersectionality Theories in Interventional Health Research in High-income Countries: A Systematic Scoping Review', *The Lancet* 400(1): S58.

background, geography, ethnicity and other characteristics;[53] and the Women's Health Strategy called for the creation of a dedicated research unit on women's reproductive health.[54] But further progress here will be essential if commissioners are to be able to avoid making policy which – although perhaps legally justifiable because of a lack of data – nonetheless disadvantages particular groups because they have been excluded from the design of the research on which policy is based.

The 'postcode lottery'

Finally, a brief note on the relevance of equality law to the 'postcode lottery' of health provision. There are currently 42 ICBs across England, each responsible for a population of between one and three million. Each will make decisions about how to spend its budget and there will be differences – often very significant differences – between the treatments available to the populations they serve, leading to a highly publicized 'postcode lottery'. Cancer drugs may be funded in one locality but not in another; more cycles of IVF may be available on the NHS or may be available for older patients in one ICB but not in its neighbour; and waiting lists for particular treatments may be significantly longer in neighbouring ICBs. The rationale for local, rather than national, priority setting is to reflect differences in the needs of different populations. We saw in Chapter 1 that geography plays a significant part in mapping health inequalities because there are very significant disparities between wealth as well as diversity of (in particular) the age and ethnicity of the populations. Local commissioning allows ICBs, working within Integrated Care Systems, to be responsive to the health needs of their populations and to prioritize resources accordingly to meet them. When suitably resourced, this is likely to be an important part of addressing health inequalities. While recent structural changes in the Health and Social Care Act were in part designed to reduce inequalities by promoting enhanced coordination and reducing the number of commissioning bodies, differences remain. Likewise, NICE was established in part to set national standards and reduce disparities in local provision. While local commissioners are not obliged to follow NICE's non-mandatory guidance, they must have regard to it in their decision making and must provide clear reasons for departing from it, which may not include simple disagreement with NICE over the current state of medical science.[55]

[53] National Institute of Health and Care Research (n 48).

[54] Department of Health and Social Care (n 51).

[55] *R (on the application of Rose) v Thanet Clinical Commissioning Group* [2014] EWHC 1182 (Admin).

When justifying policies which might indirectly (or directly in the case of age) discriminate against particular patient groups, ICBs will need to be careful to explain any divergence from NICE, and from neighbouring ICBs in terms of the different demands of their locality. One of the elements of proportionality is that a measure must normally be shown to be 'necessary' for achieving a legitimate aim in order to be proportionate. The existence of a less discriminatory policy approach in a neighbouring locality (for example, a higher upper age limit for access to IVF or funding for a breast cancer drug that would mainly benefit women) may signal that the measure in question is not 'necessary' because an alternative, less discriminatory, approach could have been chosen. This issue has arisen in the context of age discrimination in employment – as we saw earlier, in *Prigge* a departure from internationally accepted age limit for pilots, without good reason, was a reason for finding the relevant measure disproportionate. This problem can potentially be avoided for commissioners by making sure that the aim of the measure in question is expressed in terms which make specific reference to the particular needs of and priorities for the local population. We will return to this problem in relation to funding for assisted fertility in Chapter 6.

Conclusion

This chapter has identified some of the ways in which discrimination may arise in deciding what treatment to fund and which patients can access it, and has considered how the equality law framework might respond. Many of these examples arise because of the way the benefits of health care intervention are assessed – whether by policy makers in determining and comparing the cost-effectiveness of different treatments or by clinicians in deciding what is appropriate for their own patients. It is evident that in assessing whether these examples amount to lawful or unlawful discrimination, much will hinge on the application of the proportionality test – what aims are legitimate in this context and what factors will be relevant in determining whether the policy or decision in question is a proportionate means of achieving these aims? The likely approach of the courts to these questions is considered further in Chapter 4. The next chapter now turns to consider the circumstances under which commissioners and others may be under *positive obligations* or may otherwise be free to take positive steps, to address the disadvantages faced by groups and individuals in relation to their health, or their access to health care. If a policy decision to not fund a particular treatment disadvantages a particular group, for example, under what circumstances are commissioners permitted, or required, to make an exception for that group, or for individual patients belonging to it?

3

Making Exceptions

Introduction

It was seen in Chapter 2 that, while an analysis of the cost-effectiveness of an intervention is usually the starting point for policy recommendations or decisions about which treatment to fund, this may be modified in some circumstances. Both National Institute for Health and Care Excellence (NICE) principles and NICE guidance make clear that other relevant factors – including considerations of equity and equality – will be considered and that this may sometimes result in interventions that are less cost-effective being made generally available. The question this chapter now considers is the circumstances under which it will be possible to make interventions available *only* to certain subgroups of patients or to individuals where they would be particularly disadvantaged, in ways related to their protected characteristics, by a policy not to fund them. It will aim to identify, as far as possible, the circumstances under which equality law will permit or require the personal characteristics of patients to be taken into account in determining whether an exception for a specific group or for an individual should be made. It will also highlight a number of challenges the equality law framework presents for commissioners and other health professionals in making decisions about how to allocate resources.

The chapter is divided into two main sections. The first outlines the existing policy approaches taken to making exceptions for groups, and for individuals in the context of Individual Funding Requests (IFRs), the reasons underpinning these policy choices, and the approach the courts have taken to assessing the legality of policy approaches to IFRs in the context of public law challenges to rejection of IFRs by health authorities. The second section then turns to the bearing that equality law may have on these issues. It considers in detail three sets of circumstances in which commissioners may be permitted, or required, to take personal characteristics into account when deciding on an approach to exceptions for groups or individuals: positive action, reasonable adjustments and indirect discrimination.

Making exceptions for groups

NICE makes clear in its principles that there will be circumstances under which it will consider recommending an intervention only for a particular group (even though there may be other patients who would benefit from it):

> 32 NICE's guidance aims to serve the interests of the population as a whole. But sometimes the available evidence shows differences in the effectiveness and cost effectiveness of an intervention for a particular group of people. Certain groups may also be at a disadvantage compared with others, including those covered by the Equalities Act 2010 [sic]. In such cases, it may be appropriate for us to make recommendations for specific groups of people.
>
> 33 NICE may recommend an intervention for a specific group of people only if there is: enough relevant evidence that the intervention is more effective or cost effective in the subgroup, or a legal requirement to act in this way, or other reasons relating to fairness for society as a whole.[1]

NICE guidance manuals also make reference throughout to the need for its decision-making committees to be mindful of equality considerations (including but not limited to legal obligations under the Equality Act and Human Rights Act) but leaves the ways these are to be incorporated into decision-making frameworks to the discretion of the committee, noting that '[t]here are no hard-and-fast rules or mechanisms for doing this: the committee should make conscious and explicit use of its members' skills and expertise'.[2] The NICE manual for Technology Appraisal Guidance (mandatory funding) is more detailed and notes that recommendations for particular subgroups should be made only where:

> there is clear evidence that the characteristics defining the subgroup influence the effectiveness or value for money of the technology. It can only do this based on an appropriate consideration of subgroups, to make sure that the decision is clinically justifiable, methodologically robust, ethical, and lawful under equalities legislation. The committee should be particularly aware of the benefits and harms (to

1 National Institute for Health and Care Excellence (nd) *Our Principles*, available at: https://www.nice.org.uk/about/who-we-are/our-principles (accessed December 2024).

2 National Institute for Health and Care Excellence (2014) *Developing NICE Guidelines: The Manual (PMG 20)*, updated 29 May 2024 at 193, available at: https://www.nice.org.uk/process/pmg20 (accessed December 2024).

> individuals and to the NHS as a whole) of including or excluding a given subgroup.[3]

In a recent comprehensive review of its policies and procedures, NICE considered going further by introducing a 'health equalities modifier' in its assessment of the cost-effectiveness of an intervention but has decided that more work is needed to develop an appropriate model and is therefore something to be addressed in a future work programme.[4] In much the same way as the 'severity modifier' discussed in Chapter 2, a health inequalities modifier would, presumably, be a mechanism to give extra weight to Quality Adjusted Life Years generated by interventions that are judged particularly significant or effective in reducing known health inequalities. It may therefore result in technologies being recommended for subgroups who are particularly disadvantaged in relevant respects.

Commissioners will also need to consider whether and when to make exceptions for subgroups and fund interventions that are otherwise deemed low priority. Integrated Care Boards (ICBs) generally refer to the need for equality issues to be taken into account in their ethical frameworks but it is often unclear how this will be done. Some use a 'scorecard' for treatments where equality considerations can attract points and make it more likely that a treatment will be funded but the circumstances under which a group exception will be made are not clear.[5] Far more detail is usually available on the circumstances in which individual patients may receive exceptional funding, as explained in what follows.

There is certainly an argument that, in many cases at least, making proactive policy-based exceptions for whole groups is a more transparent and fairer approach than reactive exceptions for individuals who request them (although, as we will see, the possibility of making individual exceptions is something required by law). NHS England takes this view, noting that:

---

3 National Institute for Health and Care Excellence (2023) *Health Technology Evaluations: The Manual*, at 6.2.29, available at: https://www.nice.org.uk/process/pmg36/resources/nice-health-technology-evaluations-the-manual-pdf-72286779244741 (accessed December 2024).

4 National Institute for Health and Care Excellence (2021) *Review of Methods for Health Technology Evaluation Programmes: Consultation 2*, available at: NICE Review of Methods - Proposals for Change (1).pdf (accessed December 2024).

5 For example, Staffordshire and Stoke Integrated Care Board (8 July 2022) *Policy on the Prioritisation of Healthcare Resources*, available at: https://staffsstoke.icb.nhs.uk/your-nhs-integrated-care-board/our-publications/governance-handbook/all-policies/commissioning/icb-policy-on-the-prioritisation-of-healthcare-resourcesmaster/?layout=file (accessed February 2025).

> Either a treatment or service is funded in order to create the opportunity for all patients with equal need to be treated or, if this cannot be afforded, it should not be commissioned as part of NHS treatment for any patients. The NHS CB considers that if funding for a treatment cannot be justified as an investment for all patients in a particular cohort, the treatment should not be offered to only some of the patients unless it is possible to differentiate between groups of patients on clinical grounds. A decision to treat some patients but not others has the potential to be unfair, arbitrary and possibly discriminatory.[6]

Making exceptions for individual patients: Individual Funding Requests

Where health care commissioners decide, as a general policy, that they will not generally fund a particular medical treatment or intervention (or will restrict its availability to those meeting certain criteria), individual patients, denied under the policy, can ask for an exception to be made. This is generally done by means of an IFR, whereby the patient, typically with the support of their medical team, can make a case for individual funding on the basis that there are significant and relevant differences between their circumstances and those of other patients who might need or want the treatment in question. The openness of public decision makers to making exceptions to a general policy is a central requirement of public law – decision makers must not fetter their own discretion by applying policies rigidly and must be willing to consider whether to depart from the policy in an individual case.[7]

The approach of health care commissioners to deciding on IFRs is normally to take into account clinical factors only. The key question is whether the individual patient – clinically speaking – is likely to benefit significantly more from the treatment in question, or to suffer considerably more if denied, than other patients in their cohort. This is often no easy task for a patient to demonstrate. According to NHS England:

> Very few patients have clinical circumstances which are genuinely exceptional. To justify funding for treatment for a patient which is not available to other patients, and is not part of the established care pathway, the IFR Panel needs to be satisfied that the clinician has

6 NHS England (2013) *Commissioning Policy Ethical Framework*, available at: https://www.england.nhs.uk/wp-content/uploads/2013/04/cp-01.pdf (accessed December 2024).

7 *R (A) v Secretary of State for the Home Office* [2021] UKSC 37.

> demonstrated that this patient's individual clinical circumstances are clearly different to those of other patients, and that because of this difference, the general policies should not be applied. Simply put, the consideration is whether it is fair to fund this patient's treatment when the treatment is not available to others.[8]

IFR policies tend to make clear that they will not take into account 'social factors' in deciding whether or not to make an exception. Where 'social factors' are defined in policies they tend to embrace two different categories. First are value judgements about factors related to the role of the individual in society – whether the patient is an employee or parent or carer – and value judgements about the behaviour of the patient – for example the lifestyle of the patient and the extent to which they may bear some responsibility for bringing about their need for medical treatment. The second category – and that of interest here – includes the personal characteristics of the patient – sex, age, disability and so on. For example, one current IFR policy states that '[n]on-clinical social factors (for example, but not limited to, age, gender, ethnicity, employment status, parental status, marital status, carer status, religious/cultural factors) will not be taken into account in determining whether exceptionality has been established'.[9] Another states that 'IFRs should not be made on the basis of non-clinical social factors, personal or protected characteristics'.[10]

The position is complicated by the fact that some personal characteristics – including age, sex and disability, may sometimes be highly relevant to the clinical benefit an intervention is likely to produce. Accordingly, some IFR policies may make clear that where personal characteristics are relevant to the clinical effectiveness of a treatment then they may be taken into account as part of this assessment.[11] The scope of this is not clear, however, and in relation to comorbidities (concurrent health conditions, some of which may amount to disabilities and are therefore a protected characteristic under the Equality Act) NHS England suggests that:

---

8 NHS England (8 February 2023) *Commissioning Policy: Individual Funding Requests* (Version 3), https://www.england.nhs.uk/publication/commissioning-policy-individual-funding-requests/ (accessed February 2025).

9 NHS Staffordshire and Stoke-on-Trent Integrated Care Board (8 July 2022) *Individual Funding Request Policy*, 4.2.5.

10 NHS Cornwall and Isles of Scilly (2022) *Individual Funding Requests Policy and Procedures*, CISICB, 5, available at: https://docs.cios.icb.nhs.uk/DocumentsLibrary/NHSCornwallAndIslesOfScilly/Services/IndividualFundingRequests/Individualfundingrequestpolicyandprocedures.pdf (accessed December 2024).

11 For an example see Nottingham and Nottinghamshire Integrated Care Board *Individual Funding Requests (IFR) Commissioning Policy* (June 2024–June 2027) at 7.5.

> If the usual treatment cannot be given because of a pre-existing comorbidity which is unrelated to the condition for which the treatment is being sought under the IFR or is not unusual in the relevant patient group or generally, the fact that the co-morbidity is present in this patient and its impact on treatment options for this patient is unlikely to make the patient clinically exceptional.[12]

Finally, some IFR policies make express reference to the need to improve health inequalities, and the need to sometimes give priority to health services which target population groups who tend to have poorer than average health outcomes or who are disadvantaged in some way in relation to access to health care.[13] It is not obvious how this is envisaged working in the context of considering IFRs (rather than, say, in the context of an overall strategic approach to priority setting where resources may be targeted to disadvantaged groups from the outset). It is not clear, for example, whether patients from groups with poorer health outcomes generally are more likely to be given individual funding – and if so whether this would be the case for those with poorer outcomes related to the specific conditions for which treatment is sought or for those with poorer health outcomes more generally.

At best, therefore, there is lack of clarity as to the way personal characteristics will, if ever, be relevant to determining when to make an exception to a funding policy and the criteria for determining whether and when they will. The focus on clinical reasons for exceptionality, and the broad rejection of the relevance of social factors, including personal characteristics, appears to stem from a number of related concerns. First, it is clear there is some worry that treating social factors as relevant to decisions about individual funding risks discrimination. The decision to treat social utility, personal responsibility or personal characteristics as irrelevant stems, at least in part, from concern to ensure that the health of one individual is not valued any more or less highly than that of another. Thus, for example, one ICB states that '[t]he ICB considers all lives of all patients to be of equal value and in making decisions about funding treatments will seek not to discriminate on the grounds of age, sex, sexuality, race, religion' and so on;[14]

---

12 NHS England (2023) *Commissioning Policy: Individual Funding Requests*, NHS England, 9, available at: https://www.england.nhs.uk/wp-content/uploads/2017/11/B2086-commissioning-policy-individual-funding-requests-v3.pdf (accessed December 2024).

13 For an example see NHS Kent and Medway Integrated Care Board (2022) *Principles and Guidance for Dealing with Individual Funding Requests*, KMICB, 22, available at: https://www.kentandmedway.icb.nhs.uk/application/files/1116/7085/0695/Principles_and_Guidance_for_dealing_with_Individual_Funding_Requests_Part_I_ICB.pdf (accessed December 2024).

14 Nottingham and Nottinghamshire Integrated Care Board (n 11).

and NHS England notes that '[as] a central principle, the NHS does not make judgements about the worth of different individuals and seeks to treat everyone fairly and equitably. Consideration of these non-clinical factors would introduce this concept of "worth" into clinical decision making'.[15] There is also a more practical problem. Commissioners will usually lack the data and expertise to evaluate non-clinical evidence and to compare this across individuals and populations.[16] While initial cost-effectiveness reviews of the relevant treatment or drug, based on published trial data, for example, will have given a good idea of the average and typical range of clinical responses – allowing clinical exceptions to be identified with more confidence – the same is not true of social factors.

Underlying these concerns is a desire to treat patients fairly. This includes both fairness between those who are denied under an IFR and those who are successful; and fairness to those patients from whose treatment the money spent on making an exception in a particular case might be divested. While those deciding on IFR requests (and indeed the courts adjudicating claims made by individual patients refused under an IFR) are able to know the circumstances of the individual asking for an exception to be made, they will not be similarly aware of the needs and circumstances of those whose heath care may be compromised by the consequent reduction in budget. The difficulty with this – often apparently blanket – approach to the (ir)relevance of personal characteristics, however, is that it ignores the disadvantage that can be caused to (or reinforced in) members of protected groups by adopting 'characteristic blind' decision-making criteria. Sole focus on clinical response, while apparently fair, may ignore both underlying differences in ability to access treatment and underlying disadvantage, which may itself result from other forms of discrimination and will be compounded by lack of access to treatment. The following sections now turn to consider the circumstances under which the legal framework may in fact require, or permit, departure from an equal treatment or characteristic blind model so that personal characteristics are taken into account in commissioning decisions in order to avoid or reduce substantive inequalities.

Individual Funding Requests in public law

In common with all public bodies, health care commissioners are under a public law duty to not fetter their own discretion. In deciding which medical interventions to fund, and the access criteria for these, they must therefore remain open to the possibility of making exceptions to a general policy in

[15] NHS England (n 12).

[16] NHS Staffordshire and Stoke-on-Trent Integrated Care Board (n 9).

response to individual patient circumstances. This duty was explained in *R v North West Lancashire*, a case concerning the refusal of gender reassignment surgery, where Auld LJ held that 'it is proper for an authority to adopt a general policy for the exercise of such an administrative discretion, to allow for exceptions from it in "exceptional circumstances" and to leave those circumstances undefined'.[17]

Case law subsequent to *Lancashire* has addressed questions about the scope of this duty but has failed to produce clear guidance. Commissioners must make decisions about whether individual patients are 'exceptional' in accordance with the general principles of public law – and, in particular, in this context, in accordance with the principle of rationality – but what rationality requires has proved difficult to pin down. As a result the criteria for determining the circumstances under which an exception should be made – and the factors relevant to making these decisions – remain fraught with uncertainty. In particular it remains unclear how 'unusual' a patient has to be, and in what respects. Indeed the lack of clear guidance from the courts or elsewhere on this issue has resulted in what has been described as a 'legal farce', creating uncertainty for patients, clinicians and commissioners.[18]

One aspect of exceptionality on which the courts have sent a much clearer message, however, is in relation to the exclusion of 'social factors' from decision making on IFRs. The courts have sanctioned the approach to exceptionality which treats non-clinical factors as irrelevant. The leading case is *Condliff*, a case which did not itself involve any claims of discrimination.[19] Mr Condliff was morbidly obese and wanted laparoscopic gastric bypass surgery. The policy of North Staffordshire Primary Care Trust (PCT) was then to fund this surgery only for those patients whose body mass index exceeded 50 and Mr Condliff was not eligible because his body mass index was below this threshold. He therefore made an IFR, supported by his GP and by a number of other specialists, which noted the serious impact of his condition on his mental and physical wellbeing, and on his lifestyle, but his request was turned down by the PCT, whose IFR policy stated that social factors (including personal characteristics such as age, gender and ethnicity as well as employment, parental and marital status, and religious or cultural factors) would not be taken into account in deciding whether or not a patient was exceptional. Mr Condliff challenged the social factors exclusion, arguing, among other things, that it was in breach of Article 8 of

17 *R v North West Lancashire Health Authority ex parte A* [2000] 1WLR 977 at 991.

18 A. Ford (2012) 'The Concept of Exceptionalilty: A Legal Farce?', *Medical Law Review* 20(3): 304–336.

19 *R (on the application of Condliff) v North Staffordshire Primary Care Trust* [2011] EWHC 872 (Admin); [2011] EWCA Civ 910.

the European Convention on Human Rights (ECHR) because it failed to take into account all factors relevant to his Article 8 right to a private life.

Neither the High Court nor the Court of Appeal found any breach of Article 8. In the first place, it was doubted that Article 8 founded any positive right to treatment in the circumstances; even it if did, it was held that the approach of the PCT would amount to a justified interference with Mr Condliff's Article 8 rights because it had struck a fair balance between the rights of individual patients and the needs of the community. The Court of Appeal noted that:

> The policy of allocating scarce medical resources on a basis of the comparative assessment of clinical needs is intentionally non-discriminatory. The statutory function of the PCT is to use the limited resources provided to it for the purposes of the provision of healthcare. … To perform that function by allocating those resources strictly according to the PCT's assessment of medical need … is to do no more than to apply the resources for the purpose for which they are provided without giving preferential treatment to one patient over another on non-medical grounds.[20]

A similar approach was taken in *Longstaff* – a case concerning a patient who wanted access to artificial blood products which were not routinely funded.[21] His reason for rejecting human blood was a phobia developed as a result of his brother's death from contaminated blood products. The Court suggested that there is a difference in kind between a refusal of treatment for clinical reasons and a refusal based on other factors including phobia or religious belief.[22] While neither of these cases involved claims of discrimination, the remainder of this chapter now turns to consider what equality law might require of commissioners in determining their approach to these kind of decisions where personal characteristics are involved. Under what circumstances may, or must, personal characteristics be taken into account when deciding whether or not to make an exception from a general rule or policy to not fund a particular medical intervention?

---

[20] *R (on the application of Condliff) v North Staffordshire Primary Care Trust* [2011] EWCA Civ 910 at 36. At first instance, Waksman LJ suggested that some social factors were directly relevant to clinical outcomes – but that these would then constitute clinical factors themselves and so not be caught by the policy. On the facts, Mr Condliff's circumstances did not fall into this category: *R (on the application of Condliff) v North Staffordshire Primary Care Trust* [2011] EWHC 872 at 23.

[21] *R (on the application of Longstaff) v Newcastle NHS Primary Care Trust* [2003] EWHC 3252 (Admin).

[22] Ibid at 56.

Equality law

There are three sets of obligations under the Equality Act and Article 14 of the ECHR which are of particular relevance to the issues under consideration here and which will be explored in what follows. These are positive action, as a form of exception to the prohibition on direct discrimination; the duty to make reasonable adjustments in the case of disability; and indirect discrimination which arises where an apparently neutral policy or practice serves to disadvantage those sharing a protected characteristic, and cannot be justified. The relevance of the Public Sector Equality Duty (PSED) to the question of exceptionality is also considered briefly.

Positive action under the Equality Act

The Equality Act provides that positive action is permitted in certain circumstances. Positive action involves the use of steps to help those facing particular disadvantages, connected to a protected characteristic, to overcome them.[23] It is normally distinguished from positive or 'reverse' discrimination, which is generally unlawful in the UK, and is normally characterized as preferential treatment of an individual because of a protected characteristic – although the division between these two concepts is not always clear. Positive action in any form is controversial because it can involve the perception that it creates unfair advantage for some groups at the expense of others; the boundary between redressing disadvantage and creating unfair advantage is sometimes hard to draw. On the other hand, it is widely acknowledged that some form of positive action is often necessary to achieve substantive equality and to ensure that society is sufficiently responsive to the different needs and experiences of different groups.[24]

Section 158 of the Equality Act provides that positive action will be lawful where service providers, or those carrying out public functions, reasonably think that individuals who share a particular protected characteristic are at a disadvantage connected to the characteristic, or have needs that are different from those who don't have the characteristic. When this is the case, it is lawful for service providers to take *proportionate* steps to help them to overcome the disadvantage or to meet those needs.

There are, as yet, no cases considering the application of Section 158 in relation to health care resources, but a first judgment on the scope of

---

[23] For a helpful categorization of different forms of positive action see C. McCrudden (1986) 'Rethinking Positive Action', *Industrial Law Journal* 15(4): 219–243.

[24] For a useful summary of the debate on positive action see S. Fredman (2022) *Discrimination Law (3rd Edition)*, Oxford: Oxford University Press, chapter 7.

these provisions by the Supreme Court in 2020 in *R (Z) v Hackney*, in the context of social housing, gives a useful example of how the provision may operate in the context of public services.[25] A portion of the social housing stock in Hackney was owned by the Agudas Israel Housing Association (AIHA), whose policy was to prioritize its housing stock for members of the Orthodox Jewish community. The claimant, who had young children, including two with autism, was considered by Hackney Council to be among the group with the highest need for housing but was not nominated by the Council for a series of suitable properties owned by AIHA because of their priority policy. She claimed that she had suffered direct discrimination on grounds of religion and race under the Equality Act as she had been treated less favourably because she was not Jewish. The Supreme Court found that there had been no discrimination because (among other things) the Council and the AIHA were able to rely on the positive action provisions in Section 158. There was undisputed evidence that the Orthodox Jewish community faced 'real and substantial disadvantage' connected with their religion in relation to housing, as well as having different needs to those who were not members of the community. The Court held that the correct approach to determining the proportionality of a positive measure was to weigh the disadvantage to the group in question – here the Orthodox Jewish community – against the disadvantage other groups would face in consequence of the disputed measure.[26] On the facts, although the individual claimant in this case was significantly disadvantaged by the measure because of her particular circumstances, the evidence suggested that the wider group of those in need of social housing were not because the housing stock of the AIHA formed such a small proportion of the overall housing stock available to the Council. The measure was therefore proportionate.

In the context of commissioning health care, the positive action provisions should therefore allow an approach which takes into account the protected characteristics of patients in some circumstances. Where it is recognized that a decision not to fund a particular treatment is likely to disadvantage members of a particular group, commissioners are unlikely to be acting unlawfully if they allow for exceptions to be made for those within that group, provided that this is proportionate. Arguably this could be achieved *either* by carving out an exception as part of the funding policy itself – for example, by generally funding a drug or intervention *only* for members of the relevant

[25] *R (Z)* v *Hackney London Borough Council and another* [2020] UKSC 40.

[26] Ibid at 79. This accords with the guidance in the Equality and Human Rights Commission (2011) *Equality Act 2010 Statutory Code of Practice: Services, Public Functions and Associations*, EHRC, which notes at 10.22 that '[t]he seriousness of the relevant disadvantage, the degree to which the need is different … need to be balanced against the impact of the action on other protected groups, and the relative disadvantage, [or] need … of these groups'.

group – *or*, alternatively, by having an IFR policy which makes clear that protected characteristics may be relevant to individual decisions where the positive action provisions of the Act apply. There are good reasons to take the first approach wherever possible, not least because, as argued by Sheehan, identifying exceptional groups at the policy stage is likely to prove fairer, more effective and more transparent.[27] The exercise of the PSED should equip commissioners to consider needs and disadvantage at an early stage of policy making. On the other hand, there may be situations where it is more challenging to identify in advance the groups whose needs may be different to others affected by the policy or who may be particularly disadvantaged in relation to it, for reasons connected to a protected characteristic. In these circumstances, allowing the disadvantage to be overcome or needs met through the mechanism of the IFR process may be another way of utilizing the positive action provisions for commissioners wishing to do so.

While positive action is possible, therefore, commissioners may nonetheless have understandable reservations about taking such action when they are not required to. This has certainly proved true in other contexts. In relation to employment, for example, research suggests that 'organizations prefer to steer clear of this opportunity to address disadvantage suffered by protected groups'[28] and that a lack of clarity as to the boundaries of permissible positive action, and resulting lack of confidence, may be to blame.[29] It would be unsurprising if this was also true of policy makers in the NHS.

Clarity and confidence aside, a second challenge for policy makers is to determine an approach for voluntary positive action that accords with their broader ethical framework (as well as the legal one) and is compatible with the principles that underscore their approach to resource allocation. In line with the legal framework, this exercise will involve at least two elements. The first is identifying the respects in which a group would be disadvantaged (or have different needs) in order to trigger the use of permissible positive action in the first place. The Equality Act appears to allow a broad definition of relevant disadvantage in this context which could include both disadvantage related to a particular policy or funding decision, or a broader conception

27 M. Sheehan, 'Exceptionality in the Context of Individual Funding Requests', a paper presented at 'A Community of Healthcare Lawyers: A Symposium in Honour of Professor Chris Newdick', University of Reading, April 2022.

28 C.M. Davies and M. Robison (2016) 'Bridging the Gap: An Exploration of the Use and Impact of Positive Action in the United Kingdom', *International Journal of Discrimination and the Law* 16(2–3): 83–101.

29 C. Davies (2019) *Exploring Positive Action as a Tool to Address Under-representation in Apprenticeships*, EHRC Research Report 123, available at: https://www.equalityhumanrights.com/sites/default/files/research-report-123-positive-action-apprenticeships.pdf (accessed February 2024).

of disadvantage embracing disadvantage in relation to access to health care or health care outcomes more generally, although the boundaries remain unclear. The answer to this question will be highly significant to deciding whether and when positive action in access to health care may be used as a mechanism to address health inequalities more broadly. A second step comes in relation to deciding whether making a group exception to a particular funding decision is a proportionate response. Following the Supreme Court's guidance in *R (Z)*, it is clear that this will involve a weighing of the disadvantage to the protected group which has triggered the need for positive action in the first place (here, Orthodox Jews in need of housing) against any disadvantage caused *by* the positive action to those not in the protected group. In *R (Z)*, the group disadvantaged by the positive action were those, like the claimant, also seeking housing in the borough and were therefore relatively easy to identify. When it comes to health care commissioning, this weighing exercise is potentially much more challenging. Money spent on funding exceptions may need to be divested from health care provision which may be entirely separate from the treatment and cohort being considered and as a result it is likely to be much more difficult for commissioners to identify who is likely to be impacted. If I need access to more expensive drug B because my religion prevents me from using cheaper and generally available drug A, the money spent on eliminating my disadvantage (and that of others in my position) in relation to that treatment may be taken from others who are disadvantaged, in different ways (and indeed in relation to other protected characteristics) in relation to health outcomes and access to health care. Arguably, at least, this will therefore require a different and potentially more complicated weighing exercise than required of Hackney Council in *R (Z)* and a clear and transparent process will be needed.[30]

Positive action under the Human Rights Act

Under the Human Rights Act, positive action is not only permitted but may sometimes be required. The European Court of Human Rights made clear in *Thlimmenos v Greece* that it is possible for a breach of Article 14 to arise because of a failure to treat individuals differently, without justification, where there are relevant differences between them.[31] Mr Thlimmenos had been refused appointment as a chartered accountant because of a criminal conviction for refusing to wear a military uniform because of his religious

[30] See Fredman (n 24) chapter 7, for useful comparative discussion of the difficulties of demarcating the relevant beneficiary group for positive action, and of determining the scope of the relevant disadvantage on both sides of the scales.

[31] *Thlimmenos v Greece* (App no 34369/97) ECtHR 6 April 2000.

beliefs. In finding that this failure to make an exception for individuals in the position of Mr Thlimmenos was a violation of Article 14, in conjunction with Article 9, the Court held that '[t]he right not to be discriminated against in the enjoyment of the rights guaranteed under the Convention is also violated when States without an objective and reasonable justification fail to treat differently persons whose situations are significantly different'.[32]

In common with all claims under Article 14, when determining whether a failure to treat people differently in this way amounts to unjustified discrimination, the domestic courts engage in varying intensity of review which will determine the approach taken to proportionality and the extent to which the assertions of policy makers will be accepted by the courts without the need for close scrutiny. The approach to be taken in any particular case depends on a complex matrix of factors including the ground of discrimination (with some grounds calling for a more intense review than others), the seriousness of the disadvantage created by the contested policy or treatment, and whether or not the relevant policy involves questions of socio-economic policy and the allocation of resources.[33] In cases involving difficult decisions about the allocation of resources – as will normally be the case in relation to health care commissioning – the courts tend to take a deferential approach, although this is not automatic and stricter scrutiny may still be called for in some circumstances.[34] This is discussed in detail in Chapter 4.

Deference was very much in evidence in a rare case involving claims of 'Thlimmenos' discrimination in the context of health care commissioning. In *R (AC) v Berkshire* the claimant, a male to female transexual, sought judicial review of a decision by Berkshire West PCT to refuse her breast augmentation surgery.[35] It was the policy of the PCT to treat breast augmentation surgery as low priority and it was only funded for those who could demonstrate exceptional clinical need or benefit. The claimant had made a number of requests for funding which had been rejected. Her claim included an argument that by failing to make an exception for her, by agreeing to her IFR, the PCT was in breach of Article 14, together with Article 8 of the ECHR.[36] The claimant argued that there were relevant differences between her need for surgery and those of a natal woman because, as the Equality

[32] Ibid at 44.

[33] *R (SC) v Secretary of State for Work and Pensions* [2021] UKSC 26.

[34] Ibid.

[35] *R (AC) v Berkshire West Primary Care Trust* [2010] EWHC 1162 (Admin); *R (AC) v Berkshire West Primary Care Trust* [2011] EWCA Civ 247.

[36] At the time the facts of the claim arose, there was no legal protection from indirect discrimination on grounds of gender reassignment under the Sex Discrimination Act 1995 – a claim which may be now advanced on the same facts.

and Human Rights Commission (EHRC) (intervening) put it in their submission, 'only a transgender woman needs breasts to address the very condition from which she suffers, and only transsexuals suffer, of living in a body which is not the gender which they feel themselves to be'.[37] In rejecting her claim, however, the Court of Appeal effectively delegated the decision on the question of which differences between individuals are relevant to the PCT.[38] As the PCT had decided it was not relevant that 'one of the women seeking treatment was born a woman whereas the other has become a woman or seeks to become a woman', that was the end of the matter.[39]

Using Article 14 to argue successfully that exceptions should be made may therefore prove a difficult task for patients. More recently, however, a less deferential approach to the scope of Thlimmenos discrimination was taken by the court in *R (Adath Yisroel Burial Society) v HM Senior Coroner for North London*,[40] which concerned religious belief and therefore concerned Article 9 (freedom of religion) as well as Article 14. The case offers some useful insights as to how obligations to make exceptions might arise. It concerned a policy of the Senior Coroner not to prioritize deaths because of the religious belief of the deceased or their families – where, for example, their religion required that burial take place as soon as possible after death. Instead, deaths would be dealt with in the order in which they were referred – described by the defendant as the 'cab rank rule'. The only basis on which prioritization was permitted was for homicide and organ donation. Prioritization for religious – or any other reason – had been described by the defendant as 'queue jumping' and she had expressed concern about the impact of prioritizing one group on the families of others who were therefore pushed further back in the queue.[41] It was also suggested in argument that, among other things, one of the reasons for the coroner's refusal to prioritize deaths on religious grounds was a fear of discriminating under the Equality Act,[42] concerns which echo those seen in IFR policies.

The claimants successfully challenged the policy on a number of grounds, including that it was a breach of the claimant's Article 9 and Article 14

[37] *R (AC) v Berkshire West Primary Care Trust* [2011] EWCA Civ 247 at 41.

[38] While a deferential approach is not surprising here, given the context of resource allocation, it is arguable that the appropriate sphere of deference should have arisen in relation to the question of whether a decision to not treat the claimant differently here was justified here, rather than the question of whether or not there was potential discrimination requiring justification in the first place. See, for example, *Burnip v Birmingham City Council* [2012] EWCA Civ 629.

[39] *R (AC) v Berkshire West Primary Care Trust* (n 37).

[40] *R (Adath Yisroel Burial Society) v HM Senior Coroner for North London* [2018] EWHC 969.

[41] Ibid at 50.

[42] Ibid at 108.

rights. In relation to Article 9, the Court held the policy constituted a prima facie interference with the right to freedom of religion which could not be justified. In particular, it noted that it was relevant to justification that prioritization on grounds of religious belief is not unlawful under the Equality Act because it is consistent with the positive action provisions of Section 158, discussed earlier. The coroner's concerns about giving priority to one person over another on religious grounds were therefore 'misguided'.[43] In relation to Article 14, having established that this was a prima facie case of *Thlimmenos* discrimination – because there were significant relevant differences between those requiring expedited burial for religious reasons and others using the services of the coroner – the Court considered whether there could be any 'objective and reasonable' justification for the coroner's policy of not allowing exceptions to be made on religious grounds. On the facts, there was not. The coroner had advanced two justifications – the first that a 'bright line rule' was easier to understand and to administer; the second that the resources of the coroner's office were limited. The Court dismissed both. The fact that the coroner allowed for exceptions in other circumstances undermined the argument about administrative workability.[44] In relation to concerns about managing finite resources – perhaps of particular resonance in the context of thinking about the approach to commissioning health care – the Court noted that:

> Limits on resources may explain why it is not possible to help a particular family to achieve expedition (whatever the reason for their request for expedition, whether or not it is based on a religious belief) but they cannot justify discrimination of this kind, which means that certain reasons for a request for expedition (religious ones) are excluded from consideration altogether.[45]

R (Adath Yisroel Burial Society) remains a relatively rare case of a successful argument based on *Thlimmenos* discrimination in the context of public services. Given a diversity of judicial approach in considering Article 14, and general reluctance of the courts to direct authorities on the way they should balance competing demands for resources, discussed in detail in the next chapter, the scope of the obligation on public bodies therefore remains unclear. It is certainly plausible, however, that commissioners might be required *at least* to be open to the possibility of making exceptions for patients whose religious beliefs or other characteristics underlie their need

[43] Ibid at 112.

[44] Ibid at 123.

[45] Ibid at 124.

to access generally unfunded treatment options. While concerns about the impact on funding for others may justify a particular decision not to make a policy exception for those from a particular group – or refuse an exception for a particular individual – these wider impacts would be factors to be weighed in the balance when considering the question of justification. IFR policies which rule out the relevance of personal characteristics may fall foul of Article 14.

The duty to make reasonable adjustments

Sometimes a patient may be unable to access available treatment for their condition because of an unrelated health condition or 'comorbidity' – because, for example, that treatment may exacerbate their comorbidity or interact badly with medication taken for it or because the available treatment is in some other way inaccessible. If alternative treatments, which would be accessible, are not normally funded, then the patient my need to make an IFR to ask that the unfunded treatment be made available to them instead. Commissioners may agree to an IFR where, because of comorbidity, the patient can demonstrate that they are able to derive significantly more clinical benefit from the unfunded treatment and are therefore clinically exceptional. However, NHS England policy suggests that it will not usually be enough simply to demonstrate inability to access a treatment because of a comorbidity, particularly where the condition is a common one because 'a patient cannot be exceptional by virtue of also having a comorbidity which is common in the general population'.[46]

The Court considered what common law rationality requires of decisions in this type of situation in *R (SB) v NHS England*.[47] Here the claimant was a severely autistic child who also had a rare condition called Phenylketonuria (PKU) which inhibits the ability to ingest protein and can cause serious disabilities if not treated. The usual treatment for PKU is dietary management – involving a very restrictive diet. Because of his severe autism, the claimant was unable to cope with the required dietary restrictions and so – supported by his doctors – had requested to be treated with the drug Kuvan. This request had been rejected by NHS England (the relevant commissioning body). The Court held that their rejection was irrational for a number of reasons. In particular, they noted that given the rarity of the combination of conditions, their severity, and the evidence that Kuvan would prove a clinically effective option 'it is difficult to see how

46 NHS England (n 8).

47 *R (on the application of SB) (by his father and litigation friend PB) v NHS England* [2017] EWHC 2000 (Admin).

the Panel could reach any other rational conclusion than that he was likely to gain significantly more clinical benefit from taking Kuvan than other children with PKU whose condition could be managed by the conventional treatment alone'.[48]

The combination of severe autism and PKU in this case was very rare indeed – only one or two individuals in the whole of the UK, including the claimant, were both affected by the two conditions and responsive to Kuvan.[49] It remains unclear how rare a case – and how significant the clinical benefit – would have to be before a refusal to treat as exceptional is irrational.

However where – as will sometimes be the case – the comorbidity in question amounts to a disability within the meaning of the Equality Act, additional legal obligations will arise which do not depend on how common or rare that condition is in the population. Separate from the positive action provisions, the Equality Act includes an obligation on service providers and those charged with public functions to treat individuals with disabilities differently in some circumstances by making reasonable adjustments. Section 20 of the Act provides that where there is a policy, criterion or practice which puts disabled persons at a substantial disadvantage in comparison with persons who are not disabled, service providers are obliged to take such steps as are reasonable to avoid the disadvantage. Failure to do so amounts to unlawful discrimination.[50] The purpose of reasonable adjustments is to eliminate, as far as possible, the disadvantage attaching to that disability in order to improve equality of access and opportunity and the duty is generally seen as a transformative legal tool which has significant potential to improve inclusion across the areas in which it applies.[51] There have been instances – mainly in an employment context where most of the case law still is – where courts have taken a very expansive approach to interpretation of the duty.[52] Importantly, unlike with rationality at common law, the existence of the obligation to make reasonable adjustments to policy will apply irrespective of how rare or common the relevant disability is.

An adjustment will only be required if it is reasonable. Reasonableness is left undefined by statute. The EHRC Code of Practice provides some guidance, suggesting that of particular relevance will be the extent to which a proposed adjustment would overcome the disadvantage and the practicability and cost of the adjustment.[53] Of particular concern in this context will of course be

---

[48] Ibid at 49.

[49] Ibid at 43.

[50] Equality Act 2010, s 29(7).

[51] For a comprehensive account of the duty see A. Lawson (2008) *Disability and Equality Law in Britain: The Role of Reasonable Adjustment*, Oxford: Hart.

[52] See, for example, *Archibald v Fife Council* [2004] IRLR 651.

[53] Equality and Human Rights Commission (2011) *Equality Act 2010 Statutory Code of Practice: Services, Public Functions and Associations*, EHRC, at 7.29–7.30.

the extent to which budgetary considerations are relevant to the question of reasonableness – will it be reasonable to make an exception irrespective of the implications of diverting resources away from other patients? The Code of Practice notes that '[t]he resources available to the service provider as a whole are likely to be taken into account as well as other demands on those resources'.[54]

There is little case law to assist in assessing reasonableness in the context of public services. In an employment context it is clear that, while cost alone is unlikely to disqualify a potential adjustment from being reasonable, the relative cost of the adjustment might be. Laws LJ in *Sanders v Newham Sixth Form College*[55] (an employment case) made clear that it was not possible to assess the reasonableness of an adjustment separately from the question of how significant the disadvantage caused by the policy is. The more significant the disadvantage, the greater the resources that are required to be spent before the cost prevents the adjustment from being a reasonable one. In *Cordell v Foreign and Commonwealth Office* the (very high) cost of the adjustment in question – the provision of a lip reading service in Kazakhstan – was considered relative to the overall budget available for reasonable adjustments. The Foreign and Commonwealth Office had a budget set aside for reasonable adjustments and the impact on that budget was to be taken into account according to their own policy. The Employment Appeal Tribunal decided that while the size of this budget could not be decisive (as the size of the budget was itself a decision of the employer and an employer cannot be permitted to avoid its legal obligations simply by selecting a smaller budget for adjustments) it was nonetheless a relevant factor. It was also held that the general resources of the employer were relevant to the question of reasonableness as 'no-one's resources, not even the government's, are infinite'.[56]

In relation to commissioning health care, the cost of making an adjustment and the impact of doing so on the overall commissioning budget, will therefore be factors likely to be relevant to the question of reasonableness – but only when considered in relation to the nature of the disadvantage faced by the individual patient whose disability means they cannot access a funded course of treatment in the same way as can other patients. For this reason, where a disability is – in the words of NHS England – 'common in the general population', this *may* have a bearing on whether or not commissioners are obliged to make adjustments or exceptions for this group. But the prevalence of that disability will have no bearing on whether or not the duty to make reasonable adjustments arises in the first place.

---

54 Ibid at 7.32.

55 *Sanders v Newham Sixth Form College* [2014] EWCA Civ 734.

56 *Cordell v Foreign and Commonwealth Office* [2012] I.C.R. 280 (2011) 32–33.

In contrast to employment, the duty is an anticipatory one.[57] Commissioners (and other service providers) cannot wait for individuals with disabilities to present themselves but must consider in advance what adjustments to policies and practices might be reasonable in relation to disabled services users generally. While it may be easiest to do so by identifying in advance a set of alternative arrangements for the relevant group at the stage of determining funding policy, it is arguable that this duty could also be met by ensuring that there is a route to access alternatives by means of an IFR. In any case, in addition to the anticipatory duty, it is likely that the duty to make reasonable adjustments will also apply in a reactive way – as it does in other contexts such as employment and education – in response to specific difficulties faced by specific individuals who become known to commissioners.[58] In these circumstances, making an exception to the original funding policy may well amount to a reasonable adjustment and IFR policies should reflect this.[59]

Indirect discrimination

In determining the approach to take in dealing with requests for individual funding, commissioners should also be mindful that their approach to dealing with IFRs may also be relevant to whether or not the *original* funding policy from which an exception is sought – such as a decision not to fund a particular drug – is itself discriminatory. Most funding policies do not directly discriminate, although some do – the use of age limits for access to in vitro fertilization would be an example of potential direct age discrimination, for example, although it will be remembered that, unlike for other characteristics, direct age discrimination can be justified under the Equality Act. Funding policies are more likely to be susceptible to charges of indirect discrimination – prohibited both under Section 19 of the Equality Act and Article 14 of the ECHR. A policy will be *potentially* indirectly discriminatory where it is apparently neutral, and applies equally to those with and without the relevant protected characteristic, but in fact serves to disadvantage those sharing a characteristic more than it does those without it. For example, a policy which determines that artificial blood products will not generally be funded applies equally to all but may disadvantage those who are unable to be treated with human blood because of their religious beliefs; and a policy which determines that only one hearing aid, rather than two, will generally

[57] Equality Act 2010, Schedule 2, 2(2), stipulates that the duty arises in respect of 'disabled persons generally'.

[58] Recently confirmed, in the context of higher education, in *The University of Bristol v Dr Robert Abrahart* [2024] EWHC 299 (KB).

[59] See Equality and Human Rights Commission (n 53) 7.7 and 7.8.

be funded will disadvantage older age groups because they are more likely to benefit from having access to two hearing aids. Importantly the impact, or disadvantage, which is relevant to identifying indirect discrimination will be broader than one relating solely to clinical considerations. Nor will the size of the group affected be relevant here. There is no need to show that the impact on the individual is unusual or exceptional. Indeed, part of the point of indirect discrimination is to understand the disadvantage faced by an individual in the context of the disadvantage faced by a much wider group with a shared protected characteristic.

Where policies have disparate impact, they can be justified where the policy makers can show that the policy is a proportionate means of achieving a legitimate aim. Behind many or most decisions to restrict access to health interventions is of course the need to ration limited resources and to target those limited resources towards interventions which commissioners believe will be most cost-effective or otherwise beneficial. It is important to note in this particular context that while discrimination cannot be justified simply because it is cheaper, courts have recognized that the imperative of meeting wider budgetary constraints is likely to amount to a legitimate aim.[60] However, commissioners will still be obliged to demonstrate that the policy choices made to achieve that aim are proportionate because while 'saving cost is a legitimate objective of public policy … if a benefit is to be limited to save costs it must be limited in a non-discriminatory way'.[61]

To what extent is a willingness to make exceptions capable of 'saving' the original policy from being indirectly discriminatory? Given that the possibility of making exceptions to a general rule means that the harmful impacts of the rule may be reduced, and further, that a willingness to make exceptions will sometimes amount to a less discriminatory way of achieving the overall aim, it seems plausible that it should be a relevant factor. Identifying and considering disparate impact on protected groups is of course required of commissioners to ensure they comply with the PSED to have 'due regard' to the need to avoid discrimination and promote equality. Indeed Fredman has argued that, where disparate impact has been identified as part of the exercise of the PSED, pre-emptive action may be required in order to correct any practices identified as potentially discriminatory, amounting to a form of mandatory positive action.[62] In relation to reasonable adjustments, the EHRC Code of Practice makes clear that it will be difficult to establish

---

[60] *R (Coll) v Secretary of State for Justice* [2017] UKSC 40.

[61] Ibid at para 40.

[62] S. Fredman (2014) 'Addressing Disparate Impact: Indirect Discrimination and the Public Sector Equality Duty', *Industrial Law Journal* 43(3): 349–363 at 354; and see discussion in Davies and Robison (n 28).

proportionality, and therefore justification, where there has been a failure to make reasonable adjustments to the policy or practice in question.[63]

There is case law to suggest that a willingness to make exceptions will be relevant to whether or not a policy is indirectly discriminatory. In *Watkins-Singh*, a uniform policy at a school which prohibited the wearing of jewellery was indirectly discriminatory on grounds of race and religion *because* the school had refused to make an exception to the policy in the case of a Sikh pupil who needed to wear jewellery for religious reasons.[64] Similar considerations are also evident in the context of Article 14 of the ECHR. In *AL (Serbia)*, for example, it was one of the features that led the Court to conclude that the government policy of using family status to determine eligibility for indefinite leave to remain was justified. The measure was proportionate because, among other things, 'it permitted compelling claims by those falling outside the policy to be recognised and accommodated'.[65]

On the other hand, it is unlikely that a mere willingness to make exceptions in principle will always be enough to prevent a funding policy amounting to indirect discrimination. In *Eisai v NICE*, there was a challenge to NICE guidance which had recommended that Aricept, a drug manufactured by Eisai to alleviate symptoms in those with mild to moderate Alzheimer's disease, should only be funded for patients whose scores fell within a certain range on a cognitive test. Eisai argued, among other things, that the guidance was indirectly discriminatory on grounds of race and disability because the test disadvantaged those with learning difficulties and those for whom English was not a first language. NICE accepted this but argued that there was unlikely to be discriminatory impact in practice because the guidance made clear it was not to be followed slavishly – clinicians were able to identify these anomalies and funding policies and decisions could reflect this accordingly. NICE argued that this flexibility should be enough to defeat any charge of discrimination. Dobbs J in the High Court disagreed. He found that the issue of atypical groups had been dealt with in an unsatisfactory way in the guidance because 'instead of looking at how NICE as a public body could itself promote equal opportunity, having accepted that the Guidance could have a discriminatory effect if applied slavishly, the approach taken was to leave it to others to sort out in the hope and expectation that they would'.[66] This failure to deal adequately with disadvantaged groups in the guidance meant that the guidance did amount to indirect discrimination.

---

63 Equality and Human Rights Commission (n 53).

64 *R (on the application of Watkins-Singh) v Governing Body of Abderdare Girls' High School* [2008] EWHC 1865.

65 *AL (Serbia) v Secretary of State for the Home Department* [2008] UKHL 42 at 3.

66 *Eisai Limited v The National Institute for Health and Clinical Excellence (NICE)* [2007] EWHC 1941 (Admin) at 83.

Making exceptions for a group – or being open to making exceptions for individuals – on the basis of personal characteristics may also undermine the aim of the original funding policy decision in some circumstances. This is most obviously the case where the original policy relates to a treatment which would be wholly or mainly likely to benefit a protected group if it were available – but where a decision has been made that the resources to fund that treatment would be better spent elsewhere. In these circumstances the onus will be on commissioners to justify the original policy as proportionate in the context of wider funding priorities. Even where this is not the case the likely size of the group for which exceptions are potentially appropriate should – arguably at least – have a bearing on whether or not they need to be made in order to justify the original funding policy. The likely cost of making exceptions will have a direct bearing on the reduction in resources available for other patients and should therefore be relevant to any proportionality assessment which involves the weighing of disadvantage to those who will be impacted by the measure.

Conclusion

Equality law has long recognized that the requirement to treat likes alike can only go so far in eliminating unfair discrimination and promoting equality. Being blind to personal characteristics will often create or entrench disadvantage where those characteristics inhibit access to available services or are otherwise relevant to the impact a policy will have on those to whom it applies. In the ways described earlier, therefore, the law sometimes permits, and sometimes requires, service providers and others subject to equality law to make exceptions to general rules so as to eliminate disadvantage experienced by particular groups in access to health care. Using, or complying, with these provisions presents a number of challenges for policy makers, however.

It will have become apparent in the discussion in this chapter that there is still some uncertainty over the boundaries of both required and permissible positive action and the question of what will amount to a reasonable adjustment. One thing does seem clear however: an IFR policy, or an approach to identifying exceptions to a funding policy, which excludes altogether the relevance of protected characteristics from considerations of exceptionality is likely to be legally problematic. As well as identifying the likely disparate impact of funding policies on protected groups as part of the exercise of the PSED, commissioners should consider whether exceptions can or should be made for protected groups. Exceptionality policies should make clear that exceptions will be made for individuals disadvantaged by protected characteristics where required by law. Consideration should also be given to the circumstances under which use will be made of the optional positive action provisions to redress disadvantage or meet needs.

As Chris Newdick has long argued, there is a need to balance the compelling cases of individuals against the health care needs and outcomes of the wider population – and as a result the legal framework needs to permit commissioners to find an appropriate compromise between realizing individual rights and addressing communitarian concerns. This was recognized by the High Court in *Condliff* where it was held that 'it is impossible to see how the Social Factors Exclusion, as part of the PCT policy of medical resource allocation, does not amount to a fair balance between the individuals seeking treatment under the IFRs and the medical requirements of the community as a whole'.[67] One of the challenges posed by the equality law framework, and in particular the provisions discussed earlier, however, is that it requires commissioners to also consider a third dimension in arriving at this balance – that of groups whose shared characteristics disadvantage them, or give rise to particular needs, in relation to individual treatments or interventions or more generally in relation to access to health care or health outcomes. This is not to suggest that groups disadvantaged by protected characteristics need be prioritized or treated more favourably than those disadvantaged in other ways – as was seen earlier there is scope to consider the impact of making exceptions for protected groups and individuals on other patients in the context of determining proportionality (for positive action and indirect discrimination) or reasonableness (for reasonable adjustments). But consideration of the needs of these groups should at least be part of the balancing act.

Acknowledgements

Chapter 3 substantially reproduces the contents of an article published as Horton, R. (2025) 'Equality, discrimination and exceptionality in access to healthcare' *Northern Ireland Legal Quarterly* Vol 76 No. 1: 24–28 and appears here with kind permission of the journal.

[67] Waksman, J. in *R. (on the application of Condliff) v North Staffordshire Primary Care Trust* [2011] EWHC 872 (Admin) at 67.

4

Reviewing Decisions

Introduction

We have seen that the scope of many of the obligations imposed by equality law depend on the interpretation and application of tests of proportionality and comparison. Comparison requires us to take a view on the respects in which two individuals or groups are similar or different, and which of the differences between them should be discounted and which are relevant. Proportionality, as we have seen, often involves not only assessment of the legitimacy of the aim for which a measure has been adopted, and whether the measure is appropriate and necessary to achieve it, but also a balancing of the impacts of the measure on those affected against its wider aims. The Public Sector Equality Duty (PSED) requires an understanding of what is meant by 'due regard'. The approach of the courts is therefore key. In particular, the extent to which the courts are willing to engage in scrutiny of decision making, or, by contrast, to defer to the judgement of the decision makers, will shape the strength and effectiveness of the legal framework.

In reviewing the acts of the executive, the judiciary have long recognized an important concern as to the proper scope of their intervention. Traditionally, this has manifested itself in a culture of 'deference' and a reluctance to scrutinize the decision making of public authorities beyond an assessment of rationality, legality or procedural impropriety.[1] In particular, there has been a strong reluctance to substitute the views of the court for those of the public authority, provided that the latter complies with these basic minimum standards. Broadly speaking, two main reasons are normally given as to why (some degree of) deference is appropriate and necessary in the context of public law.[2]

---

[1] *Council of Civil Service Unions v Minister for the Civil Service* [1985] A.C. 374.

[2] K. Syrett (2014) 'Courts, Expertise and Resource Allocation: Is there a Judicial "Legitimacy Problem"?', *Public Health Ethics* 7(2): 112–122.

The first of these relates to the separation of powers and to democratic accountability. The concern is that in exercising too intense a scrutiny of matters of public policy, the judiciary may be overstepping their constitutional function and usurping the role of democratically elected decision makers (or those to whom authority to decide has been devolved by elected bodies). This anxiety is often manifest where highly sensitive or 'political' issues such as national security or resource allocation are at stake. The view is that resource related decisions should be made by those who are democratically answerable to the electorate. The second, though related, concern of the judiciary in scrutinizing decisions of public authorities relates to what is often termed 'institutional competence'. Significantly, judges will express concern that they lack the perspective necessary to understand the full implications of resource allocation decisions which represent a balance struck between a very wide range of interests. As Fredman puts it: 'The bipolar, reactive, dispute-based nature of judicial processes means that judges cannot achieve the wide lens necessary to make polycentric decisions.'[3]

This chapter assesses the approach (or likely approach) of the courts to reviewing resource allocation decisions involving potential discrimination and what this may mean for our understanding of the scope of the obligations which bind those commissioning health care, and for the ability of the law to address inequality and disadvantage which relates to our protected characteristics in this context. Given that there is only limited case law, to date, on discrimination in health care resource allocation, it will consider both 'ordinary' judicial review of health care resource allocation decisions and case law which deals with discrimination in a range of resource allocation contexts.

Deference in 'ordinary' judicial review

An often cited example of the reluctance of the judiciary to involve themselves in decisions which set priorities in health care is *R v Cambridge Health Authority ex parte B.*[4] The case concerned a challenge to a decision of Cambridge Health Authority to not fund experimental treatment for a ten-year-old leukaemia patient because, among other things, the view of the clinicians was that the treatment would be ineffective. As Syrett notes, while clinical considerations appear to have been at the heart of the decision, the Authority had also been concerned with the resource implications of funding the treatment and the funding that would be displaced from other patients

[3] S. Fredman (2008) *Human Rights Transformed: Positive Rights and Positive Duties*, Oxford: Oxford University Press.

[4] *R v Cambridge Health Authority, ex parte B* [1995] EWCA Civ 49.

as a result.[5] At first instance, the High Court had quashed the decision of the Health Authority, noting the importance of the interest at stake, and holding that in such circumstances the Health Authority 'must do more than toll the bell of tight resources' and 'must explain the priorities that have led it to decline to fund the treatment', something it found the Authority had failed to do in this case.[6] In disagreeing with the High Court and upholding the Health Authority's appeal, the Court of Appeal famously stated that:

> [D]ifficult and agonising judgments have to be made as to how a limited budget is best allocated to the maximum advantage of the maximum number of patients. That is not a judgment which the court can make. In my judgment, it is not something that a health authority such as this authority can be fairly criticised for not advancing before the court.[7]

Almost 30 years on from *Cambridge*, there is evidence that the courts have become more willing to review resourcing decisions made by health commissioners, as we will see in this chapter.[8] Nonetheless, significant deference remains in evidence, at least in relation to the substance of the decisions, in common with resource allocation decisions in other contexts. Deference stems from two types of concerns – competence and democratic role.

A useful example of concerns about competence arose in *Servier*, a case concerning a challenge by Servier Laboratories to a refusal by the National Institute for Health and Care Excellence (NICE) to recommend for funding its drug 'Protelos' which was intended for the prevention of fractures in patients with osteoporosis. The High Court began its assessment by noting that 'it is important to stress at the outset that NICE is the specialist, expert body, charged with making appraisals and decisions of this type. The court is not. I have neither the right, still less the expertise, to review the decisions as to their substance'.[9] The decision was overturned on appeal – the Court of Appeal found that NICE had not properly explained its reasons for rejecting the methods employed by the pharmaceutical company – but the approach of the High Court is indicative of a nervousness to scrutinize the reasoning behind decisions of this sort. It is true that allocation decisions, as

5 Syrett (n 2).

6 *R. v Cambridge Health Authority, ex parte B* [1995] 1 FLR 1055 (QBD) at paras 1064–5.

7 *R v Cambridge Health Authority, ex parte B* [1995] 1 WLR 898 (CA) at para 906.

8 See, for example, K. Syrett (2007) *Law, Legitimacy and the Rationing of Health Care: A Contextual and Comparative Perspective*, Cambridge: Cambridge University Press; and D. Wang (2017) 'From Wednesbury Unreasonableness to Accountability for Reasonableness', *Cambridge Law Journal* 76(3): 642–670.

9 *R (Servier Laboratories Ltd.) v NICE* (2009) EWHC 281 (Admin), [6].

we saw in Chapter 2, often rest on economic analysis which is beyond the usual expertise of the judiciary. Determining whether – for example – all relevant considerations have been taken into account in these circumstances may be a relatively technical task, made more challenging by the fact that courts are generally more reticent to admit expert evidence in judicial review proceedings.[10]

Syrett argues, however, that courts are not inherently incapable in these matters. There are plenty of examples of courts successfully grappling with epidemiological and health economic evidence (including, in the end, on appeal in *Servier*) and indeed judges are generally well placed to deal with the context of administrative and managerial decision making.[11] Some parallels may perhaps be drawn with the approach of the courts to making decisions which involve clinical considerations in respect of individual patients. It is notable, for example, that in the Court of Protection, where decisions about the capacity and best interests of incapacitous patients are made, there has been a noticeable shift in the willingness of the judiciary to recognize that the questions at issue often involve assessment not only of clinical factors but of broader values and interests of the patient, where deference to the medical profession would be misplaced.[12] As Butler Sloss stated in *Re A* – where it was necessary to determine whether sterilization was in the best interests of the patient – 'it is the judge, not the doctor, who makes the decision that it is in the best interests of the patient that the operation be performed'.[13] The same may also be said of the approach of the civil courts to questions of medical negligence, particularly in the arena of informed consent.[14]

A second 'competence' problem is really a knowledge problem. In matters of priority setting the courts are conscious that it is rarely possible for them to identify the opportunity cost involved in the decision to allocate funding to a particular intervention and that they therefore lack the necessary 'wide lens', only available to the relevant decision-making authority, to assess competing claims on funding against often unknown 'others'. While there may appear to be compelling reasons to allocate funds to the particular individual or group bringing the legal challenge before the court, it is not possible to assess the strength of the claim without identifying those from

---

10 *R (Gardner) v Secretary of State for Health and Social Care* [2021] EWHC 2946 (Admin).

11 Syrett (n 2).

12 Although it is important to note that the Court of Protection does not, in this context, make decisions about resource allocation – it determines only whether available treatment options are in the best interests of patients and has no power to order that additional treatments be resourced or provided.

13 *Re A (medical treatment: male sterilisation)* [2000] 1 F.L.R. 549.

14 See, for example, discussion in S. Devaney and S. Holm (2018) 'The Transmutation of Deference in Medicine: An Ethico-Legal Perspective', *Medical Law Review* 26(2): 202–224.

whom funding would be divested as a result. As Lord Hoffmann put it in a different context, a court

> has no way of knowing whether this means that other people dependent upon social security, police protection and so on will have to make sacrifices because there is less money for them. The only people who can make such decisions are the democratically elected bodies who are in charge of the budget as a whole.[15]

This difficulty was expressed very clearly by the High Court recently in a judicial review bought against the failure of NHS England to keep waiting times for gender identity services within required limits. Noting, among other things, the opportunity cost involved in increasing resources for the service, the Court held that in respect of any order it might give, 'the result might be to divert resources from other important health service purposes in circumstances where the court could not gauge whether or not such a diversion would be beneficial overall'.[16]

Even if it were possible for authorities and courts to identify with any certainty the opportunity cost that would result from a requirement to fund a particular intervention for a particular patient or patients, the deference issue would remain. This is because, as Syrett argues, it is ultimately 'the profundity of the moral convictions which are held, the absence of consensus on a socially acceptable basis for distribution and the incommensurability of the positions adopted by different parties, which give rise to the "legitimacy problem" in the allocation of scarce healthcare resources'.[17] The question of which principles should underlie resource allocation decisions in health care is one which has given rise to profound and consistent disagreement among both ethicists and policy makers over decades and one on which it may not be possible to reach consensus.[18] Certainly, then, these are questions which the judiciary may feel are best left to the democratically elected, and those to whom they delegate decision making.

Notwithstanding these reservations, however, in the context of decisions about health care rationing generally (not discrimination specific) the courts have moved from the highly deferential approach seen by the Court of Appeal in *Cambridge*, to one where – within an area of comfort at least – they are much more willing to engage in more intense scrutiny of allocation

15 L. Hoffmann (2002) 'Separation of Powers', *Judicial Review* 7: 137–145.
16 *R (AA) v NHS Commissioning Board* [2023] EWHC 43 (Admin) at 97.
17 Syrett (n 2).
18 N. Daniels (2008) *Just Health: Meeting Health Needs Fairly*, Cambridge: Cambridge University Press.

decisions.[19] This area of comfort is the procedural aspects of decision making (rather than the substantive merits of the decision) where there are fewer concerns about overstepping their constitutional role. Thus, according to Wang, 'courts have started to require administrative decisions to be based on explicit and rational reasons, and made through transparent and fair processes … and have become increasingly demanding and stringent when assessing these reasons and processes'.[20] Indeed, Wang argues that the structure of this enhanced scrutiny reflects the 'accountability for reasonableness' framework for decision making, proposed by Daniels and Sabin as a way forward in the absence of consensus on principles of rationing and is a structure which – partly a cause of and partly in consequence of this approach to judicial scrutiny – has been adopted by many decision makers including, explicitly, NICE.[21] In particular, accountability for reasonableness requires both that decision making be transparent and that the grounds for decision making be relevant – this latter condition is also familiar as it is central to the approach courts take to assessment of rationality in judicial review.[22] This approach does not rid courts of concerns of legitimacy and competence entirely, however – decisions about the factors that may or may not be relevant to a decision are themselves often value-laden (for example, whether or not 'social' factors should be taken into account, discussed in the last chapter) and may be questions on which courts defer to the view of the public authority.

Equality law

The next part of this chapter reviews the scope for deference in the application of equality law – both under the Human Rights Act and the Equality Act – to questions of resource allocation. In doing so two aspects of the legal tests for discrimination will be particularly significant. First is the question of comparison. In determining whether or not a policy or decision gives rise to prima facie discrimination (such that the question of justification must be addressed) the court is first required to decide whether or not an appropriate comparison can be drawn between an individual or group and a comparator or comparators. This requires an assessment of whether or not the differences between them are relevant (such that different treatment or impact can be explained other than by discrimination) or irrelevant and gives rise to questions about who is best placed to make that judgement – the public authority or the court. Second is the

19 See, for example Syrett (n 8) and Wang (n 8).

20 Wang (n 8).

21 M. Rawlins (2012) 'Playing Fair on Treatments', *Health Service Journal* 122(6315): 18.

22 *R v Devon Health Authority, ex parte Coughlan* [2001] QB 213.

proportionality test. Proportionality – whether a policy or decision amounts to a 'proportionate means to achieve a legitimate aim' – is the test normally used in the Equality Act to determine whether treatment or decisions that would otherwise amount to discrimination can be justified. It applies in respect of both indirect discrimination[23] and direct age discrimination.[24] It is also the test used to determine the permissible scope of positive action and applies to a range of other relevant exceptions, such as the provision of single-sex services. Likewise, proportionality is a test used under the European Convention on Human Rights (ECHR) to decide whether treatment or legislation which is prima facie discriminatory under Article 14 is justified.

The scope for different degrees of deference in the application of the proportionality test manifests itself in two main ways. First, there are a number of different variants of the proportionality test itself which may entail different standards of review. Broadly speaking, there are four different approaches found to the application of the proportionality test across the various legal contexts under consideration here. Assuming the alleged discriminator has established the existence of a legitimate aim, the question then turns to the issue of whether the means chosen to achieve that end were proportionate. The first, and weakest, form of the test is that of whether the means chosen to achieve the end are appropriate to it. A stronger version of the test asks whether the means chosen are not only appropriate but necessary. Thus, even where appropriate, action may not be proportionate where it goes further than necessary in order to achieve the aim (and therefore results, perhaps, in discriminatory impacts which could have been avoided without compromising the achievement of the aim). A third form of the test requires the court to establish whether an appropriate balance has been struck between the importance of the aim and the discriminatory impact of the action taken to achieve it. The final version of the test requires both necessity and balance. Where applied, it is likely to result in the most 'intense' form of proportionality review. Even means necessary to achieve an aim may not be justified where the discriminatory impact outweighs the importance of the aim. The courts have not been consistent in their approach to the choice of test either when adjudicating claims under the Equality Act, or under Article 14 of the ECHR.

A second issue relates to the approach the judiciary take to the question of establishing proportionality in terms of the rigour with which the claims of the state (or claimant) are examined and the weight given by the judiciary to the views of the primary decision maker. These two issues are clearly related – a court will be more likely to need persuasive evidence from a

---

23 Equality Act 2010, s 19.

24 Ibid, s 13.

respondent needing to show that their chosen means of achieving a legitimate aim is necessary rather than simply that it is appropriate. Separate, although conceptually related to the form of test used by the judiciary, is the issue of the weight afforded to the initial decision maker in determining whether the proportionality test is satisfied.

Proportionality poses a challenge for determining the appropriate scope of judicial intervention. In some respects it engages with questions that may be classed as 'procedural' and therefore within the traditional area of comfort for judicial scrutiny – such as, for example, whether a decision that a measure is 'appropriate' or 'necessary' to achieve an aim is based on evidence. On the other hand, particularly in its strongest form, the proportionality test invites the judiciary to engage in a weighing of the interests at stake, an activity which is often argued to be beyond the proper scope of their intervention where questions of resource allocation for the public good are involved. Lord Hoffmann, for example, argued in both his judicial and extra-judicial writing that while certain basic and human rights cannot be overridden by utilitarian concerns (or can be only in restricted circumstances) and that courts have a role in ensuring this does not happen, 'outside these basic rights, there are many decisions which have to be made everyday (for example, about the allocation of resources) in which the only fair method of decision is by some person or body accountable to the electorate'.[25] The problem does not only arise in the context of utilitarian decision making but in any context – including health care commissioning - where policy makers must determine which from a range of competing principles to deploy in prioritizing resources.[26] Given the nature of these decisions the courts are understandably reluctant to substitute their own views for the appropriate weight to be given to a range of competing – and potentially equally valid – considerations. Against this backdrop, however, Fredman, among others, has argued that, in the context of developing jurisprudence under the Human Rights Act, the judiciary have recently begun to shift their approach to deference in recognition that protection of individual human rights is an essential part of democracy rather than something necessarily ranged against it.[27] Indeed, King argues that in consequence of the Human Rights Act, issues of resource allocation have ceased to be 'non-justiciable'. Instead, where human rights are involved, the relevant debate has now shifted to the question of what intensity of review

[25] *(R (Alconbury Developments Ltd) v Secretary of State for the Environment, Transport and the Regions* [2001] UKHL 23 at 70.

[26] For a useful discussion of this point see also Syrett (n 2).

[27] S. Fredman (2006) 'From Deference to Democracy: The Role of Equality under the Human Rights Act 1998', *Law Quarterly Review* 122: 53–81.

is appropriate.[28] What follows will explore the intensity of review applied in relation to claims under Article 14 of the ECHR and then the Equality Act where issues of health care resource allocation and the right not to be subject to discrimination are both engaged. The main focus will be on proportionality but the chapter also considers the scope for deference at an earlier stage of a claim for discrimination – in establishing a comparator – and in an assessment of compliance with the PSED.

Article 14 of the European Convention on Human Rights

Proportionality

The usual approach of the European Court of Human Rights (ECtHR) to proportionality has been to ask whether there is objective and reasonable justification, a question normally answered in turn by asking whether there is a 'reasonable relationship of proportionality between the means employed and the [legitimate] aim sought to be realised'.[29] The national courts have tended to apply the test in a more structured way, often but not always working through all four of the elements of the test identified above.[30]

The intensity of review applied to the application of the test in relation to Article 14 has been the subject of much recent judicial attention. The ECtHR has always applied a 'margin of appreciation' – a doctrine of judicial 'self-restraint' which determines the degree of discretion afforded to member states. The width of the margin is determined by a range of factors, including the seriousness of the impact of the policy or decision at issue, and whether the measure involves social or economic policy or the allocation of resources (in which case a wider margin is likely to be given). On the other hand, a narrower margin is usually applied where the characteristic in question is 'suspect' – these are held to be particularly sensitive grounds demanding more intense review.

In the national courts, the intensity of review, or deference, afforded to public authorities has been complicated by the adoption of what is known as the 'manifestly without reasonable foundation' (MWRF) test, the use of which had remained unclear and inconsistent until clarity was recently provided by the Supreme Court. This test suggests that courts should defer to the policy choices of public bodies in respect of matters of social and economic policy unless these are 'manifestly without reasonable

[28] J. King (2007) 'The Justiciability of Resource Allocation', *Modern Law Review* 70(2): 197–224.

[29] *Carson v United Kingdom* (2010) 51 EHRR 369, para 61.

[30] *Bank Mellat v HM Treasury (No 2)* [2013] UKSC 39, 72–76.

foundation'.[31] It was unclear whether the MWRF was intended as an *alternative* and weaker form of proportionality test, or rather simply an approach to deciding the appropriate *weight* to be afforded to the views of public authorities in applying the more conventional proportionality test.[32] There was also dispute about the circumstances in which the test should apply. In *Stec* it was suggested that it would apply as a matter of course in any case involving economic and social policy, irrespective of the ground of discrimination, whereas in *JD & A v UK* the ECtHR suggested it would only be applicable in cases concerning the adoption of positive action.[33]

The Supreme Court recently considered the issue at length in *R (SC) v Secretary of State for Work and Pensions* – a case concerning a challenge to legislation that limited child tax credit to two children on the basis that it discriminated against women (as primary carers) as well as against children (and in particular children living in households with more than two children) contrary to Article 14 (in conjunction with Article 8 and Article 1, Protocol 1).[34] It confirmed that the MWRF standard is not a separate test but rather a way of describing a wider margin of appreciation; and it made clear that there are no hard and fast 'rules' which determine the circumstances in which the MWRF standard will be applied. Rather, whatever the context, the degree of intensity of review required will depend on a complex matrix of factors, all of which are relevant. These factors largely match those used by the ECtHR to determine the margin of appreciation and include, in particular, the ground of discrimination and whether or not the decision in question concerns economic and social policy.

Most of the characteristics protected under the Equality Act have been held to be suspect characteristics by the ECtHR. These include disability,[35] sex,[36] sexual orientation,[37] religion,[38] and race, ethnic origin and nationality.[39] Gender reassignment has not yet been considered by the Strasbourg Court but it seems unlikely that it would not be found to be suspect also. Certainly, it fits the criteria of Lord Reed, who suggested in *SC* that the sensitivity of a characteristic rested on the link between the characteristic and 'problems of stereotyping, stigma and social exclusion'.[40] Given the open-ended list

[31] *Stec v United Kingdom* [2006] 4 WLUK 341, 52.

[32] See, for example, *R (Drexler) v Leicestershire CC* [2020] EWCA Civ 502.

[33] *Stec v United Kingdom* [2006] 4 WLUK 341; *JD v United Kingdom* [2019] 10 WLUK 436.

[34] *R (SC and others) v Secretary of State for Work and Pensions* [2021] UKSC 26.

[35] *Kiss v Hungary* [2013] 56 EHRR 38; *JD v United Kingdom* [2019] 48 BHRC 36.

[36] *Petrovic v Austria* [2001] 33 EHRR 14.

[37] *EB v France* [2008] 47 EHRR 21.

[38] *Vojnity v Hungary* [2013] 2 FCR 495.

[39] *Timishev v Russia* [2007] 44 EHRR 37.

[40] *SC* (n 34) at para 103.

in Article 14 it is possible that the list of suspect characteristics could be further extended by the ECtHR, or in the national courts according to the test in *SC*.

Importantly, however, age has not been deemed a suspect ground. The issue has not yet been considered by the ECtHR and the UK courts have failed to offer much clarity. In *Carson* age was identified as a 'contemporary example of a borderline case' between the two categories of 'suspect' and 'non suspect' characteristics.[41] In *AL (Serbia)* Lord Brown suggested, obiter, that age was a suspect characteristic, on a par with sex and race,[42] whereas the Court of Appeal, in considering Gurkha pensions entitlements, decided that 'stronger justification' would be required for discrimination on grounds of nationality than it was on grounds of age.[43] In *Drexler* the Court of Appeal was clear that 'age is not a suspect ground of discrimination, such as race or sex'[44] but in *SC*, decided later, the Supreme Court appears to suggest that the answer may depend on the context, noting that 'although age has not been treated as a "suspect" ground, the best interests of children have been treated by the European court as an important factor in assessing proportionality under art 14 … reflecting the fact that individuals in that age group have particular needs and vulnerabilities'.[45] Certainly age appears to meet the criteria – stereotyping, stigma and exclusion – which the Supreme Court in *SC* found to be behind the decisions of the Strasbourg court to require 'weighty reasons' for justification. There is evidence of stereotyping, stigma and exclusion related to age in all contexts, including the provision of health care.[46]

In relation to the policy context, the Supreme Court noted in *SC* that 'the ordinary approach to proportionality gives appropriate weight to the judgment of the primary decision-maker: a degree of weight which will normally be substantial in fields such as economic and social policy, national security, penal policy, and matters raising sensitive moral or ethical issues'.[47] It was clear, however, that this was not a 'rule' and that there remains scope for courts to engage in more intensive review, even in these

41 *R (Carson) v Secretary of State for Work and Pensions and R (Reynolds) v Secretary of State for Work and Pensions* [2006] 1 AC 173.

42 *AL (Serbia) v Secretary of State for the Home Department* [2008] UKHL 42 at 50: 'It involved no discrimination on any "suspect" ground. It was not sexist, nor racist, nor ageist.'

43 *R (British Gurkha Welfare Society and Others) v Ministry of Defence* [2010] EWCA 1098 at 11.

44 *R (Drexler) v Leicestershire CC* [2020] EWCA Civ 502 at 78.

45 *SC* (n 34) at 114.

46 See, for example, S. Fredman and S. Spencer (eds) (2003) *Age as an Equality Issue*, Oxford: Hart.

47 *SC* (n 34) at 161.

circumstances, where appropriate. When that might be appropriate is unclear. In particular, it is unclear how the appropriate sphere of discretion is to be decided where – as would be the case in most claims of discrimination in health care commissioning – what needs to be justified is discrimination on a suspect ground but in the context of social and economic policy. In *Carson* Lord Hoffmann had suggested that where suspect grounds were involved, differences in treatment 'cannot be justified merely on utilitarian grounds'.[48] However, in *SC* the Supreme Court suggested that the picture is more nuanced than this. Neither the ground nor the policy context will act as trumps to determine the correct approach, but rather remain two considerations among others which a court will need to take into account. Other relevant considerations may include the type of discrimination – with direct discrimination likely to call for closer scrutiny than indirect discrimination[49] – as well as the nature of the disadvantage created.[50] How this matrix of factors is to be navigated remains unclear.

SC, then, leaves open the possibility of more intense review of claims of discrimination, even in matters of economic and social policy, including prioritization and rationing of health care resources. However, as McColgan notes, this may amount to a 'pyrric victory'[51] as there has been little success in subsequent Article 14 decisions that have relied on the reasoning in *SC*. Certainly the Supreme Court took the opportunity to make clear that, in respect of primary legislation at least, Article 14 should not be seen as an easy option for campaigning organizations who had failed to influence policy at its formation:

> In practice, challenges to legislation on the ground of discrimination have become increasingly common in the United Kingdom. They are usually brought by campaigning organisations which lobbied unsuccessfully against the measure when it was being considered in Parliament. … The favoured ground of challenge is usually article 14, because it is so easy to establish differential treatment of some category of persons, especially if the concept of indirect discrimination is given a wide scope. Since the principle of proportionality confers on the courts a very broad discretionary power, such cases present a risk of undue interference by the courts in the sphere of political choices. That risk can only be avoided if the courts apply the principle in a manner which respects the boundaries between legality and the political process.[52]

---

48 *R (on the application of Carson) v Secretary of State for Wok and Pensions* [2006] 1 AC 173.

49 See discussion in A. McColgan (2023) *Discrimination Law*, Oxford: Hart, p 102.

50 *A v Secretary of State for the Home Department* [2004] UKHL 56.

51 McColgan (n 49) p 111.

52 *SC* (n 34) at 162, per Lord Reid.

Comparison

Questions of deference and intensity of review may also arise at an earlier stage of the analysis – where a prima facie case of discrimination needs to be made out. While Article 14 does not make the requirement for a comparator explicit, and the courts have generally taken a flexible approach, claimants will normally be required to show that they are in an 'analogous' situation to those in a comparator group.

The approach taken by the House of Lords in *Carson*, a case brought under Article 14, illustrates why deference on the question of comparison matters. The claimant, a UK national resident in South Africa, argued that she had been discriminated against on the grounds of her place of residence because, unlike pensioners resident in the UK, she was not entitled to annual cost of living increases in her pension payments. UK resident pensioners were, she argued, the appropriate comparators because, like them, she had a full record of social security contributions. While acknowledging the potential relevance of her contributions, Lord Hoffman argued that this was not sufficient to put her in an analogous position with her chosen comparator. Her contributions had to be considered in the context of the complex social security system which involved an interlocking system of obligations and entitlements and which itself distinguished between residents and non-residents. Therefore, he argued, the position of residents and non-residents was materially different. Rather than accepting prima facie discrimination on grounds of residence and proceeding to consider whether the reasons for treating resident and non-resident pensioners differently was justified as a proportionate means of achieving a legitimate aim, the case was disposed of by deciding that the state's purported reasons for drawing the distinction meant that there was no discrimination to justify.

Another very recent instance of judicial deference on the determination of the comparator issue was in *R (on the application of AC)*.[53] The claimant, a male to female transexual, sought judicial review of a decision by Berkshire West Primary Care Trust (PCT) to refuse her breast augmentation surgery. It was, she argued, incumbent on the PCT to treat her differently from, rather than the same as, natal females, in respect of their cosmetic surgery policy. The claim was not that the PCT had acted illegally by discriminating directly or indirectly on grounds of gender reassignment under the Sex Discrimination Act 1975 (SDA), but was brought on the basis that the PCT had acted irrationally in failing to distinguish between the needs of natal and transgender females and, further, had in doing so failed to comply with its obligations under the Gender Equality Duty under the SDA (the

[53] *R (on the application of AC) v Berkshire West Primary Care Trust (Equality and Human Rights Commission Intervening)* [2011] EWCA Civ 247.

forerunner of the PSED). There was also a claim under Articles 8 and 14 of the ECHR. It is noteworthy that, having concluded that the PCT had done nothing irrational in treating trans and natal females the same for the purposes of their policy on breast augmentation, Hooper LJ considered this conclusion to also settle the questions arising under Article 14 of the ECHR and the gender equality duty (because, given there was no 'unlawful discrimination', he argued, the PCT could not have failed in their duty to eliminate it).[54] In doing so he clearly equates rationality at common law with a lack of unlawful discrimination under the SDA. In this respect the case is indicative of the potential for common law approaches in public law to influence the interpretation of the Equality Act.

The comparator issue arose because the claimant argued that transgender and natal females seeking breast enhancement were not relevantly alike because 'only a transgendered woman needs breasts to address the very condition from which she suffers'.[55] In considering this argument, Lord Justice Hooper noted that there was a divergence in the evidence as to whether status as a trans or natal female was clinically relevant to an assessment of the need for treatment. Given this, he reasoned that 'the issue may thus come down to a choice of points of view' and that

> the court is not appropriately placed to make either clinical or budgetary judgments about publicly funded healthcare … the material legal criteria are that gender and clinical needs are both relevant characteristics … but what are more critically relevant are the ethical and clinical judgment of the PCT, provided these do not transgress the law.[56]

Thus, having determined that transgender status was a potentially relevant difference, the Court of Appeal then deferred to the PCT on the issue of weight, allowing them to weigh the potential relevance of transgender status against other policy and budgetary considerations. There was no need for them to demonstrate that this approach was proportionate.

On the other hand in *R (Coll)* the Supreme Court was more willing to scrutinize – and ultimately reject – the claim of the Secretary of State for Justice that there was no sex direct discrimination between male and female prisoners who needed to live in approved premises on release. There were only six such premises for women compared with 94 for men, which meant that women were much more likely to have to live a long way from family,

[54] Ibid at 58.
[55] Ibid at 45.
[56] Ibid at 56.

as was the case for the claimant. The Secretary of State had argued that there were material differences between men and women in these circumstances – male prisoners were much more likely to be high or very high risk – which meant that their cases were not comparable and no discrimination arose. Rejecting this argument, the Supreme Court agreed with the assessment of the Court of Appeal that these differences were not material in the context of the issue at stake, which was the need to accommodate prisoners close to home on their release. In this respect there was no relevant difference between them. In reaching its assessment the Supreme Court stated that:

> The question of comparing like with like must always be treated with great care – men and women are different from one another in many ways, but that does not mean that the relevant circumstances cannot be the same for the purpose of deciding whether one has been treated less favourably than the other.[57]

The case law is therefore inconsistent and gives rise to considerable uncertainty.

The Equality Act

It would be wrong to suggest that there is an established doctrine of deference or intensity of review under the Equality Act. Most reported cases involving the Act relate to employment – where the evolution of legal protection from discrimination had its beginnings – and while there are also important questions in this context about the extent to which employment tribunals and courts should scrutinize the evidence and arguments put forward by employers in justifying any prima facie discrimination, the underlying issues are clearly very different. Questions of the constitutional role of the judiciary are not at issue.

Claims of discrimination in the provision of public services under the Equality Act (as distinct from claims involving the PSED) are still relatively uncommon. While claims for damages arising from discrimination in the provision of public services can be brought in the county courts, most reported claims about discrimination in this context have been brought in the administrative court by way of judicial review. Commonly, claims will involve arguments both that there have been breaches of the Equality Act (that there has been unlawful discrimination and/or that the authority has failed in its obligations under the PSED) *and* that the authority is in breach of their obligations under Article 14 of the ECHR. Arguments may also be made that the decision or policy under challenge is unlawful or

---

57 *R (Coll) v Secretary of State for Justice* [2017] UKSC 40 at 32.

unreasonable at common law. The understandable tendency of the courts in these cases is to approach the claims for discrimination under different provisions – Equality Act Section 29 and Article 14 of the ECHR – in the same way. If no discrimination is found under Article 14, the same will be true for Article 29.[58] This approach, as it were, tends to 'import' the margin of appreciation developed in a public law and human rights context into adjudication under the Equality Act. It is arguable that it is right that is does so – adjudication of discrimination claims under Article 29 have much in common with public law claims for judicial review of under Article 14 where deference is well established. On the other hand, there are some potentially important differences between the Equality Act and Article 14 which give rise to questions as to whether, and how, this approach should be modified.

First, the Equality Act provides protection from discrimination across various areas of life in both 'public' and 'private' contexts including employment, education, housing and the provision of both public and private services. The protection afforded in each context is not identical – the Act provides a detailed set of exceptions specific to each area – but the courts have generally indicated that the core provisions of the Act, including the tests for direct and indirect discrimination and the proportionality test, have the same meaning irrespective of the context in which they are applied. Although the approach of the courts to proportionality has been inconsistent,[59] there has certainly been no suggestion that a different test, or degree of scrutiny, should apply depending on the context. On the contrary, courts have made clear that tests are the same across all of the different areas of life regulated by the Act. Thus, by way of example, the House of Lords, in the disability discrimination case of *Lewisham v Malcolm*, concluded that the test for establishing 'disability related discrimination' must mean the same in relation to housing and to employment, despite the different overall scheme of the different sections of the (then) Disability Discrimination Act 1995.[60] Likewise, in *Elias*, a case concerning indirect race discrimination in the administration of a government compensation scheme for prisoners of war brought under the 1976 Race Relations Act, it was held that the appropriate test of proportionality was the one established by the European Court of Justice in *Bilka* in the context of a claim of sex discrimination in the workplace, even though the claim in *Elias* was not one to which European

[58] See, for example, *R (on the application of McDonald) v Royal Borough of Kensington and Chelsea* [2011] UKSC 33.

[59] J. Lane and R. Ingleby (2018) 'Indirect Discrimination, Justification and Proportionality: Are UK Claimants at a Disadvantage?', *Industrial Law Journal* 47(4): 531–553.

[60] *London Borough of Lewisham v Malcolm* [2008] UKHL 43.

Union anti-discrimination law applied.[61] It has nowhere been articulated by the judiciary that a lower standard of review should apply when considering a claim arising in one context than it should in another. Any attempt to apply a 'weaker' form of proportionality test for claims made under the Equality Act in respect of public services therefore risks also diluting the protection available in other contexts.

The second possible difference relates to the protected characteristics. We saw that the court differentiates between 'suspect' and 'non-suspect' characteristics in adjudicating Article 14 claims. No such distinction has been made by the courts in relation to the characteristics protected under the Equality Act. It is worth noting, however, that differences between age and other protected characteristics arise both in the nature of the protection from discrimination provided by the Act and in the way the courts have interpreted its requirements. Most notably, direct age discrimination can be justified under Section 13 where it is a proportionate means of achieving a legitimate aim. This is not possible for the other characteristics other than in relation to positive action or where a specific exception exists. In considering the justification of direct age discrimination in an employment context, the UK courts – following the European Court of Justice – have had to grapple with the idea that less favourable treatment on grounds of age is therefore permissible in some circumstances in which, and for reasons that, less favourable treatment on other protected grounds such as race and sex would simply not be. As Lady Hale put it when considering this problem in *Seldon*, 'the answer must be that age is different'.[62] For this reason a less intense review of the justification for potential age discrimination in the provision of public services than is afforded in respect of other characteristics would not be entirely out of step with the approach taken more generally in age based claims under the Act. Nonetheless it would be helpful if the courts would address directly the differences and similarities between the Equality Act and Article 14 when both are being considered together.

The courts have been prepared to engage in much greater scrutiny of decisions of public authorities in relation to the PSED. This, it will be remembered, requires public authorities, in the exercise of their functions, to have 'due regard' to the need to eliminate unlawful discrimination and to advance equality of opportunity. While not always consistent in their approach to the duty, the courts have nevertheless been ready to establish that compliance with the duty involves some reasonably demanding procedural standards: the Court must be able to satisfy itself that the duty has been

---

61 *Secretary of State for Defence v Elias* [2006] EWCA Civ 1293; *Bilka-Kaufhaus GmbH v Weber von Hartz*, C-170/84 [1987] ICR 110.

62 *Seldon v Clarkson, Wright and Jakes (a Partnership)* [2012] UKSC 16 at 4.

'exercised in substance, with rigour and with an open mind'.[63] This is a matter of substance and not just a 'tick box exercise' although at the same time 'courts must ensure that they do not micro-manage the exercise'.[64] Further, it is non-delegable and continuous and includes a duty to seek out relevant information, if it is not already available, which may require consultation with appropriate groups.[65] Alongside this willingness to set procedural standards, however, the courts have simultaneously emphasized that the duty imposes neither obligations to take steps to eliminate discrimination and advance equality, nor to achieve any particular outcome. As a result, the weight given by authorities to considerations of discrimination and equality, following the 'proper and conscientious' exercise of the duty, is a matter for them and not something with which the Court is prepared to interfere.[66]

It is worth noting that little is required of authorities in relation to transparency – one of the aspects of the 'accountability for reasonableness' framework – in their exercise of the PSED. While separate regulations require authorities in Scotland and Wales to produce Equality Impact Assessments, this is not the case in England where authorities are obliged only to publish annual information to demonstrate compliance with the PSED and to publish equality objectives every four years.[67] While authorities may choose to document the steps taken to comply with the duty in particular cases and the deliberations that evidence their engagement with it, in order to be able to evidence compliance in the event of judicial review, there is no obligation to do so. The duty is one of substance rather than form. In *McDonald*, for example, a case concerning the provision of night time care support, the Supreme Court rejected the argument that the authority had failed to comply with the then Disability Equality Duty in Section 49 of the Disability Discrimination Act 1995 because they had nowhere made reference to it. Express discussion of the duty was, it was held, 'entirely superfluous' where the decision in question concerned a person with disabilities and the authority was acting under statutory obligations which directed its attention to the needs of disabled persons.[68] Arguably, these weaker requirements undermine both the ability of the public both to understand the weights given to equality considerations in decision making and, where necessary, to hold authorities to account in respect of their implementation of the duty.

---

63 *R (Bridges) v Chief Constable of South Wales Police* [2020] EWCA Civ 1058 at 175.

64 *R (Greenwich Community Law Centre) v London Borough of Greenwich* [2012] EWCA Civ 496 at 30.

65 *R (Bridges) v Chief Constable of South Wales Police* [2020] EWCA Civ 1058 at 175.

66 *R (Hurley) v Secretary of State for Business, Innovation and Skills* [2012] EWHC 201 (Admin) at 77.

67 Equality Act 2010 (Specific Duties) Regulations 2011, SI 2011/2260.

68 *R (on the application of McDonald) v Royal Borough of Kensington and Chelsea* [2011] UKSC 33.

Conclusion

The reluctance (with a few notable exceptions) of the judiciary to engage in more intense scrutiny of decisions involving the allocation of limited resources, even where this involves potential discrimination, is unsurprising. While the ruling in *SC* has opened the door for courts to engage in strict scrutiny, at least for claims made under Article 14, there has been little subsequent evidence of their willingness to do so. There is insufficient case law, to date, involving claims of direct or indirect discrimination under the Equality Act in the allocation of health care resources by public authorities, to be able to reach any firm conclusions about the approach of the judiciary to assessing questions of comparison, or justification, in this context. But in the case law we do have, there is nothing to suggest a significant departure from the approach taken to claims of discrimination, in similar contexts, under the Human Rights Act. What this means in practice is that commissioners are likely to have considerable discretion both to determine the way in which they make distinctions between patients and groups of patients and in the way they then choose to balance the needs of individuals, and groups against other groups or the wider population in deciding how to prioritize health care spending, even where the decisions they make disadvantage patients in ways that amount to prima facie discrimination. On the one hand, this may undermine the potential of equality law to require commissioners to address, in particular, the discriminatory impacts of their policy decisions or to treat patients differently, because of their protected characteristics, where a failure to do so creates or reinforces disadvantage. More optimistically, perhaps, this discretion may also afford space and encouragement for decision makers who are minded to do so to choose to engage in positive action without anxiety that they will thereby be breaching their legal obligations to not discriminate. It should also be remembered, as is evident from the discussion of some of the case law on indirect discrimination in earlier chapters, that courts may prove more willing to look closely at claims that contested measures are 'appropriate' or 'necessary' - questions which will often give rise to issues that are more procedural (the existence and accuracy of evidence, for example) than substantive.

The greater willingness for the courts to scrutinize the wholly procedural demands of the PSED is also, perhaps, unsurprising. It reflects the approach taken by courts to judicial review of commissioning decisions more generally, where, as we have seen, there is an increased willingness to engage with questions of procedural fairness alongside a continued reluctance to intervene in substantive resource allocation. The duty fits neatly too, with the accountability for reasonableness framework. Essentially, it directs policy makers to treat discrimination and inequality, related to protected characteristics, as *always* being relevant in policy making.

5

Public Health

Introduction

Public health policy is usually understood as a concern with improving population health by the prevention of disease and injury. It is broad in scope and embraces vaccination and screening programmes; initiatives to discourage smoking, excessive consumption of alcohol, gambling addiction or obesity through the taxation or regulation of marketing of products that are bad for us; encouraging healthy diet and exercise; and the containment and management of infectious disease. Policies which aim to address the social determinants of health such as clean air or adequate housing may also be understood to fall within its remit.

Coggon[1] argues that public health is 'public' both in the sense that achieving it is a collective endeavour, mediated by the state and engaging deeply political questions as to the basis for and limits of intervention and interference, and because the goal of public health policy is the public or wider population rather than simply the individuals within it (although it is a matter for debate whether public health simply amounts to an aggregation of the health of the individuals within it or is, additionally, also a good in its own right).[2] It is a central dimension of health policy in its own right and its success will have a direct impact on individual access to health care. In 2022 the government estimated that the annual cost to the National Health Service (NHS) of obesity was £6 billion, projected to rise to over £9.7 billion by 2050.[3] The cost of smoking to the NHS (in additional hospital

---

[1] J. Coggon (2012) *What Makes Health Public?* Cambridge: Cambridge University Press.

[2] R. Faden S. Shebaya and A. Siegel (2019) 'Distinctive Challenges of Public Health Ethics' in A. Mastroianni, J. Kahn and N. Kass (eds) *The Oxford Handbook of Public Health Ethics*, Oxford: Oxford University Press, pp 12–20.

[3] Department of Health and Social Care (2022) *New Obesity Treatments and Technology to Save the NHS Billions*, DHSC, available at: https://www.gov.uk/government/news/new-obesity-treatments-and-technology-to-save-the-nhs-billions (accessed December 2024).

admissions and the costs of treating smoking related conditions in a primary care setting) is estimated in the UK at around £2.2 billion.[4] In 2014 the estimate of the cost to the NHS of late diagnosed cancers was estimated to be £210 million a year, reinforcing the benefits of screening programmes for the NHS and its patients more widely, as well as the individuals themselves.[5]

Managing public health gives rise to some difficult theoretical questions, because strategies for improving population health may constrain or otherwise disadvantage individual members of the population. One key focus of public health literature, for example, is on the appropriate role of paternalism and the circumstances in which – if ever – it is appropriate to compel individuals to behave in a particular way (or at least to make it very difficult for individuals to not comply). Public health policy also gives rise to important questions relating to equality and discrimination. It may assist in tackling injustice arising from personal or structural discrimination in other areas of life because it can serve as a mechanism to shine a spotlight on the social determinants of poor health. In this respect, Powers et al argue that 'the role of public health, grounded in social justice, is to draw attention to any aspect of the social structure that exerts a pervasive and profound effect on the development and preservation of health'.[6] But public health strategies may also create or reinforce patterns of disadvantage, because the interests of individuals or groups may be secondary to the interests of the population as a whole. The burdens of effective public health policy may fall disproportionately on groups who are already disadvantaged in some way, including in relation to their protected characteristics. Some public health measures target 'lifestyle illnesses', for example, including sexually transmitted disease, obesity or smoking related illnesses, which, as seen in Chapter 1, can intersect with both poverty and status inequalities. Some approaches to addressing these challenges may bring stigma or threats to dignity.[7] The problem is perhaps particularly evident in relation to the management of infectious disease. The public health response to COVID-19, discussed in more detail later in the chapter, shone a spotlight on the nature of the

[4] H. Reed (January 2025) *Cost Benefit and Public Finance Model of Smoking in the UK, Version 2.3. A report commissioned by Action on Smoking and Health (ASH) from Landman Economics* available at: https://ash.org.uk/uploads/CBPF-model-January-2025.pdf?v=1737456620 (accessed February 2025.)

[5] Z. Kmietowicz (2014) 'NHS Could Save £210m a Year if All Cancers were Diagnosed as Early as in Best Areas', *British Medical Journal* 349: 5776.

[6] M. Powers and R. Faden (2006) *Social Justice: The Moral Foundations of Public Health and Health Policy*, Oxford: Oxford University Press, p 83.

[7] N. Kass, K. Hecht, A. Paul and K. Birnbach (2014) 'Ethics and Obesity Prevention: Ethical Considerations in 3 Approaches to Reducing Consumption of Sugar-Sweetened Beverages', *American Journal of Public Health* 104(5): 787–795.

difficulty of achieving a balance between the rights of individuals, the needs of groups, and the health and wellbeing of the population as a whole.

This chapter will look at two aspects of public health policy that raise interesting questions and challenges for equality law. First, screening programmes aiming to catch serious disease at an early stage. These provide an interesting case study because public health screening is one of the few contexts in which it is common to find explicit use of age limits (or occasionally sex) to determine eligibility for treatment. Second, the chapter explores aspects of the public health response to COVID-19, the way this served to disadvantage some groups, and the role of the Public Sector Equality Duty (PSED) in informing the policy choices that needed to be made.

Screening programmes

Current policy and evidence

Several of the few remaining examples of explicit rationing by age within the NHS relate to national screening programmes. Existing national screening programmes for adults screen for breast, bowel and cervical cancer and for vascular disease. All include both upper and age limits for access, although in some cases those outside the age band are able to request screening tests despite being excluded from routine screening invitations.[8]

Women between the ages of 50 and 71 (and trans men and women and non-binary patients registered with their GP as female in the same age group) are invited for breast cancer screening every three years. Women outside this age range do not currently receive an invitation for screening but may be able to access screening after referral by their GP for specialist intervention, where, for example, family history or other clinical factors suggest this would be beneficial.[9] In addition, the AgeX trial, involving over four million women, is currently assessing the benefits of offering an additional screen to women aged 47–49 and, separately, of offering an additional screen to women aged 71–73. The results on mortality effects are anticipated from 2026 onwards.[10] Men (and trans men and women and

[8] There is some minor variation in the upper and lower age limits in England, Scotland, Wales and Northern Ireland – the age limits given in the following are those which apply in England.

[9] NHS England (2023) *NHS Breast Screening (BSP) Programme*, available at: https://www.gov.uk/government/collections/nhs-breast-screening-bsp-programme (accessed December 2024); NHS England (2023) *NHS Population Screening: Information for Trans and Non-binary People*, available at: https://www.gov.uk/government/publications/nhs-population-screening-information-for-transgender-people/nhs-population-screening-information-for-trans-people (accessed December 2024).

[10] Oxford Population Health, *AgeX Trial*, available at: https://www.ceu.ox.ac.uk/research/agex-trial/agex-trial (accessed December 2024).

non-binary patients registered with their GP as male) are not invited for breast cancer screening. Men get breast cancer too, although in very much smaller numbers – according to Cancer Research UK approximately 390 of the 56,000 people who are diagnosed with breast cancer each year are men. The risk for trans men and trans women is still under-researched but a recent study suggests that trans women who have undergone hormone treatment have an increased risk of breast cancer compared to cis men and a lower risk compared to cis women and that trans men who have undergone hormone treatment have a reduced breast cancer risk compared to cis women but are at higher risk compared to cis men.[11] Cervical cancer screening is currently offered to 'women and people with a cervix' between the ages of 25 and 64, or beyond for those who have a history of abnormality or who have never been screened.[12] People aged 25 to 49 receive invitations every three years and this frequency drops to every five years for those aged 50 to 64. Age limits are applied to the NHS Health Check programme that is available to those aged 40 to 74 without a pre-existing medical condition. This assesses cardiovascular risk, among other things, with a heavy emphasis on lifestyle changes that might bring health benefits.[13]

Bowel cancer screening is currently offered every two years to those between the ages of 54 and 74 while those over 74 can request to be screened on a biannual basis. Following a decision taken by ministers in August 2018, the NHS has begun to reduce the lower age limit with a view to ensuring that bowel cancer screening will start at the age of 50.[14] Screening for the risk of abdominal aortic aneurysm (AAA) is offered to men (and trans women and men and non-binary patients registered with their GP as male) over the age of 65. The test involves a straightforward ultrasound. Where AAA is undetected it may lead to rupture and fatality.

In addition to these uses of age limits and sex to determine access to screening, it is also worth noting that the UK National Screening Committee, based on a review that occurred in November 2020, does not currently

---

11 C.J.M. De Blok, C. Wiepjes, N. Nota, K. van Engelen, M. Adank, K. Dreijerink et al (2019) 'Breast Cancer Risk in Transgender People Receiving Hormone Treatment: Nationwide Cohort Study in the Netherlands', *British Medical Journal* 365: 1652–1658.

12 NHS England (2015) *Cervical Screening: Programme Overview*, NHS England, updated 8 July 2024, available at: https://www.gov.uk/guidance/cervical-screening-programme-overview#target-population (accessed December 2024).

13 NHS (nd) *NHS Health Check*, available at: https://www.nhs.uk/conditions/nhs-health-check/ (accessed December 2024).

14 NHS England (2015) *Bowel Cancer Screening: Programme Overview*, updated 8 July 2024, available at: https://www.gov.uk/guidance/bowel-cancer-screening-programme overview#target-population (accessed December 2024).

recommend prostate cancer screening,[15] although a large scale trial has recently commenced.[16] While clearly this applies to all age groups, and thus does not involve any direct age discrimination, prostate cancer is a disease which is particularly prevalent in older men and thus the decision not to provide a national screening programme for this particular cancer is an example of potential indirect discrimination on grounds of age (or age and sex where an intersectional approach is taken).

It is not easy to find clear explanations for the use of sex or age limits in each case – or of the particular age limits used – in the available public policy materials. However, what follows attempts to summarize the reasons that are provided. First, the limits chosen may reflect the evidence on the incidence of the relevant disease in particular sexes or age groups. Chronological age and sex are both used as a proxy for the likelihood of an individual developing the condition that the screening programme is intended to detect. For example, the national cancer screening website suggests that the incidence of the disease is the reason for the upper age limit for cervical cancer screening: 'Generally speaking, the natural history and progression of cervical cancer means it is highly unlikely that women of 65 and over will go on to develop the disease.'[17] Similarly, the Department of Health explains that 'eight out of ten people who get bowel cancer are over the age of sixty'.[18]

Second, even where evidence suggests that those in a particular age group may be at risk of developing the condition, screening tests may be unavailable because of evidence that the screening test itself is likely to be ineffective in that age group due to the changes in the body associated with changes in age. This appears relevant particularly in the case of cervical and breast cancer where the lower age limits are both justified by reference to the inability of existing screening tests to generate reliable results in particular age groups. In relation to breast cancer, there is evidence that the current screening test (conventional mammography) is less effective in pre-menopausal breast tissue;

[15] UK National Screening Committee, *Adult Screening Programme: Prostate Cancer*, available at: https://view-health-screening-recommendations.service.gov.uk/prostate-cancer/ (accessed December 2024).

[16] Department of Health and Social Care (2023) *Biggest Prostate Cancer Screening Trial in Decades to Start in UK*, available at: https://www.gov.uk/government/news/biggest-prostate-cancer-screening-trial-in-decades-to-start-in-uk (accessed December 2024).

[17] NHS England (10 October 2024) *Guidance, Topic 1: The NHS Cervical Screening Programme (NHSCSP)*, available at: https://www.gov.uk/government/publications/cervical-screening-cervical-sample-taker-training/topic-1-the-nhs-cervical-screening-programme-nhscsp (accessed December 2024).

[18] UK National Screening Committee, *Adult Screening Programme: Bowel Cancer*, available at: https://view-health-screening-recommendations.service.gov.uk/bowel-cancer/ (accessed December 2024).

the lower age limit is therefore used as a proxy for the end of menopause.[19] In relation to cervical screening, the lower age limit reflects concern that normal changes in the younger cervix may result in a high rate of 'false positives' should routine screening be extended to younger women.[20]

Third, and related, there is concern that, in certain age groups or sexes, the risks and disadvantages of the screening tests may outweigh the benefits. There is a concern both that 'false positives' (generated by screening in age groups where the screening test is less reliable) may increase anxiety and lead to unnecessary and potentially harmful treatment; and that 'true positives' may likewise result in avoidable anxiety and intervention where the age of the patient and the normal progression of the disease mean that the disease would be unlikely to manifest itself naturally during the lifetime of the patient. Thus, a review of the lower age limit for cervical cancer concluded that extending testing to women below the age of 25 could lead to adverse psychological impacts and to an increase in unnecessary treatment which in turn could have harmful side effects in relation to future childbearing.[21] Similarly, for both bowel[22] and prostate[23] cancer screening it has been argued that, given that most older patients in whom screening would detect cancer are likely to die of something else before the cancer reaches its advanced stages, the negative impacts of screening in older age outweigh the benefits.

Fourth, it has been argued, at least in relation to cervical cancer screening, that using age as the entry point into the screening programme, rather than determining when screening is appropriate for an individual patient based on other factors, ensures that the system is fair, consistent and workable. There was a real danger of stigmatizing women if the first screen was to be based on sexual activity or smoking – lifestyle based risk factors which

---

19 UK National Screening Committee, *Adult Screening Programme: Breast Cancer*, available at: https://view-health-screening-recommendations.service.gov.uk/breast-cancer/ (accessed December 2024).

20 Minutes of the Advisory Committee on Cervical Screening (19 May 2009) available at: http://www.cancerscreening.nhs.uk/cervical/cervical-review-minutes-20090519.pdf (accessed December 2023); for similar concerns about the risk and impact of false positives in breast cancer screening in younger women, see A. Rawdin and J. Madan (2008) 'An Initial Assessment of the Merits of Extending Breast Cancer Screening Aged 47–49 Years to Assist the Appraisal of Options for Extending the NHSBSP with Appendix Considering Women Aged 71–73', Sheffield: School of Health and Related Research.

21 Minutes of the Advisory Committee on Cervical Screening (19 May 2009).

22 C. Quarini and M. Gosney (2009) 'Review of Evidence for a Colorectal Cancer Screening Programme in Elderly People', *Age and Ageing* 38(5): 503–508.

23 D. Burford, M. Kirby and J. Austoker (2010) *Prostate Cancer Risk Management Programme: Information for Primary Care: PSA Testing in Asymptomatic Men: Evidence Document*, NHS Cancer Screening Programmes.

would in fact be the best indicator for when the first cervical screen would be beneficial.[24]

Fifth, there is lack of evidence as to the impact of screening in some cases. In relation to breast cancer this is now being remedied through a large scale trial to test the benefits of additional screening at either end of the current age spectrum. This potential policy change is part of a broader programme to improve UK statistics on cancer mortality and does not appear motivated by any particular concerns about the use of age limits for access. In relation to AAA, research has suggested in addition to sex and age, smoking is a highly relevant risk factor. Given the high prevalence of smoking among women, not enough is yet known about the risk to women smokers and the benefits of screening this particular group.[25]

Finally, there is cost-effectiveness. The national screening programmes do not come under the auspices of National Institute for Health and Care Excellence guidance and there is no clear explanation of how cost-effectiveness is determined in relation to the various screening programmes, nor how information on cost-effectiveness is then used in decision making in relation to age limits. Clearly, many of the other reasons discussed are relevant to cost-effectiveness. Cost-effectiveness is certainly evident in research which informs the decisions about the ages at which the various screening programmes should be offered. Thus, in relation to the lower age limits for both vascular and bowel cancer screening, and upper and lower age limits for breast cancer screening, Quality Adjusted Life Years (QALYs) were used to model the cost-effectiveness of a range of lower age limits.[26] Interestingly, in relation to breast cancer screening, a QALY based assessment suggested that the extension to the upper age limit was likely to be more cost-effective than the extension to the lower age limit, even though the potential QALY gain in preventing mortality from breast cancer is much larger for younger women. The reasons for this were that screening was found to generate more 'true positives' and fewer 'false positives' in older women.[27] In relation to AAA screening, modelling for the extension of screening to women suggests that it would not be cost-effective; for every 3,900 invited to screening only one life would

---

[24] Minutes of the Advisory Committee on Cervical Screening (n 20) at 7.2.

[25] P. Song, Y. He, D. Adeloye, Y. Zhu, X. Ye, Q. Yi et al (2023) 'The Global and Regional Prevalence of Abdominal Aortic Aneurysms: A Systematic Review and Modeling Analysis', *Annals of Surgery* 277(6): 912–919.

[26] Department of Health (2008) *Putting Prevention First – Vascular Checks: Risk Assessment and Management*, Department of Health; S. Whyte, J. Chilcott and S. Halloran (2011) *Reappraisal of the Options for Colorectal Cancer Screening: Report for the NHS Bowel Cancer Screening Programme*, Sheffield: ScHARR; Rawdin and Madan (n 20).

[27] Rawdin and Madan (n 20).

be saved and there was a likelihood of significant false positives. Further research on the benefits of inviting a subgroup of women at greatest risk was recommended.[28]

Some literature challenges the evidence on which some of the current screening limits are based. Indeed, a review of the literature on the use of age in access to screening programmes concluded that 'while some (screening programmes) have a sound evidence base and for others there is no available evidence, some are clearly discriminatory and are not justifiable by disease prevalence or any other clinical indicator'.[29] Thus, for example, the upper age limit for cervical cancer screening is explained – as noted earlier – as reflecting the fact that those over 65 are 'highly unlikely to go on to develop the disease' whereas research suggests that more women in their 70s die from cervical cancer than women under 30 and that there is a second 'peak' in the incidence of cervical cancer in those over the age of 85.[30] And it has been argued in relation to bowel cancer that there is a lack of any evidence base for the use of the upper age limit, or indeed for the effect of screening in the older population at all.[31]

This review suggests that chronological age and biological sex are used as a proxies for a number of different characteristics in determining access to treatment: as a proxy for the capacity of an individual to benefit from an intervention; for the type of harm which may result from an intervention; for the likelihood of such benefit or harm occurring; and, in some cases, for other indicators used to determine what may be in the patient's interest. They are normally imperfect proxies. While it is true that only those with a cervix will develop cervical cancer, the same is not true of breast cancer, which is something that men can get too.[32] Chronological age limits can only ever be imperfect approximations, no matter how good the evidence base and how strong the established correlation or cause. Instead, age and sex are used as proxies in this way where no better 'marker' for the relevant characteristic exists or where – for reasons including cost, practicality or fairness – age and sex may be used in preference to other available markers.

---

28 M. Sweeting, K. Masconi, E. Jones, P. Ulug, M. Glover, J. Michaels et al (2018) 'Analysis of Clinical Benefit, Harms and Cost-effectiveness of Screening Women for Aortic Abdominal Aneurism', *The Lancet* 392: 487–495.

29 Centre for Policy on Ageing (2009) *Ageism and Age Discrimination in Secondary Health Care in the United Kingdom: A Review from the Literature*, London: Centre for Policy on Ageing, p 22.

30 M. Law, J. Morris and N. Wald (1999) 'The importance of age in screening for cancer' *Journal of Medical Screening* 6(1): 16–20.

31 Quarini and Gosney (n 22).

32 Cancer Research UK (nd) *Breast Cancer in Men*, available at: https://www.cancerresearchuk.org/about-cancer/breast-cancer/types/male-breast-cancer (accessed December 2024).

The law

Using age limits

Restricting access to medical care by age will, as seen in Chapter 2, normally amount to prima facie direct age discrimination which will only be lawful if it can be justified as a proportionate means of achieving a legitimate aim. How might the law apply to the use of age limits in the particular context of cancer screening? It was seen earlier that there are likely to be two aims giving rise to age restrictions for screening invitations and services. The first, making use of limited resources in a way that will maximize the benefit for the population as a whole is, for reasons discussed throughout the book, highly likely to be legitimate. The second, the aim of protecting patients from distress, is perhaps more difficult. It will be remembered that commissioning decisions noted a preference for shielding patients from the anxiety of 'false positives' or of 'true positives' where the progress of the disease meant individuals were likely to die of something else before the cancer became fatal. There was also a desire to protect young women from the stigma of invitations to screening for cervical cancer based on lifestyle.

The UK Supreme Court did accept an – arguably – comparable reason as a legitimate aim in *Seldon*, an employment case involving age discrimination, following the case law of the Court of Justice of the European Union (CJEU).[33] Mr Seldon, a solicitor and partner in the respondent law firm, had been required to retire from the partnership at the age of 65. The respondent firm claimed that their treatment of Mr Seldon was justified by a number of aims, one of which was to limit the need to expel partners by way of performance management, thus contributing to a congenial and supportive culture in the respondent firm. By the time the case reached the Supreme Court, this aim was expressed in terms of a concern for preserving the dignity of Mr Seldon and others in his position by avoiding potentially humiliating future performance management and disputes about competence as he continued to age. The Supreme Court was unanimous that this aim, among others, was legitimate and indeed had been held to be so by the CJEU. This decision (and this feature of it in particular) has proved controversial, not least because it rests on assumptions about what older people may want and who is best placed to decide this. While avoiding performance management and disputes is likely to be in the interests of the employer, the aim was also expressed as being to ensure the best outcome for employees. Thus, it seemed to reinforce a stereotype of older people as being not only more vulnerable to potentially humiliating capability proceedings and in need of protection from them but also as not best placed to choose for

[33] *Seldon v Clarkson, Wright and Jakes (a Partnership)* [2012] UKSC 16.

themselves whether or not to remain in the workplace and to risk a capability assessment at some point in the future. Age UK, intervening in Seldon, had argued that the dignity of each individual was the philosophy underlying all the anti-discrimination laws and that this amounted to a right not to be treated on the basis of stereotypical assumptions. Dignity included respect for autonomy. Lady Hale expressed some sympathy with this position, but she concluded that the CJEU's acceptance of dispute avoidance/preserving dignity as a legitimate aim was the end of the matter.

In a medical context it may be relevant that – certainly in relation to medical decision making in respect of individual patients – the courts have, in the past decade or so, taken an approach which firmly rejects 'medical paternalism' and emphasizes the right of the patient to be made aware of relevant risks and to decide for themselves among available options, where competent to do so, unless the distress caused by doing so poses serious risk to their health (the so-called 'therapeutic exception'). In *Montgomery* the Supreme Court, having made clear that the therapeutic exception is

> a limited exception to the general principle that the patient should make the decision whether to undergo a proposed course of treatment: it is not intended to subvert that principle by enabling the doctor to prevent the patient from making an informed choice where she is liable to make a choice which the doctor considers to be contrary to her best interests.[34]

While there is reason, therefore, to believe such aims may be considered legitimate, they are perhaps more vulnerable to challenge in this context.

Having established legitimate aims, policy makers will then need to demonstrate that the use of age limits, and of the particular age limits chosen, is proportionate. In Chapter 2 it was suggested that a number of issues may be of particular importance here – the accuracy of the use of age as a proxy for risk or capacity to benefit and the availability of an alternative test. It was seen that there have been instances where the use of a particular age limit has been found to be disproportionate because the choice of that particular age is not well founded. In *Prigge*, for example, the Court of Justice found that an age limit of 60 for mandatory retirement of airline pilots, chosen to represent the age at which physical capacity would decline, was disproportionate as it was not supported by evidence. On the other hand, there are other examples where courts have been willing to accept that age is a suitable proxy without significant investigation into its accuracy,[35] or to accept a low threshold of

---

[34] *Montgomery v Lanarkshire Health Board* [2015] UKSC 11 at 91.

[35] *Petersen v Berufungsausschuss für Zahnärzte für den Bezirk Westfalen-Lippe* [2010] 2 CMLR 830; *Kucukdeveci v Swedex GmbH & Co KG* [2010] 2 CMLR 33.

accuracy. In *Reynolds*, which concerned an Article 14 challenge to the use of the age of 25 as a proxy for those who were (among other things) likely to have lower living costs and could thus be paid jobseeker's allowance and income support at a lower rate, Lord Hoffman held that, while any age limit was likely to prove arbitrary, all that was required for justification was that the distinction should 'reflect a difference between the substantial majority of the people on either side of the line'.[36] However, reduction in cancer mortality in the population is unlikely to be achievable without an improvement in mortality in the older population, where the highest incidence of almost every form of cancer is found.[37]

A second issue which is likely to be relevant to determining the proportionality of using age limits as proxies is whether or not there is scope to achieve the same legitimate aim through individual testing and assessment – in other words, whether the use of age as a proxy is 'necessary' or whether a less discriminatory option exists. Individual assessment is likely to prove a less discriminatory alternative wherever it may identify individuals for whom the age limit in question is a bad proxy – those whose biological age is younger than their chronological age, for example, or for whom other reasons mean that, in their particular case, age is a poorer predictor of risk or benefit. A theoretical possibility of testing each individual rather than applying an age limit is unlikely to be enough to make the use of an age limit disproportionate, however. Rather, as recognized in *Bibi*, the feasibility of administering individual testing will be highly relevant here. *Bibi* concerned an Article 14 challenge to the application of a language test to applicants for long-term residence. Nationality was used as a proxy to determine who would be exempt from the test. In assessing proportionality the possibility of an alternative approach, including individual testing, was considered but the Court held that it would be 'absurd' to require individuals to be language tested in order to decide whether or not they needed to be language tested. Even where a feasible alternative or individual test is conceivable, therefore the cost and administrative inconvenience involved may incline a court to decide that a failure to choose the alternative was not disproportionate,[38] particularly where the fair or efficient use of scarce resources is one of the legitimate aims in question. In relation to routine population-wide health screening, therefore, it seems unlikely that the theoretical possibility of

---

[36] *R (on the application of Reynolds) v Secretary of State for Work and Pensions* [2006] 1 AC 173 at 51.

[37] Department of Health (2011) *Improving Outcomes: A Strategy for Cancer*, London: Department of Health. https://assets.publishing.service.gov.uk/media/5a7ca62040f0b65b3de0a457/dh_131787.pdf

[38] See, for example, *R (Hooper) v Secretary of State for Work and Pensions* [2002] EWHC 191 (Admin).

screening everybody is likely to render the use of age limits disproportionate. On the other hand, effective mechanisms for identifying those outside the age range who may benefit from screening (such as through primary care), or to raise awareness of and encourage self-referral for those for whom age is unlikely to be as accurate a proxy, may go some way to making the current approach proportionate.

Sex discrimination

Some public health interventions are based on sex. Breast cancer affects both men and women although the risk is very much higher for women and trans men, but only those registered with their GP as female (and who fall within the relevant age bands) are routinely invited for screening. There has never been any legal challenge to the differential provision here. On the face of it, offering a service to only one sex when it might benefit both appears to be less favourable treatment because of sex. Direct sex discrimination cannot be legally justified under the Equality Act so in order for a policy such as this to be lawful it must satisfy one of two tests. Either that it is not direct discrimination because although there is 'less favourable treatment because of sex', there are 'material differences between the circumstances' relating to men and women such that they cannot be compared under Section 23; or that it is not direct discrimination because it falls within the scope of the single-sex services exemption in Schedule 3, para 27.

The Supreme Court considered the scope of both of these provisions in the case of *Coll*, discussed in Chapter 4. The case involved a claim that the Secretary of State had discriminated against women offenders by providing far fewer approved hostels for women to live in as a condition of release than for men, with the consequence that women were far more likely to be required to live far away from family. On the question of whether men and women could be compared, the Secretary of State had argued that there were material differences between their circumstances because fewer women prisoners were of high risk and the criteria for admission were therefore different. The Supreme Court disagreed. Lady Hale found that although there were indeed differences between men and women offenders, there was no differences in the *relevant* circumstances, which here was the requirement to live in an approved hostel. Interestingly she noted that relevant circumstances will usually 'be something other than the personal characteristics of the men and women concerned, something extrinsic rather than intrinsic to them'.[39] It is not certain how this would apply in relation to breast cancer screening but it is certainly plausible that the degree of risk for

[39] *R (Coll) v Secretary of State for Justice* [2017] UKSC 40 at 32.

men and women – which arises principally as a result of 'something intrinsic' to each sex – would amount to a relevant difference here, given that the purpose of the screening programme is to offer preventative intervention to the section of the population judged most at risk. This is particularly likely given, as seen in Chapter 4, the courts tend to afford a wide margin to decision makers on the relevance of clinically significant differences between groups of patients.

The single-sex services exemption provides that public services can be provided exclusively to members of one sex where the limited provision is a proportionate means of achieving a legitimate aim and where at least one of a number of specified conditions are satisfied, the most relevant in this context being that '(1) only persons of that sex have need of the service' or '(3) a joint service for persons of both sexes would be less effective, and the extent to which the service is required by persons of each sex makes it not reasonably practicable to provide separate services'.[40] There is limited case law on this provision but in *Coll* the Supreme Court considered the – very similar – exemption which permits the provision of different services to men and women where this is a proportionate means of achieving a legitimate aim. Here, the Court found, the Secretary of State had failed to demonstrate that their approach was proportionate. This was partly because, Hale noted, while saving cost (one of the reasons for the differential provision of hostels) was a legitimate aim of public policy, 'if a benefit is to be limited in order to save costs, it must be limited in a non-discriminatory way' and in this case there was no evidence that the government had taken any steps (in breach of the PSED) to consider the disadvantage caused to women by the existing provision or how this might be mitigated.[41] In relation to public health screening, the legitimate aim is likely to be expressed as more than simple cost saving – public health interventions are, by definition, usually aimed at addressing health in the population as a whole – by targeting those most at risk. But, in order to be proportionate, it will still be important that, as part of the exercise of the PSED, thought is given to whether and how disadvantage to those not eligible for invitation to screening may be mitigated – for example, by ensuring robust mechanisms for those whose risk is higher to self-refer or be referred through primary care.

Finally, it is worth noting that the policy to screen for cervical cancer which affects only women (or trans men) and not (currently) for prostate cancer which affects only men (or trans women) is highly unlikely to be direct discrimination because the 'relevant material circumstances' of men and women in this context are likely to be judged to be different. Certainly

---

[40] Equality Act 2010, Schedule 3, para 27.

[41] *R (Coll) v Secretary of State for Justice* (n 39) at 40.

this was the view of the Court in *Rose* which involved a challenge to the policy of *Thanet* Clinical Commissioning Group to offer funded services to freeze semen but not oocytes (eggs) for the purposes of future assisted fertility treatment.[42] The claimant sought the treatment as a matter of urgency before undertaking a course of chemotherapy which was likely to bring on early menopause and leave her infertile. Rejecting the claim of direct sex discrimination, the Court noted that there were 'obvious relevant differences' between semen and oocytes such that it couldn't be accepted that 'differentiating between gametes in this context means the same as differentiating between men and women'.[43] The claim did succeed at judicial review, not because it was found to be discriminatory but because it was found that there had been departure from National Institute for Health and Care Excellence guidance for reasons that were not permissible. Those commissioning public health will, however, need to continue to have due regard to the need to address cancer screening in a way that does not create inequality between the sexes in compliance with its obligations under the PSED.

COVID-19, public health and the Public Sector Equality Duty

COVID-19 posed an enormous threat to public health and a very significant challenge for all those engaged in tackling it. The government's response was multidimensional, and included vaccination, test and trace, and enforcement of mask wearing and social distancing measures, including several periods of lockdown. With the possible exception of the vaccination programme (discussed further in what follows), aspects of the response have been subject to considerable criticism, including from those in the public health community. These include that the government was poorly prepared, too slow to react, to quick (or too slow) to relax restrictive measures, and failed to be clear in communicating with the public.[44] The response is the subject of an ongoing enquiry.

One feature of the pandemic as a whole – both the virus and the response to it – was that that it did not impact everyone equally.[45] Various groups

[42] *R (on the application of Rose) v Thanet Clinical Commissioning Group* [2014] EWHC 1182 (Admin).

[43] Ibid at 122.

[44] British Medical Association (2022) *The Public Health Response by UK Governments to COVID-19*, BMA, available at: https://www.bma.org.uk/media/5980/bma-covid-review-report-4-28-july-2022.pdf (accessed December 2024).

[45] C. Bambra, J. Lynch and K. Smith (2021) *The Unequal Pandemic: COVID-19 and Health Inequalities*, Bristol: Bristol University Press.

were hit particularly hard in different respects. The risk of mortality was highest among the elderly, with those locked down within the close confines of care settings particularly vulnerable, and those with serious underlying health conditions; the risk of infection was particularly high among frontline health and social care workers. And the patterns of disadvantage caused by lockdown – economic, social and health related – were related to characteristics including race, sex and disability. In large part this can be explained by the interaction of the nature of the virus and the response to it with pre-existing structural inequalities in almost every aspect of society. For example, the Women and Equalities Committee noted that:

> Throughout the coronavirus pandemic, Black, Asian, and minority ethnic (BAME) people have been acutely affected by pre-existing inequalities across a huge range of areas, including health, employment, accessing Universal Credit, housing and the no recourse to public funds policy. As the pandemic progressed, many of these underlying inequalities made the impact of the pandemic far more severe for BAME people than their White counterparts.[46]

Unequal impact on health was caused not only by the virus itself but also by the public health response itself. The need for hospitals and other health services to prioritize the treatment of those affected most severely by COVID-19 (predominantly older adults) meant that the delivery of ordinary health care and elective surgery was severely disrupted. In addition there was evidence that patients were not presenting in primary care settings for non-COVID-19 related problems, because of the perception that services would be unavailable or because they didn't want to 'bother' GPs, resulting in missed or late diagnosis and treatment for a wide range of conditions.[47] Routine care for those with long-term conditions and disabilities was also severely disrupted.[48] For example, the Women and Equalities Committee found that the stalling of routine annual health checks for patients with learning disabilities risked compounding disadvantage for those who already faced difficulties in accessing accurate diagnoses and treatment for physical illness.[49] It is clear too that there was a sharp fall in the number of patients referred and diagnosed

---

46 Women and Equalities Committee (2020) *Unequal Impact? Coronavirus and BAME People: Third Report of Session 2019–21*, House of Commons, HC 384, 15 December 2020, available at: https://committees.parliament.uk/publications/3965/documents/39887/default/ (accessed December 2024).

47 Bambra et al (n 45) p 37.

48 British Medical Association (n 44).

49 Women and Equalities Committee (2020) *Unequal Impact: Coronavirus, Disability and Access to Services: Fourth Report of Session 2019–21*, House of Commons, HC 1050, 22

with cancer,[50] with an inevitable negative impact on prognosis. Given the relationship between underlying conditions and susceptibility to COVID-19, many suffered twice – from COVID-19 and from disruption to normal health services. And as Bambra et al note, 'since the burden of chronic illness largely follows the social gradient of health … the impacts of these wider health challenges will inevitably be unequal'.[51] However, the health burden of COVID-19 was not restricted to those who were most at risk from the disease itself. Some of the very serious – and in some cases fatal – outcomes fell to those whose personal risk from COVID-19 was relatively low. Another indirect health impact was on mental health. Research in the UK suggests that mental health worsened, in particular for women and young people, as well as for those with pre-existing mental health conditions and those from socially disadvantaged backgrounds.[52] Reasons for disproportionate impact are again linked, in many cases, to pre-existing disadvantage.

Even the vaccination programme, widely praised as the success story of the pandemic, was not without difficulties from an equalities perspective.[53] The vaccine was developed with remarkable speed and large stocks rapidly secured by high income countries, including the UK, amid concerns about global vaccine equity.[54] Rollout in the UK began in December 2020 and by the end of May 2022 90 per cent of the adult population had been vaccinated with two doses.[55] The scale of the administrative task involved in the vaccine rollout meant that it was necessary to establish an order of priority to determine the order in which different population groups would be offered access to the vaccine. Advising on priority setting was the task of the Joint Committee on Vaccination and Immunisation (JCVI), which had to consider a number of strategies in order to strike the optimal balance between prevention of transmission and protection of the most vulnerable individuals. Ultimately, given the lack of epidemiological information on the effect of the vaccine on transmission at that stage of the pandemic, the JCVI concluded that the

December 2020, available at: committees.parliament.uk/publications/4068/documents/40461/default/ (accessed December 2024).

50 E. Morris, R. Goldacre, E. Spata, M. Mafham, P. Finan, J. Shelton et al (2021) 'Impact of the COVID-19 Pandemic on the Detection and Management of Colorectal Cancer in England: A Population-based Study', *The Lancet (Gastroenterology and Hepatology)* 6(3): 199–208.

51 Bambra et al (n 45).

52 Ibid.

53 Ibid.

54 By May 2021 high income countries had administered 69 more doses per inhabitant than low income countries: T. Burkhi (2021) 'Global COVID-19 Vaccine Inequity', *The Lancet Infectious Diseases* 21(7): 922–923.

55 House of Commons Committee of Public Accounts (2022) *The Rollout of the COVID-19 Vaccine Programme in England: Eleventh Report of Session 2022–23*, House of Commons, HC 258, 13 July 2022.

first priority should be targeting protection at those most at risk of mortality and morbidity. Other relevant priorities included prevention of transmission through protection, for example, of health care workers who were most likely to come into contact with both the disease and with those most vulnerable to it; ease of implementation in order to ensure maximal vaccine uptake; protection of the health and social care service; and maintaining resilience in essential public services. Based on these priorities it was decided that access to the vaccine should be organized largely by age, with those residing in care homes for older adults (because they had both a high risk of infection and a higher risk of severe disease and mortality) and their carers as first priority. Frontline health and care workers were in the second group along with those aged 80 and over, then came the over 75s. Those deemed 'extremely clinically vulnerable' were in group four along with the over 70s, followed by the over 65s and then, in group six, those between 16 and 65 with underlying health conditions which put them at higher risk of serious disease and mortality. Below this group were adults over the age of 50, in descending age order.[56]

While the prioritization strategy itself attracted little criticism, there were nonetheless some concerns with the way it worked in practice. Perhaps the most significant of these was that adults with learning disabilities had not been properly considered. This group were particularly badly affected by the pandemic: early research found that adults with learning disabilities who contracted COVID-19 were five times more likely to be admitted to hospital and eight times more likely to die.[57] These disparities in health outcomes existed before the pandemic and were then magnified by it.[58] It has been suggested that this high susceptibility to COVID-19 arose as a result of high prevalence of comorbidity and was compounded by difficulties in accessing appropriate health and social care and support.[59] While many adults with learning difficulties fell into group six of the JCVI prioritization scheme – those with underlying health conditions that put them at higher risk – lots were not invited in practice when the vaccination programme reached this stage. This happened because

[56] Department of Health and Social Care, *Joint Committee on Vaccination and Immunisation: Advice on Priority Groups for COVID-19 Vaccination, 30 December 2020* available at: https://www.gov.uk/government/publications/priority-groups-for-coronavirus-covid-19-vaccination-advice-from-the-jcvi-30-december-2020/joint-committee-on-vaccination-and-immunisation-advice-on-priority-groups-for-covid-19-vaccination-30-december-2020#vaccine-priority-groups-advice-on-30-december-2020 (accessed February 2025).

[57] K. Courtenay and V. Cooper (2021) 'COVID 19: People with Learning Disabilities are Highly Vulnerable', *British Medical Journal* 374: 1701–172.

[58] N. Scherer, P. Wiseman, N. Watson, R. Brunner, J. Cullingworth, S. Hameed et al (2022) '"Do They Ever Think about People Like Us?": The Experiences of People with Learning Disabilities in England and Scotland during the COVID 19 Pandemic', *Critical Social Policy* 43(3): 423–447.

[59] Ibid; Courtenay and Cooper (n 56).

GP systems did not always accurately capture the severity of disability and many individuals with learning disabilities were therefore not properly identified as being at high risk and were missed.[60] Following a high profile media campaign in early 2021, the JCVI issued guidance that anyone on the GP Learning Disability Register should be invited immediately for vaccination as part of priority group 6 and that efforts should be made to identify individuals who should be on the Register but were not.[61] Research by Scherer et al into the experiences of those with learning disabilities and their carers during the pandemic found that not only was this recognition of priority status very hard won, but that in many cases inaccessibility and failures to make reasonable adjustments in the administration of vaccines meant that many of those with learning difficulties faced additional barriers to taking it up.[62]

Equality law in the pandemic

What was, or should have been, the role of equality law in addressing these patterns of disadvantage? First, as seen in this chapter, it is evident that much of the disproportionate disadvantage arose not simply as a result of the public health policy response to the pandemic but because patterns of pre-existing, health related disadvantage were then exacerbated. As Fredman puts it, 'we could have weathered the pandemic better in a more equal society'.[63] The need for public health policy (construed in its very widest sense) to address the wider determinants of health inequality and the role of equality law in addressing this was the subject of Chapter 1. Tackling health inequalities in 'ordinary' times will be fundamental to ensuring a less inequitable distribution of the burden of ill health in a future crisis.

Second, the uneven impact of the public health response to the virus reinforces the need for those making and implementing policy to pay attention to those groups – such as those with learning difficulties in the context of the vaccination programme – who may be particularly disadvantaged, whether as a result of pre-existing disadvantage or as a result of the response, or both. Ensuring due consideration of the needs of disadvantaged or marginalized groups in policy making is, as was explored in Chapter 1, a key rationale

[60] E. Mahese (2021) 'COVID-19: All Adults on Learning Disability Register Should be Prioritised for Vaccination, Says Advisory Committee', *British Medical Journal* 372: 547.

[61] Public Health England (2021) *JCVI Advises Inviting People on Learning Disability Register for Vaccine*, PHE, available at: https://www.gov.uk/government/news/jcvi-advises-inviting-people-on-learning-disability-register-for-vaccine (accessed December 2024).

[62] Scherer et al (n 58).

[63] M. Campbell, S. Fredman and A. Reeves (2020) 'Palliation or Protection: How Should the Right to Equality Inform the Government's Response to COVID-19?', *International Journal of Discrimination and the Law* 20(4): 183–202.

behind the PSED. There has yet to be a comprehensive review of the effectiveness of the PSED in shaping the law and policy that developed through the pandemic, but there is certainly evidence that it did not, or at least did not always, function in the way intended. On the one hand, there is evidence of at least formal compliance with the PSED by key agencies in their decision-making process. Equality Impact Assessments exist in relation to the (many) different regulatory and policy decisions, many of which identify the potential negative impact of proposed measures on various protected groups and consider what mitigations may alleviate these. On the other hand, concerns have been raised that these duties were not fully understood, or not taken sufficiently seriously, by those taking the lead on key decisions.

In an enquiry into the gendered impact of the government's COVID-19 response, the Women and Equalities Committee expressed disappointment that they had found the (then) Minister for Equalities to 'appear dismissive of the imperative to consider the effects of policies on those with protected characteristics under the Equality Act', preferring instead to consider the effects of policies 'in the round'.[64] This suggests a lack of systematic consideration to the different groups protected by the Act. Also of concern was a lack of – at least initial – transparency in relation the Equality Impact Assessments carried out in relation to Coronavirus legislation. The Government was slow to publish its Equality Impact Assessment for the Coronavirus Act apparently because, as explained in evidence given to the Women and Equalities Committee, there was concern that publicity could result in a 'chilling effect on being frank in those assessments'. This led the chair of the Women and Equalities Committee to write to the Minister to urge the need for greater transparency because 'in a fair and democratic society, it is only right that we are able to have an open conversation about the equality assessment; to allow Committees such as ours, individuals and other groups to scrutinize the Government's work and contribute to mitigating any negative consequences'.[65] This seems right. The PSED, it will be remembered, is an obligation to have due regard to the need to avoid unlawful discrimination and to achieve equality. It is not an obligation to achieve any particular outcome and (provided there is no unlawful discrimination under

[64] Women and Equalities Committee (2021) *Unequal Impact? Coronavirus and the Gendered Economic Impact: Fifth Report of Session 2019–21*, House of Commons, HC 385, 26 January 2021, available at: https://committees.parliament.uk/work/319/unequal-impact-coronavirus-and-the-gendered-economic-impact/ (accessed December 2024).

[65] Women and Equalities Committee (30 April 2020) *COVID-19: Committee Calls on Govt to Publish Equalities Assessment of Coronavirus Act*, available at: https://committees.parliament.uk/work/227/unequal-impact-coronavirus-covid19-and-the-impact-on-people-with-protected-characteristics/news/115186/covid19-committee-calls-on-govt-to-publish-equalities-assessment-of-coronavirus-act/ (accessed December 2024).

the Equality Act or Article 14 of the European Convention on Human Rights) should not serve to constrain policy makers in making difficult policy choices about the distribution of the burdens of a pandemic. What the PSED can achieve, however, when properly implemented, is to ensure that disadvantage is not caused *inadvertently* through a failure by policy makers to focus attention on the likely impact to particular groups. While, in times of non-emergency, evidence on the potential impact of policy will often arise through formal consultation with relevant groups, there is less, or no, opportunity for this to happen when decisions are urgent. In these circumstances, therefore, transparency is particularly important as it affords opportunity for public scrutiny and contribution by those affected and their representatives.

A related point is that, in order to make it less likely that the needs of some groups are overlooked, there needs to be ready access to a diverse range of experience, which may include diversity among decision makers themselves.[66] In an emergency, when decisions may need to be taken without time for careful consultation and research, it becomes even more important that a range of voices are easily accessible to decision makers and included in decision making not least because, as Kamunge notes, 'the question of whose voice is heard, and its corollary – whose voice is not being heard – prompts us to recognise the value-laden nature of decision making'.[67] While diversity among decision makers, or access to diverse perspectives by decision makers, may not result in a change of approach as to difficult trade-offs that need to be made, it may ensure that where burdens cannot be avoided, due consideration is given to how they might be mitigated. In *R (Good Law Project)* the High Court recognized that taking diversity into account during the recruitment process was part of the proper exercise of the PSED. The case concerned a challenge to the appointment process for positions critical to the government's response to the COVID-19 pandemic amid concerns that key appointments had been made on the basis of personal connection and without open competition. The claimants argued that, in these circumstances, proper exercise of the PSED had the potential to enable the decision makers to take straightforward steps to avoid the risk of discriminatory impact. The Court agreed that while the PSED does not require a particular outcome, such as an open recruitment policy, 'nevertheless, there must be some evidence of what precisely the decision-maker did in the circumstances of these cases to discharge the obligation

66 Campbell et al (n 63); B. Kamunge (2021) *Which Inequalities Should We Focus on in Evaluating Health Policy Before, During, and Following COVID-19?*, UK Pandemic Ethics Accelerator, available at: www.ukpandemicethics.org (accessed December 2024).

67 Kamunge (n 66).

when deciding the method by which each relevant appointment was to be made'.[68]

Thus, while equality law played some part in shaping the response to COVID-19, with some limited success as a result of threatened or actual judicial review involving claims under the Equality Act, avoidable disadvantage to some groups sharing protected characteristics nonetheless resulted, suggesting a need for a more robust approach to ensuring the PSED is well understood and used appropriately. In Chapter 1 we saw that there are some inherent limitations in the duty – in relation to intersectionality and socio-economic disadvantage in particular – both important factors in the patterns of disadvantage that were created or reinforced by the pandemic. But the experience of the pandemic also shone a light on weaknesses in leadership and implementation, including at the top of government.[69]

Conclusion

In public health – perhaps more than in any other health care context – it is evident that the health of the wider population will often take priority over the needs of individuals or of groups. A focus on population health may involve limiting access to public health programmes to the subset of the population whose health is judged to be at greatest risk or imposing obligations or restrictions which lead to unequal disadvantage. This chapter has argued that while to do this may be well be justifiable in some circumstances, decision makers will need to take steps to ensure that they actively monitor – in their exercise of the PSED – any patterns of uneven disadvantage which may result and then consider what steps may be taken to mitigate these. In particular, they should be alert to pre-existing disadvantage, resulting from a history of structural discrimination or exclusion, which – as in COVID-19 – public health measures may entrench or make worse.

[68] *R (on the application of the Good Law Project, Runneymede Trust) v The Prime Minister, Secretary of State for Health and Social Care* [2022] EWHC 298 (Admin) at 112.

[69] See also M. Bell (2023) 'More than an Afterthought? Equality Law in Ireland during the Pandemic' in S. Fredman and S. Atrey (eds) *Exponential Inequalities*, Oxford: Oxford University Press, pp 145–160.

6

Infertility

Introduction

Around one in seven couples in the UK have difficulty conceiving.[1] Yet fertility treatment – and in particular the public funding of fertility treatment – is controversial and raises interesting issues about the boundaries of 'health' and the extent of state obligations to support what may be among our most fundamental and important goals.[2] Those seeking fertility treatment form a broad group including not only those with a recognized medical condition or disease of the reproductive system but also those unable to conceive for physiological reasons not amounting to disease such as older age; those unable to engage in sexual intercourse for psychological reasons or because of unrelated physical disability; and those who have no partner, or who have a partner of the same sex or who need assistance to conceive because they have undergone treatment for gender dysphoria. Indeed, the most recent data from the Human Fertilisation and Embryo Authority (HFEA) for 2022 notes the biggest rise in demand for in vitro fertilization (IVF) has been among single women and women in same-sex relationships.[3] While the inability to conceive without assistance in these cases will not amount to disease, the mental and emotional toll will usually be no different than for those who are unable to have a child because of 'clinical' infertility.[4]

[1] National Institute for Health and Care Excellence (2013) *Fertility Problems: Assessment and Treatment*, NICE, Clinical Guideline CG156, updated September 2017, available at: https://www.nice.org.uk/guidance/cg156 (accessed December 2024).

[2] See, for example, E. McTernan (2015) 'Should Fertility Treatment be State Funded?', *Journal of Applied Philosophy* 32(3): 227–240.

[3] Human Fertilisation and Embryology Authority (2024) *Family Formations in Fertility Treatment 2022*, available at: https://www.hfea.gov.uk/about-us/publications/research-and-data/family-formations-in-fertility-treatment-2022/ (accessed December 2024)

[4] G. Cavaliere (2023) 'Involuntary Childlessness, Suffering and Equality of Resources: An Argument for Expanding State Funded Fertility Treatment Provision', *The Journal of Medicine and Philosophy* 48: 335–347.

As the World Health Organization notes, infertility is also a gender equality issue in cultures and settings where there is a particularly high social value placed on childbearing and can have 'significant negative social impacts on the lives of infertile couples and particularly women, who frequently experience violence, divorce, social stigma, emotional stress, depression, anxiety and low self-esteem'.[5]

Definitions of infertility vary. The World Health Organization defines infertility as 'a disease of the male or female reproductive system defined by the failure to achieve a pregnancy after 12 months or more of regular unprotected sexual intercourse'.[6] Guidance from the National Institute for Health and Care Excellence (NICE) avoids referring to infertility as a disease, but like the WHO, defines it by reference to a period of unsuccessful attempt at conception as 'the period of time people have been trying to conceive without success after which formal investigation is justified and possible treatment implemented'.[7] By contrast the American Society of Reproductive Medicine now defines infertility as a 'disease, condition or status' based on any of a number of factors including simply the need for medical intervention to achieve successful pregnancy.[8] This also erodes the distinction between those who are unable to conceive without assistance for biological or social reasons, or a combination of the two. An added complication is that infertility may affect – and assistance with conception may be available to – both couples and individuals. One, or both, of a couple may have a disease of the reproductive system but sometimes it is the particular combination – couples rather than individuals - who are infertile and may be not be able to conceive together but may not have difficulty conceiving with other partners. This makes the exercise of comparison, for the purposes of determining whether or not unlawful discrimination may have taken place, particularly difficult.

Given the context of this book, it is also worth noting that, so far at least, infertility has not been recognized by the courts as meeting the definition of disability under the Equality Act 2010 because no relevant claims have arisen. There are two potential difficulties here. First, the definition of disability under the Equality Act is a medical one, requiring in most cases that claimants establish the presence of 'a physical or mental impairment' which would serve to exclude those seeking assistance to conceive for 'social

[5] World Health Organization (2024) *Infertility*, available at: https://www.who.int/news-room/fact-sheets/detail/infertility (accessed December 2024).

[6] Ibid.

[7] NICE (n 1) 1.2.13.4.

[8] ASRM (2023) *Definition of Infertility: A Committee Opinion*, available at: https://www.asrm.org/globalassets/_asrm/practice-guidance/practice-guidelines/pdf/definition-of-infertility.pdf (accessed December 2024).

reasons' – because they are in a same-sex couple or are single. Second, even where such an impairment can be established, the definition then requires the claimant to show substantial adverse impact on the ability to carry out 'normal day to day activities'. It is not clear whether or not an inability to conceive naturally would satisfy this test.[9] As a result, as Weldon Johns explains, while some argue for recognition of (some forms of) infertility as disability, others are resistant to this approach because it may act to widen existing gaps in protection for certain groups.[10] In a health care context, recognition of infertility (or some forms of infertility) as a disability would not necessarily result in an obligation – or increased willingness – to fund infertility treatment for all. Many drugs and other interventions which are deemed too expensive and not cost-effective also treat conditions which are disabilities, including drugs for cancer, which is deemed a disability under the Equality Act, irrespective of the current impact of the disease on the activities of the patient.[11] But the debate gives rise to important questions as to whether the trigger for funding health care should be on the cause or the consequences (and, if so, which ones) of infertility. It is also a useful example to challenge to the current and highly contested definition of disability under the Equality Act where disability is generally rooted in a medical impairment.[12]

The definition of infertility is important for two reasons. First, because it may impact the willingness of the state to fund assisted conception – if infertility is a disease or form of ill health, it may be easier to make a case for using the National Health Service (NHS) budget to address it. As Kukla puts it: 'infertility ... purportedly deserves treatment because it is a disease, and it is a disease because it is recognized as one'.[13] The definition of

9 Equality Act 2010, s 6. Although NB in *Bragdon v Abbott* 524 US 624 (1998), a US Court, found that the Americans with Disabilities Act 1990 protects those living with HIV and AIDS from discrimination because those conditions substantially limit the major life activity of reproduction – see R. Storrow (2012) 'Marital Status and Sexual Orientation Discrimination in Infertility Care', *Law Journal for Social Justice* 3: 99–120.

10 M. Weldon-Johns (2020) *Assisted Reproduction, Discrimination and the Law*, London: Routledge; see also HC Deb, 1 November 2022, vol 721, *Fertility Treatment and Employment Rights*, available at: https://hansard.parliament.uk/commons/2022-11-01/debates/8589EBA3-231B-4370-A696-12726760EEE9/FertilityTreatmentAndEmploymentRights (accessed December 2024).

11 Equality Act, Schedule 1, para 6; see also *R (McDonald) v Royal Borough of Kensington and Chelsea* [2011] UKSC 33.

12 For a useful overview of this debate see: C. Woodhams and S. Corby (2003) 'Defining Disability in Theory and Practice: A Critique of the British Disability Discrimination Act 1995', *Journal of Social Policy* 32(2): 159–178; T. Shakespeare (2006) *Disability Rights and Wrongs*, London: Routledge.

13 R. Kukla (2019) 'Infertility, Epistemic Risk, and Disease Definitions', *Synthese* 196(11): 4409–4422.

infertility serves as a gatekeeper for access to funding because it will decide whether treatment should be funded at all and, most importantly in the current context, who among those unable to conceive without assistance should be eligible for state resources. The challenge for commissioners is to decide whether to fund treatment based on the health and other negative *consequences* of infertility or involuntary childlessness (where there may be little to distinguish between those affected) or based on the *causes* of the infertility – and particularly whether it arises as a result of a medical condition or for some other reason. If funding for everyone that might wish to access assistance with conception is impossible, because it divests too much money from treatment for other conditions, then a decision must be made as to whether to fund it at all (which will involve consideration about how it ranks against other calls on NHS resources), or whether to fund it for only some of those who seek it (and, if so, how to prioritize between these groups). Second, definition matters because, as we will see, it will be highly relevant to the exercise of comparing the relevant circumstances of those who are eligible for funding, and those who are not.

This chapter assesses the impact of restrictions on access to fertility treatment on two groups protected by equality law in particular – older women and same-sex couples. Existing policies, as we will see, often contain eligibility criteria which either exclude or restrict access to funded treatment for these groups. Having first outlined the existing policy landscape in the UK – which, as will be seen, varies significantly across different Integrated Care Boards (ICBs) – the chapter will consider whether these policy approaches are likely to be consistent with the requirements of equality law.

The existing policy landscape in the UK

The National Institute for Health and Care Excellence

Fertility treatment covers a range of interventions, the most common among which are IVF and interuterine insemination (IUI). The majority of fertility treatment in the UK is undertaken privately. According to data from the HFEA, which regulates fertility treatment in the UK, the proportion of NHS-funded IVF cycles decreased across the UK in 2022 to the lowest level since 2008, with only 27 per cent of the estimated 77,000 IVF cycles (representing just over 50,000 patients) undertaken being NHS-funded, compared to 40 per cent in 2012.[14] The number of NHS-funded IVF cycles

[14] Human Fertilisation and Embryo Authority (2024) *Fertility Treatment 2022: Preliminary Trends and Figures. Preliminary UK Statistics for IVF DI Treatment, Storage and Donation*, available at: https://www.hfea.gov.uk/about-us/publications/research-and-data/fertility-treatment-2022-preliminary-trends-and-figures/ (accessed December 2024).

carried out continued to vary by region across the UK, with decreases of 17 per cent in England, 16 per cent in Wales, and 7 per cent in Scotland from 2019 to 2022. The chances of success from a single cycle vary significantly with age. For patients aged 18–34 the pregnancy rate per embryo transferred was 42 per cent. For patients aged 40–42 it was 16 per cent, although HFEA notes that the success rate has improved significantly in all age groups due to improved clinical and laboratory practice.[15] The likelihood of success for a single cycle means that several cycles usually need to be undertaken before a successful pregnancy results. Even where initial treatment is available on the NHS, many individuals and couples supplement this with private fertility treatment where (as is true across the UK) the number of funded cycles is limited.[16] In 2018 the estimated annual cost to the NHS of IVF treatment was reported to be £68 million.[17]

In February 2013 (updated in 2017) NICE published revised guidance on access to IVF and other fertility treatment.[18] It is silent on surrogacy. Among other recommendations, the revised guidance suggests that IUI be first considered for those who cannot have vaginal intercourse because they have disabilities or psychosexual problems which make intercourse difficult or impossible; for those who have conditions which require special consideration (such as the need for sperm washing where the man is HIV positive); and for same-sex couples. The recommended approach is to offer six cycles of funded IUI where a patient has not conceived after six months of donor or partner IUI.[19] IUI is not recommended for those with unexplained infertility and able to have unprotected vaginal intercourse other than in exceptional circumstances, including where there is a religious or cultural reason why IVF is not an option.[20]

There is a well-established correlation between age and fertility in women because the quantity and quality of a woman's ovarian reserve declines as she gets older. In relation to IVF, the guidance suggests that where other clinical criteria are met, women under 40 should be offered up to three cycles of IVF treatment if they have not conceived after two years of regular unprotected intercourse or 12 cycles of artificial insemination (of which, as noted earlier, six will be funded and six self-funded). Women between the ages of 40 and 42 should be offered one free cycle of IVF treatment

15 Ibid.

16 J. Hamper and M. Perrotta (2023) 'Blurring the Divide: Navigating the Public/Private Landscape of Fertility Treatment in the UK', *Health and Place* 80: 102992.

17 S. Howard (2018) 'The Hidden Costs of Infertility Treatment', *British Medical Journal* 361: 2204–2205.

18 NICE (n 1).

19 Ibid at 1.9.1.2.

20 Ibid at 1.9.

while women aged 43 and over are not eligible for treatment. There is no lower age limit (the previous recommended lower and upper age limits for access to treatment had been 23 and 39). Where evidence suggests that IVF is likely to be the only effective treatment, and where investigations show there is no chance of pregnancy through 'expectant management' (defined as unprotected vaginal intercourse) the guidance recommends the woman should be referred for IVF directly.[21]

In revising its guidance on access to IVF in 2013, NICE used a new economic model specially developed for determining access criteria. This model compared the cost-effectiveness of one, two or three cycles of IVF with 'expectant management' (waiting to see whether conception occurs naturally). Treatment effectiveness was measured in Quality Adjusted Life Years (QALYs) and cost-effectiveness was measured for each of these four treatment options, for 198 clinical scenarios across the age range 20 (chosen as representing two years infertility from the age of 18) to 45 (chosen as a good estimate of end of natural reproductive ability). QALY gains related to improvements in health states for couples hoping to conceive and did not take into account new lives created as a result of treatment (although this was acknowledged to be a difficult task owing partly to a lack of research on changes in heath states produced by infertility/its reversal). This meant that, for the first time, the remaining life expectancy of the woman undergoing the treatment was a factor in determining the cost-effectiveness of providing IVF at a given age. Age (along with a range of other factors including cause of infertility, reproductive history) was also used to predict the likelihood of success of the treatment. In other words, age was used to calculate cost-effectiveness by using it as a proxy *both* for the likelihood of success *and*, if successful, for the duration of any health benefit thereby produced.[22] At the time of writing NICE is reviewing its guidelines on fertility due for publication in 2025, partly in response to the Women's Health Strategy for England, discussed further later in this chapter, which called for an end to all non-clinical eligibility access criteria

Integrated Care Board policies

As seen in Chapter 2, local commissioners are not obliged to follow NICE guidance and many currently do not. In particular – for the purposes of this chapter – local policies tend to diverge from NICE guidance and from each other, in two key ways: in relation to the age limits imposed for eligibility (and how many cycles of IVF each age group may be entitled to); and

21 Ibid at 1.11.

22 Ibid, Appendix M.

in relation to how those who are unable to engage in sexual intercourse must demonstrate infertility before funded treatment becomes available. Where reasons for divergence are given, these tend to refer to local funding priorities, one policy noting, for example, that 'whilst the panel recognised the considered expert advice of NICE in their recommendation, the panel also had a duty to prioritise spending of a finite resource locally and made a decision which it felt gave the most equitable and effective use of investment'.[23] In recent history, a number of Clinical Commissioning Groups (CCGs) decided (or considered whether) not to fund assisted fertility at all in the face of extreme budgetary pressures.[24] At present, however, all ICBs offer some form of funded fertility treatment although none funds treatment as part of surrogacy arrangements.

In relation to age, some ICBs use minimum age limits for the woman (ranging from 18 to 25) whereas others do not and some ICBs set upper age limits for access to IVF (ranging from 35 to 42) which differ from those suggested by NICE, or offer fewer funded IVF cycles than NICE recommend for the older age groups.[25] A few ICBs include age limits for men, although this is unusual.[26] Where reasons are given for the use of upper age limits for women these invariably relate to cost-effectiveness – because the effectiveness of IVF declines significantly after the age of 35 – rather than cost alone.[27] Interestingly, a public consultation carried out by Portsmouth CCG in 2015, before one such decision was taken, suggests that the majority (86 per cent) of the public locally supported either use of the NICE age limits or an upper boundary of at least 38.[28]

A second area where local policies may diverge is on how infertility must be demonstrated in order to access treatment. Where this is not

23 SHIP8 Clinical Commissioning Groups' Priorities Committee, *Policy Recommendation 002* 2014 (revised 2019), available at: https://fundingrequests.scwcsu.nhs.uk/wp-content/uploads/2023/05/002-Assisted-Conception-Services-Policy-Recommendation-SHIP8-review-July-2019.pdf (accessed February 2025).

24 M. Limb (2017) 'Croydon CCG Stops Funding IVF Treatment to Save £800 000 a Year', *British Medical Journal* 356: 1403.

25 See summary of different policy approaches to age limits across the majority of ICBs at Department of Health and Social Care (2024) *NHS-Funded In Vitro Fertilisation (IVF) in England*, available at: https://www.gov.uk/government/publications/nhs-funded-ivf-in-england/nhs-funded-in-vitro-fertilisation-ivf-in-england (accessed December 2024).

26 See, for example, Bath and North East Somerset, Swindon and Wiltshire ICB (nd) *Assisted Conception Policy for Infertile Patients* (Version 5.4), available at: https://bsw.icb.nhs.uk/document/bsw-cp022-assisted-conception-ivf-policy/ (accessed December 2024).

27 For example, Portsmouth CCG, AI 03 Minutes of Governing Board Meeting of 21 January 2015, 210115, GB180315, item 13.

28 Portsmouth CCG, AI 13 Assisted Conception Appendix 4, Papers for Governing Board Meeting, 21 January 2015, GB210115.

possible to achieve through a period of unprotected sexual intercourse, there are three options: providing funding for the necessary course of IUI; requiring patients to prove infertility privately; or a combination of the two where, following a course of private treatment, patients may then access funded treatment (IVF or further IUI then IVF if needed). It will be remembered that the NICE recommendation is that all individuals and couples in this category, for whatever reason, should normally be able to demonstrate 12 rounds of unsuccessful IUI, of which the second six may be funded. Some ICB policies are currently less generous than this. Some ICBs will fund some – but not six – rounds of IUI (for example, one ICB will fund two rounds of IUI for patients who have undertaken ten unsuccessful rounds privately).[29] And some ICBs determine the degree of funded support for IUI based on the reason donor sperm is needed in the first place. For example, one ICB will fund 12 rounds of IUI for 'heterosexual couples who are unable to, or who find it very difficult to have vaginal intercourse because of a clinically diagnosed physical disability or psychosexual problems formally diagnosed' (provided other access criteria are met) but state that they do not routinely fund IUI for same-sex female couples and single women.[30] It is also worth noting that most policies include a range of other eligibility criteria, including smoking and body mass index, which relate to the probability of successful treatment, as well as some non-clinical criteria. It is common, for example, for policies to restrict treatment to couples and individuals who do not already have children. This last requirement sits oddly with the policy approaches, discussed at length in Chapter 3, which reject any non-clinical criteria or social factors as irrelevant and unfair in making decisions about when to make exceptions for individual patients.

Potential for unlawful discrimination

Sexual orientation

There are no examples of policies which explicitly restrict access to IVF or other fertility treatment for same-sex couples, although the fact that surrogacy itself is simply not available of course leaves very few options for male same-sex couples. Surrogacy is discussed further in the next section. The key concern about unequal access to infertility treatment for female same-sex couples arises as a result of the eligibility requirements which

[29] Bath and North East Somerset, Swindon and Wiltshire ICB (n 26).

[30] Southwest London ICB, *Evidence Based Interventions Policy 4.1 – April 2023* 22.1 and 22.2, available at: https://www.southwestlondon.icb.nhs.uk/wp-content/uploads/2022/07/NHS-South-West-London-evidence-based-interventions-policy-4.1.pdf (accessed December 2024).

require couples (or individuals) to evidence infertility. For most heterosexual couples this involves a period of unprotected sexual intercourse (typically two years) without conception, although this requirement is dispensed with for couples where there exists an already established medical condition which precludes any possibility of natural conception. For female couples, however, most policies will allow access to funded IVF only once the 'couple' have demonstrated infertility by going through a certain number of rounds of IUI, which often needs to be wholly or partly self-funded, putting these couples at financial disadvantage. This is sometimes explained as necessary to establish some 'equivalence' with couples required to demonstrate infertility through a period of unprotected intercourse before access to funded assistance is available.[31] In relation to same-sex couples, of course, what is being demonstrated here is not the infertility of the couple who are to be parents, whose inability to conceive without assistance needs no evidence, but of the 'couple' comprised of the woman who is seeking to be pregnant and the sperm donor(s).

These policies run the risk of both direct and indirect discrimination on grounds of sexual orientation. A number of such claims have been initiated in the UK but have been settled or withdrawn before the courts have had an opportunity to consider their merits.[32] In relation to direct discrimination, the position is complicated by the need to identify the correct comparator. There are a number of possibilities. These include single women who are usually subject to the same eligibility requirements as female same-sex couples and with whom comparison is therefore unlikely to give rise to less favourable treatment; heterosexual couples unable to conceive without assistance because sexual intercourse is impossible for physical or psychological reasons (about whom many policies are silent); or heterosexual couples who require donor sperm because the male partner is known to be infertile (where IVF is often made available, provided other eligibility criteria are met, without the need to undergo self-funded IUI to demonstrate infertility). It will be remembered that in order to serve as a comparator for a claim of direct discrimination, the Equality Act requires that there be no material difference in the circumstances of the claimant and comparator. Therefore, if an ICB wants to make distinctions between groups of women who are not (known, as individuals, to be) infertile but who are known to need donor sperm (whether because single, part of a

[31] North East London CCG (2022) *Draft Fertility Policy Review – Health Inequality and Equality Impact Assessment*, NELCCG, available at: https://northeastlondon.icb.nhs.uk/wp-content/uploads/2023/04/Health-Inequalilty-Equality-Impact-Assessment.pdf (accessed February 2025).

[32] A. Rimmer (2021) 'Same Sex Couple Take Commissioners to Court Over "Discriminatory" IVF Policy', *British Medical Journal* 375: 2769.

lesbian couple, or part of a heterosexual couple where conception through intercourse is impossible) then it is crucial that they be able to point to relevant differences between their circumstances. Much will come down to the approach the courts take to the question of the relevant differences between individuals and the degree of deference afforded to commissioners in answering this question, discussed in Chapter 4. In turn, this may come back to the definition of infertility which the funding is intended to treat.

This issue arose in the Australian case of *JM*.[33] The claimant, a lesbian, had been refused treatment by a Queensland clinic whose semen donor programme was restricted to heterosexual couples where the male partner proved unable to produce semen of sufficient quality to achieve pregnancy. She sued under the Anti-Discrimination Act which prohibited discrimination on the basis of lawful sexual activity or partnership, arguing that the policy amounted to direct discrimination because of her status as a lesbian. Although successful at first instance, the Court of Appeal of the Supreme Court of Queensland disagreed and held that there was no direct discrimination because the reason for the refusal was not because of her sexual orientation but because she did not comply with the relevant definition of infertility, 'the inability to conceive after engaging in unprotected heterosexual intercourse over a period of 12 months'. Her inability to demonstrate that she satisfied this test meant that she could not compare her treatment to that of a heterosexual couple. As Storrow points out, the Court here were highly deferential to the role of the infertility industry in defining infertility. They did not engage with the question of whether or not the definition itself was discriminatory.[34]

A requirement that same-sex couples self-fund IUI in order to demonstrate infertility and therefore eligibility for IVF may also amount to indirect discrimination on grounds of sexual orientation. While requirement for those unable to conceive through intercourse to demonstrate infertility through unsuccessful (self-funded) IUI may apply to both homosexual and heterosexual couples and individuals (such as single women) it is a policy that, arguably at least, is likely to put lesbian couples at a particular disadvantage. The majority of heterosexual couples will be able to either conceive, or to demonstrate infertility, through sexual intercourse at no financial cost. If prima facie indirect discrimination is established, then the question will again turn to whether or not such a policy can be justified as a proportionate means of achieving a legitimate aim.

There are a number of considerations which will be relevant here. First, it is unclear what the legitimate aim would be in this case, other than cost

[33] *J.M. v. Q.F.G. & G.K.* [1998] Q.C.A. 228 (Austl.).

[34] Storrow (n 9).

saving. In this instance – and unlike in the case of age, discussed further on in this chapter – the restrictions on eligibility do not relate as obviously to an overall policy of efficient (in terms of capacity to benefit) or otherwise fair distribution of resources. While the latter, as suggested in Chapter 2, may well be recognized as legitimate aims, cost saving without more may not. Second, and if a legitimate aim is established, the significant variation in regional policy may raise questions about the necessity or proportionality of any one approach because regions who take a more generous approach (such as funding for IUI) have demonstrated the existence of a less discriminatory approach. It is likely to be necessary for individual ICBs to at least demonstrate that local priorities and funding constraints differ so that what may be proportionate for one area may not necessarily be in another. Finally, in relation to the balancing stage of the proportionality analysis, it needs to be considered what disadvantage should be weighed in the scales. In addition to the financial burden of self-funded IUI and the emotional and mental distress caused to those who are not in a position to self-fund, it is at least arguable that consideration should be given to the particular barriers – arising from historic and ongoing discrimination – faced by same-sex couples in establishing a family. Again, much will turn on the deference afforded by the courts to policy makers in this respect.

As far as the European Convention on Human Rights is concerned, it is clear from the judgment of the Court in *Lia v Malta* that Article 8 is engaged in relation to state provision of assisted fertility treatment and that therefore a challenge could be potentially be brought under Article 14.[35] Likewise in *JR176(2)*, a Judicial Review in Northern Ireland concerning surrogacy and discussed in more detail in the following section, the Court noted that a policy limiting eligibility to state-funded fertility treatment fell within the ambit of Article 8. Although Article 8 does not impose any positive obligation on states to fund infertility treatment, where a decision to fund some infertility treatment has been taken by the state it is demonstrative of 'respect for family life' within the meaning of Article 8 and must be administered in accordance with Article 14.[36] On the other hand, the Court made clear in *Lia* that this is an issue on which a wide margin of appreciation will be afforded to member states, notwithstanding that fertility treatment involves a 'particularly important facet of individual's existence or identity' because fertility treatment engages 'sensitive moral and ethical issues against a background of fast-moving medical and scientific developments' and is an

[35] *Lia v Malta* [2023] 76 EHRR 14.

[36] *In the Matter of an Application by JR176(2) for Leave to Apply for Judicial Review v In the Matter of a Decision of the Department of Health, the Belfast Health and Social Care Trust and the Health and Social Care Board* [2022] NIKB 21 at para 81.

issue on which there is an absence of consensus.[37] This may signal a lighter touch review of justification for potential discrimination in access to fertility treatment in the event a claim is brought.

As part of the Women's Health Strategy for England, the Department for Health and Social Care has committed to removing non-clinical access criteria for fertility treatment, and to requiring funding for IUI for female same-sex couples. It noted that 'the interpretation and implementation by the NHS of the access criteria for female same-sex couples has also been variable, placing greater financial burdens on female same-sex couples, and, in some instances, led to difficult choices about family formation'.[38] Given the subsequent change of government, the status of the commitment is, at the time of writing, uncertain. NICE is currently revising its guideline on assisted fertility, due for publication in 2025, which may reflect these changes and it is likely that ICBs will wait until then to review their own eligibility requirements.[39]

Surrogacy

Surrogacy is lawful in the UK although surrogacy agreements are not legally enforceable and the surrogate will be the legal parent of the child at birth unless or until alternative arrangements are made by parental order or adoption. There are two forms of surrogacy. 'Partial' or genetic surrogacy involves the mother using her own eggs and becoming impregnated with the sperm of the, or one of the, intended fathers whereas 'full' or gestational surrogacy involves an embryo, created in vitro, and transferred to the surrogate. The NICE clinical guideline on assisted fertility does not include advice on surrogacy of either form and currently no ICB in the UK offers funded assistance for those seeking any form of surrogacy arrangement. Where reasons for this policy approach are given, these tend to focus on ethical and legal concerns rather than on matters relating to the need to demonstrate infertility or to cost-effectiveness and capacity to benefit from the treatment options. Examples of reasons given include the lack of national guidance;[40] that there are 'significant medico-legal issues involved in surrogacy arrangements that would pose risks

---

37 *Lia v Malta* (n 35) at 59–60.

38 Department for Health and Social Care, (2022) *Women's Health Strategy for England*, available at: https://www.gov.uk/government/publications/womens-health-strategy-for-england/womens-health-strategy-for-england Women's Health Strategy for England - GOV.UK (accessed December 2024).

39 See, for example, North West London ICB (22 May 2024) *IVF Treatment Policy Update Statement*, available at: https://www.nwlondonicb.nhs.uk/news/news/ivf-treatment-policy-update-statement (accessed December 2024).

40 North East London CCG (n 31).

to an NHS organisation funding this intervention';[41] that there is 'an absence of evidence on the long-term psychological impact or social consequences for commissioning couples, surrogates or children born to surrogates';[42] that surrogacy agreements are not legally enforceable;[43] that 'ethical issues may arise during the course of a surrogacy arrangement including intended parents or the surrogate changing their minds, or disagreeing whether a pregnancy should continue if complications arise';[44] and that 'a surrogate is only available to those with means'.[45]

A policy decision to not fund surrogacy is likely to amount to indirect discrimination on grounds of sexual orientation unless it can be legally justified because, while couples and individuals of all sexual orientations may benefit from surrogacy arrangements, a lack of funded assistance for surrogacy is likely to disadvantage male same-sex couples in particular. As such, a decision not to fund IVF or IUI in the context of surrogacy will need to be justified as a proportionate means of achieving a legitimate aim. To what extent are the types of justification suggested in these policies likely to satisfy this test? Certainly surrogacy – and in particular commercial surrogacy – remains controversial and gives rise to a number of ethical and legal issues.[46] A recent Law Commission report on surrogacy raised concerns, for example, about the compatibility of commercial surrogacy arrangements with the UN Convention on the Elimination of All Forms of Discrimination against Women.[47] On the other hand, in *Whittington*, Lady Hale held that the costs of private surrogacy could form part of the calculation of damages awarded as a result of clinical negligence.[48] The claimant was unable to bear children as a result of damage to her womb caused by clinical negligence. The question for the court was whether or not awarding the costs of surrogacy, using either the claimant's own eggs or donor eggs, and including potential commercial surrogacy abroad, would be against public policy. Lady Hale concluded that it would not. In reaching her decision she noted the 'quite dramatic' shift over the past decades both in the law regulating surrogacy and in 'the law's idea of what constitutes a family … the law now recognises and

41 Bath and North East Somerset, Swindon and Wiltshire (n 26).

42 Ibid.

43 North East London CCG (n 31).

44 Ibid.

45 Ibid.

46 See, for example, E. Jackson (1996) 'Selling Babies? The Legal and Ethical Implications of Surrogacy', *Women: A Cultural Review* 7(3): 250–258; D. Lima (2024) 'Legal Parenthood in Surrogacy: Shifting the Focus to the Surrogate's Negative Intention', *Journal of Social Welfare and Family Law* 46(2): 245–266.

47 Law Commission (2018) *Building Families through Surrogacy: A New Law. Vol II (Full Report)* (HC 1237) Law Com No 411, 53–54.

48 *Whittington Hospital NHS Trust v XX* [2020] UKSC 14.

supports same sex relationships and parenthood in almost exactly the same way as it recognises and supports opposite sex relationships'.[49]

Refusal by the Belfast Health and Social Care Trust to fund IVF for the purposes of a surrogacy arrangement was recently challenged, unsuccessfully, on the basis that the refusal amounted to either direct or indirect discrimination under the relevant provisions of anti-discrimination legislation in Northern Ireland and under Article 14 (with Article 8) of the European Convention on Human Rights.[50] The claimants – a male couple – had identified a woman who was prepared to act as a surrogate for them. They planned to use a donor egg from another woman because their surrogate had herself undergone voluntary sterilization some years previously, meaning that IVF would be necessary. Interestingly, while (as the Court noted) there is no publicly funded surrogacy service in Northern Ireland,[51] the policy of the Belfast Health and Social Care Trust did not exclude the funding of IVF involving the use of a surrogate per se.[52] It was made clear in the judgment that 'IVF is offered to a woman irrespective of whether she is single or part of a heterosexual or same sex couple or as a surrogate acting on behalf of a same sex or heterosexual couple, as long as the eligibility criteria are met'.[53] Indeed, the Court noted that the eligibility criteria under the policy had in fact been amended a few years earlier to, among other things, improve equality of access to IVF for same-sex couples by allowing infertility to be demonstrated by means of unsuccessful artificial insemination as well as by unsuccessful intercourse. The difficulty in this case was rather that the surrogate was unable to meet the access criteria for IVF which included (1) the ability to demonstrate difficulty conceiving through either two years of unsuccessful intercourse or eight rounds of unsuccessful artificial insemination and (2) not having undergone voluntary sterilization. These exclude IVF in the context of surrogacy using a donor egg but not in the context of partial surrogacy.

The claimant argued that there was direct discrimination on the grounds of sex and sexual orientation because he had been treated less favourably than would a woman in a same-sex relationship (because it is possible to demonstrate infertility – and hence access IVF – using donor sperm whereas it is not possible to do so with a donor egg); and treated less favourably than would a male in a heterosexual relationship (because a couple who

[49] Ibid at 30–31.

[50] *JR176(2)* (n 36)

[51] Ibid at 28.

[52] Belfast Health and Social Care Trust (2019) *Eligibility for HSC Funded IVF and Related Treatments Effective from 1 June 2019*, amended 2024, available at: https://belfasttrust.hscni.net/services/rfc/first-steps/nhs-funded-treatment/ (accessed December 2024).

[53] *JR176(2)* (n 50) at 63.

have demonstrated a medical fertility issue would be eligible for IVF using a surrogate even if the surrogate themselves had no fertility issue or had been sterilized). The Court found that there was no direct discrimination because in each case there was a relevant material difference between the claimant and the comparator – in each case the comparator had demonstrated 'medical infertility' whereas the claimant had not. It was held that the claimant had conflated treatment for infertility (which was funded for any individual or couple only where medical infertility could be demonstrated) and surrogacy services (which were not funded). While there had been a deliberate expansion of eligibility criteria in 2019 to enable same-sex couples to access IVF, this change was introduced so as to provide a 'pathway for demonstration of medical infertility' and not because medical treatment should be provided for non-medical reasons.[54]

The claimant also argued that the eligibility criteria were indirectly discriminatory because, while they apply to everyone seeking fertility treatment irrespective of sex or sexual orientation, they serve to disadvantage single men or men in same-sex partnerships in particular. For these two groups will find it impossible or much more difficult to establish medical infertility (and indeed it was argued that the eligibility criteria produce an absurd situation where a male same-sex couple are better off finding a surrogate with a known fertility problem). Again the claim failed because of what the Court argued was a conflation between treatment for a medical problem (which was funded for those who meet the eligibility criteria) and surrogacy services (which are not). There was no disadvantage in relation to the service which was available, it was suggested, because what they were seeking was not treatment for a medical fertility problem but access to assistance in conception in the absence of a medical fertility problem – something that was simply not funded for anybody. This is to miss the disparate impact of the decision to not fund assisted conception in the absence of medical infertility – something far more likely to disadvantage same-sex couples requiring a surrogate and a donor egg. In any event, the court held, any disadvantage could be readily justified by the impact on the budget of the Trust of removing any requirement to demonstrate medical infertility.

There are perhaps two points of particular interest here. First is that – as is so often the case in discrimination claims – much will come down to the choice of comparator and the determination of what amounts to a relevant material difference between the comparator and the claimant. Second is that, in the course of argument or in the discussion of justification by the Court, there was no reference to legal or ethical concerns about surrogacy. Rather it was accepted that IVF would be funded in the context of a partial

[54] Ibid at 27.

surrogacy arrangement where a surrogate was using her own eggs and could demonstrate medical infertility through a course of unsuccessful IUI, or intercourse. And the policy of requiring medical fertility to be demonstrated, resulting in a lack of access to IVF in the context of full surrogacy requiring a donor egg, was justified by reference only to the wider impact on resources. Together with the comments of Lady Hale in *Whittington* this opens the opportunity for argument that any refusal to fund IVF as part of surrogacy arrangements for legal and ethical reasons, such as those seen in the policies of ICBs earlier, may not be justified as it is unclear that those aims remain legitimate. Where a man and a surrogate, who wishes to use her own eggs, present for treatment there may be no justified reason to treat them any differently from any other couple who have demonstrated infertility using artificial insemination.

Age

One of the most common restrictions on access to state-funded fertility treatment is the age of the woman seeking pregnancy. Upper and lower age limits (which differ across ICBs) are used to restrict access to treatment, or to determine the number of funded cycles that a woman will be eligible for. Some policies also include upper age limits for the male partner. The justification for these limits in the relevant policies, where any is provided, is generally cost-effectiveness. One ICB, for example, which offers funding only where the woman is aged between 25 and 40 years of age, notes in its policy that, while the relevant NICE guideline concludes that IVF is cost-effective for women aged 39 and under 'there is considerable uncertainty about whether IVF is cost-effective in any sub-groups of women aged between 40 and 42'. It goes on to explain that 'this policy decision is based on affordability grounds and prioritising treatment for patients where the woman is over the age of 35 years when the success rate of live births begins to decline'.[55]

As was discussed in Chapter 2, while cost-effectiveness, in the context of prioritizing limited resources where there is greatest capacity to benefit, is likely to be a legitimate aim, the proportionality of the use of chronological age as a criterion for access is likely to depend on a number of factors including the accuracy of the age limit chosen as a proxy for the likelihood of success; the availability of an alternative mechanism for assessing capacity to benefit; and the possibility of making exceptions. In relation to accuracy, departure from NICE guidance – and variation between different ICBs as to the age limits they adopt – may be problematic. Where courts have

[55] Bath and North East Somerset, Swindon and Wiltshire (n 26).

accepted that in most contexts any age limit will be an imperfect proxy, they have been willing to find the use of an age limit disproportionate where the choice of that age is not well evidenced. Even where upper age limits are chosen on the basis of strong evidence of the correlation between fertility and chronological age, it remains the case that 'women of the same age can have very different biological measures of ovarian reserve and reproductive potential' because both genetics and environmental factors can also have an important impact.[56] The proportionality of using an age limit to determine access to fertility treatment may also depend, therefore, on both the availability (and feasibility and potentially cost) of any alternative – less discriminatory – method to assess the quality and quantity of a female patient's ovarian reserve; or, related, to whether it is possible for those who fall outside the age limits to make individual funding requests if they can demonstrate that they have greater capacity to benefit than others of their age. At present, however, it appears that an alternative test is not available – while mechanisms exist to measure oocyte *quantity*, age is the only current marker of oocyte *quality*.[57] Of course, this may change in future.

While – provided the choice of the particular age is appropriate – upper age limits are likely to be justified, it is less obvious that minimum age limits will be. ICBs are not able to justify minimum age limits by reference to the capacity of the individual patient to benefit from intervention and NICE itself does not recommend a lower limit. Where minimum age limits are used, therefore, they need to be justified by reference to a different legitimate aim.

Age limits for access to IVF were at issue in *Lia v Malta*. The case concerned the decision to refuse the applicants' request, supported by their doctor, for *self-funded* IVF treatment because one of the applicants was 43, which was above the maximum age for access to IVF endorsed by the Maltese parliament which provided that it was 'desirable' for treatment to commence by the age of 42. The age limits had been chosen, the Court heard, not for reasons of resourcing but because of the perceived risks to the health (physical and mental) to the mother and the risk to the child. The Court reiterated that Article 8 was engaged while noting that margin of appreciation afforded on questions of assisted conception was a wide one because of the sensitive moral and ethical issues involved, the fast pace of medical developments in this area, and the lack of consensus among Member States.[58] However it found that in this case there had been a breach of Article 8 because while the relevant legal framework referred to the age limit as 'desirable', implying the

56 N. Ulrich and E. Marsh (2019) 'Ovarian Reserve Testing: A Review of the Options, Their Applications, and Their Limitations', *Clinical Obstetrics and Gynecology* 62(2): 228–237.

57 Ibid.

58 *Lia v Malta* (n 35) at 60.

scope for flexibility and discretion in its application, the age limit had been interpreted as a mandatory requirement by the health authority which had not engaged in any individual assessment of the claimant. This, in the view of the Court, made the law unacceptably uncertain and inconsistent, resulting in patients being unable to foresee how the provisions would apply to them.[59] Having found a breach of Article 8 the Court did not, unfortunately, feel it necessary to consider whether the use of the age limit was also a breach of Article 14. It is therefore unclear what approach the Court would take to the use of a – clear and mandatory – age limit for access to treatment in these circumstances. But the case perhaps serves as warning to ICBs to at least be clear about the way any discretion may be exercised in relation to requests for exceptional funding by those who fall outside the permitted age range.

Conclusion

This chapter has identified a number of equality concerns arising from existing policy approaches which restrict access to IVF. In particular, it has considered the ways in which eligibility criteria disadvantage same-sex couples – male and female – as well as older women. In respect of sexual orientation, in particular, the requirement to demonstrate 'medical infertility' through failed attempt at conception creates barriers for same-sex couples – and where surrogacy is needed these may prove insurmountable. Where these issues have arisen in court, health authorities have typically been given wide discretion to justify their approach by arguing that there is a relevant difference between couples seeking fertility treatment for medical infertility, and those who are seeking assistance for other reasons. In relation to surrogacy, however, it was argued that the justification typically given by ICBs for refusing funding – legal and ethical concerns – may not be sustainable in the light of developments in legal recognition of surrogacy in other contexts. In relation to age, it was suggested that while upper age limits – as long as well evidenced – may well be legally justifiable in the absence of an alternative test of declining fertility, the same may not be true of lower age limits. This is likely to be a policy area which is due for change – it remains to be seen whether the commitments in the Women's Health Strategy are implemented.

[59] Ibid at 67.

7

Intensive Care

Introduction

Intensive care provides an interesting context in which to consider the ways in which equality law impacts on decisions about resources for a number of reasons. First, it is an area where, as we will see, decisions about access to treatment are made principally by clinicians rather than policy makers. Second, those decisions are often made in circumstances of significant pressure on resources, meaning that decisions about one patient can have an immediate impact on treatment for another. And finally because, during the COVID-19 pandemic, pressure on intensive care beds led to public debate about the fairness of prioritization strategies that would cause disadvantage for older patients and those with disabilities.

Much of the litigation relating to decision making in intensive care concerns end of life decision making – and in particular whether or not it is in the best interests of a patient who lacks capacity to decide for themselves whether or not to continue receiving life sustaining treatment. These decisions sometimes involve disagreement between clinicians and families and, particularly in the case of young children, attract lots of media attention. These cases do not engage explicitly with questions of resources and rationing although they are sometimes incorrectly reported as doing so.[1] As Newdick and Danbury explain, 'the law has yet to be confronted by the resource allocation challenges presented by these cases. Judgments are given with no clear evidence of the extent to which promoting the autonomy of single litigants may adversely affect the access to intensive care of others in the queue'.[2]

[1] R. Hurley (2017) 'How a Fight for Charlie Gard Became a Fight Against the State', *British Medical Journal* 358: 3675–3678.

[2] C. Newdick and C. Danbury (2020) 'Promoting the Best Possible Death: Futility in Terminally Ill Patients Who Lack Capacity' in C. Danbury, C. Newdick, A. Ruck Keene

This chapter looks at the scope for discrimination to arise when making decisions about who can access intensive and other forms of emergency care and the way in which the equality law framework may respond to this. In particular it will explore the concerns about age and disability discrimination that arose in the COVID-19 pandemic, but it will also consider the scope for such discrimination to arise in 'ordinary' times. It will also explore, briefly, the extent to which the law requires religious belief to be accommodated in making decisions about end of life care.

The intensive care context

Even before the COVID-19 pandemic, intensive care was a place where there was often substantial pressure on resources. The UK lags behind the rest of Europe for intensive care bed capacity. At the start of the pandemic, and despite a rise in the number of beds available over the previous years, the UK had only 7.3 intensive care beds per 100,000 people, less than half the average in Organisation for Economic Co-operation and Development European Union nations.[3] Writing in 2018, the Faculty of Intensive Care Medicine noted that 'provision of critical care in the UK has always been behind most of the rest of Europe … a lack of critical care beds means a daily struggle, trying to find ways of admitting critically ill patients or not cancelling operations'.[4]

Pressure on critical care beds is made more challenging by a lack of hospital beds generally because those who are ready to be discharged from Intensive Care Units (ICUs) sometimes have no bed on an 'ordinary' ward to move to. A recent review of systemic pressures in intensive care concluded that bed shortages in ICU often arise because patients who are medically fit for discharge are occupying critical care beds when no longer necessary. These delayed discharges are a 'system-wide problem shared across secondary care, but one that has reached crisis point'.[5] In addition to the need for specialist equipment, intensive care patients require intensive

and C. Waldmann (eds) *Law and Ethics in Intensive Care (2nd Edition)*, Oxford: Oxford University Press, pp 111–136 at p 131.

3 British Medical Association (2022) *NHS Hospital Beds Data Analysis*, available at: https://www.bma.org.uk/advice-and-support/nhs-delivery-and-workforce/pressures/nhs-hospital-beds-data-analysis (accessed December 2024).

4 Faculty of Intensive Care Medicine (2018) *Critical Condition: Building a Sustainable Future for the Sickest Patients in the Hospital*, available at: https://www.ficm.ac.uk/sites/ficm/files/documents/2021-10/ficm-critical-condition.pdf (accessed December 2024).

5 J. Parry-Jones (2023) 'Improving Critical Care Flow: Admissions, Discharges and Systemic Pressures', *British Medical Journal* 381: 1363–1364.

staffing – often one intensive care nurse for every one or two patients.[6] As a result, management of ICU units can be very challenging. When demand surges (for example, during winter flu season) this can sometimes only be accommodated 'by reducing professional standards of care, or cancelling elective surgical admissions'.[7]

Occupying an ICU bed is therefore not neutral in terms of the impact on other patients – both because it is resource intensive and because it is a limited resource. At times of pressure, occupying an ICU bed may deprive or delay access to that resource for another patient. There is evidence that this pressure on resources influences decisions about who to treat in intensive care and that 'critical care doctors are constantly assessing the relative priority of the needs of patients for critical care facilities'.[8] In a recent review of decision making in intensive care, ICU consultants suggested that, while they try not to let bed pressures factor into their decision making for individual patients, they are inevitably sometimes required to decide which patients are most likely to benefit most from admission, one consultant noting that 'whether we like it or not and whether we admit it or not, we will make decisions based on lack of resources'.[9]

Decisions about who to admit to ICU are generally made by ICU clinicians. Where hospital policies exist, these provide a framework of relevant considerations within which clinical judgement should be exercised. One hospital policy provides, for example, that:

> [T]he decision to admit a patient to a critical care unit should be based on the concept of potential benefit. Patients who are 'too well' to benefit or those with no hope of recovery to an acceptable quality of life ('too ill to benefit') should not be admitted. This is a clinical decision based on individual circumstances.[10]

---

[6] S. Anandaciva (2020) *Critical Care Services in the English NHS*, The King's Fund, available at: https://www.kingsfund.org.uk/insight-and-analysis/long-reads/critical-care-services-nhs (accessed December 2024).

[7] Parry-Jones (n 5).

[8] Ibid.

[9] N. Power, N. Plummer, J. Baldwin, F. James and S. Laha (2018) 'Intensive Care Decision-making: Identifying the Challenges and Generating Solutions to Improve Inter-specialty Referrals to Critical Care', *Journal of the Intensive Care Society* 19(4): 287–298.

[10] University Hospitals of Leicester NHS Trust (2019) *Admission to Adult Critical Care at Leicester General Hospital* (C 40/2019), available at: https://secure.library.leicestershospitals.nhs.uk/PAGL/Shared%20Documents/Critical%20Care%20%E2%80%93%20Adult%20Admissions%20at%20Leicester%20General%20Hospital%20UHL%20Critical%20Care%20Guideline.pdf (accessed December 2024).

Another provides that admission should take place only where the patient 'has a reversible acute condition and is appropriate for advanced intervention' but not where the patient's 'co-morbidity and poor physiological reserve make the prospect of significant and sustained recovery minimal'.[11]

Clinical decisions about treatment in intensive care are 'inherently complex and exacerbated by a lack of guidance'.[12] This is, at least in part, because – as Bell notes – it is rare that clinicians will be able to predict outcome with accuracy:

> [S]ystems have been devised to improve predictive accuracy and facilitate informed choice and one would naturally incorporate factors such as age, comorbidity, and the reversibility of the triggering pathology into the prognosis and decision making ... but it can be seen that these aspects, which inevitably lack precision for the individual patient, can rarely be determinative.[13]

To compound these difficulties, it should be remembered that where patients requiring admission or ongoing treatment in ICU lack capacity to consent to treatment themselves, clinicians are also required to make a decision about whether new or ongoing ICU treatment is in the best interests of the patient under the Mental Capacity Act.[14] The legal framework for these decisions is discussed in what follows.

COVID-19

The outbreak of COVID-19 added huge pressure to already stretched critical care capacity in the UK. Even with the cancellation of elective and non-urgent surgery, rapid creation of new facilities and redeployment of staff from other specialisms to intensive care, there was real concern that there would not be enough intensive care beds, ventilators or staff for everybody who needed them during the peaks of the pandemic. In the end, the demand

---

[11] Great Western Hospitals NHS Foundation Trust (2021) *Critical Care Unit (CCU) (all Patients) Admission and Discharge Policy* (PC 00005), available at: https://www.gwh.nhs.uk/media/htvcv3rz/critical-care-unit-ccu-admission-and-discharge-policy.pdf (accessed December 2024).

[12] Power et al (n 9).

[13] D. Bell (2020) 'Consent for Intensive Care: Public and Political Expectations vs. Conceptual and Practical Hurdles' in C. Danbury, C. Newdick, A. Ruck Keene and C. Waldmann (eds) *Law and Ethics in Intensive Care (2nd Edition)*, Oxford: Oxford University Press, pp 3–24 at p 10.

[14] Mental Capacity Act 2005.

for ventilator support was less than anticipated and difficulties of choosing which patients' lives to try to save this way did not materialize in quite the same way as was feared. But, at least for a while, the National Health Service (NHS) had to turn attention to the way these precious resources would be prioritized in the event that there were simply not enough for everybody who needed them.[15]

Among other things, these anticipated pressures gave rise to debate in the media as well as the academic literature as to whether chronological age should be used as an explicit mechanism for rationing. The question of whether or not priority should be given to the younger, rather than the older, of two patients when there are not enough resources to treat both has long been a favourite hypothetical puzzle for ethicists and health economists. For a short time, at least, it suddenly became less hypothetical and a matter of live public and policy debate.[16] In the United States, for example, the *New York Times* reported that some policies adopted by states or health care systems specifically made age part of the equation in determining how medical resources should be allocated. In response, the civil rights office of the US Department of Health and Human Services stated that 'persons with disabilities should not be denied medical care on the basis of stereotypes, assessments of quality of life, or judgments about a person's relative "worth" based on the presence or absence of disabilities or age'.[17]

In the UK, there was no suggestion that the NHS would choose to use explicit age based rationing to decide access to ventilation or other forms of treatment. Instead, guidance made clear that prioritization of scarce resources in intensive care should be done on the basis of capacity to benefit. Guidance from the British Medical Association stated that 'if there is radically reduced capacity to meet all serious health needs, it is both lawful and ethical for a doctor, following appropriate prioritisation policies, to refuse someone

---

[15] See evidence given to the COVID-19 inquiry by Professor Sir Stephen Powis, Medical Director of NHS England, on 11 November 2024: UK COVID-19 Inquiry (11 November 2024) *Impact of COVID-19 Pandemic on Healthcare Systems in the 4 Nations of the UK (Module 3) – Public Hearings*, available at: https://www.COVID19.public-inquiry.uk/hearings/impact-of-COVID-19-pandemic-on-healthcare-systems-in-the-4-nations-of-the-uk-module-3-public-hearings/hdid/29360/#tabs (accessed December 2024).

[16] P. Span (31 July 2020) 'Should Youth Come First in Coronavirus Care', *New York Times*, available at: https://www.nytimes.com/2020/07/31/health/coronavirus-ethics-rationing-elderly.html (accessed December 2024); A. Hill (22 April 2020) 'Favouring Young Over Old in COVID-19 Treatment Justifiable, Says Ethicist', *The Guardian*, available at: https://www.theguardian.com/world/2020/apr/22/favouring-young-over-old-in-covid-19-treatment-justifiable-says-ethicist (accessed December 2024).

[17] See discussion in J. Savulescu, I. Persson and D. Wilkinson (2020) 'Utilitarianism and the Pandemic', *Bioethics* 34: 620–632.

potentially life-saving treatment where someone else is expected to benefit more from the available treatment'.[18]

The guidance was clear that while age may be relevant where 'directly linked to [a patient's] clinical ability to benefit', and that 'it is likely that priority will ordinarily be given to those whose conditions are the most urgent, the least complex, and who are likely to live the longest' decisions must not be based solely on age: 'Ethically, triage requires identification of clinically relevant facts about individual patients and their likelihood of benefiting from available resources. Younger patients will not automatically be prioritised over older ones.'[19] 'Benefit' is not defined but the guidance makes clear this is a clinical decision. Decisions about what is in the 'best interests' of a patient who lacks capacity, while necessary before commencing treatment, should not be relevant to the question of priority. The guidance also suggests that, once a 'medical utility' threshold for treatment in intensive care has been reached, choices between patients likely to benefit equally from intervention should be made on a different, 'egalitarian' basis such as first come, first served.[20]

At the start of the pandemic, in March 2020, the National Institute for Health and Care Excellence (NICE) produced mandatory guidance for critical care to enable those responsible for triage in hospitals and ICUs to determine which patients should be offered treatment.[21] It required those responsible for triage decisions to apply a nine-point clinical frailty scale (CFS) from 1 (very fit) to 9 (terminally ill) and suggested that it may not be appropriate to admit to critical care, nor to attempt cardiopulmonary resuscitation, for those with a score of 5 or over (5 being 'mildly frail', a 'more evident slowing' which 'impairs shopping, walking outside alone, meal preparation and housework'). This guidance caused great concern, particularly among advocates for those with disabilities. The difficulty with the CFS was that it included within its definitions of frailty not only those who were more likely to be less likely to respond well to critical care for COVID-19 but those with disabilities that increased their dependence on others but did not make them 'frail' in any sense relevant to their likely prognosis with COVID-19 and treatment for it.[22] The charity Mencap,

---

[18] British Medical Association (2020) *COVID-19 – Ethical Issues. A Guidance Note*, available at: https://www.bma.org.uk/media/2226/bma-covid-19-ethics-guidance.pdf (accessed December 2024).

[19] Ibid.

[20] Ibid.

[21] National Institute for Health and Care Excellence (2020) *COVID-19 Rapid Guideline: Critical Care in Adults*, London.

[22] E. Chong, M. Chan, H. Nuo Tan and W. Shiong Lim (2020) 'COVID-19: Use of the Clinical Frailty Scale for Critical Care Decisions', *Journal of the American Geriatrics Society* 68(6): 30–32.

for example, expressed grave concern that the guidance 'could result in patients with a learning disability not getting equal access to critical care and potentially dying avoidably'.[23] In response, NICE amended the guidance to tell decision makers that 'the CFS should not be used in younger people, people with stable long-term disabilities (for example, cerebral palsy), learning disabilities or autism. An individualised assessment is recommended in all cases where the CFS is not appropriate'.[24]

Although not an issue relevant only to intensive care, it is worth noting here that there were also concerns raised in the media about the use of blanket DNACPR (do not attempt cardiopulmonary resuscitation) notices as a form of rationing. In April 2020, for example, the *Guardian* newspaper reported concerns that some care homes were adding DNACPR notices 'en masse' to the records of patients in care homes without appropriate consultation because it was judged that these patients would be unlikely to benefit from hospital admission or because they should not be admitted to hospital at a time of scarce resource.[25] These reports caused the Care Quality Commission (CQC) to respond by issuing guidance that DNACPR notices should only ever be made following individual assessment and consultation. The CQC interim report on DNACPR in the pandemic notes that they had raised concerns about inappropriate use of DNACPR notices at an early stage and had 'reminded all providers that it was unacceptable for advance care plans, with or without DNACPR form completion, to be applied to groups of people of any description'.[26]

Deciding who to treat on the basis of their capacity to benefit has, as was discussed in Chapter 2, the potential to give rise to indirect discrimination on grounds of age or disability in particular. Judgements about the likelihood of recovery to some minimally acceptable quality (or length) of life mean that those less likely to recover, or to recover sufficiently – including because of age or underlying comorbidity – may be less likely to receive treatment.

---

23 Mencap (2 April 2020) *Mencap Responds to Revised Critical Care Guidance from NICE*, available at: https://www.mencap.org.uk/press-release/mencap-responds-deeply-troubling-new-nice-COVID-19-guidance (accessed December 2024).

24 NICE (n 21).

25 R. Booth (1 April 2020) 'UK Healthcare Regulator Brands Resuscitation Strategy Unacceptable', *The Guardian*, available at: https://www.theguardian.com/world/2020/apr/01/uk-healthcare-regulator-brands-resuscitation-strategy-unacceptable (accessed December 2024).

26 Care Quality Commission (November 2020) *Review of Do Not Attempt Cardio Pulmonary Resuscitation Decisions during the COVID-19 Pandemic: Interim Report*, available at: https://www.cqc.org.uk/sites/default/files/20201204%20DNACPR%20Interim%20Report%20-%20FINAL.pdf (accessed December 2024).

This was recognized by the British Medical Association, which noted in its guidance:

> During the peak of the pandemic, doctors are likely to be required to assess a person's eligibility for treatment based on a 'capacity to benefit quickly' basis. As such, some of the most unwell patients may be denied access to treatment such as intensive care or artificial ventilation. This will inevitably be indirectly discriminatory against both the elderly and those with long-term health conditions, with the latter being denied access to life-saving treatment as a result of their pre-existing health problems. … Although a 'capacity to benefit quickly' test would be indirect discrimination, in our view it would be lawful in the circumstances of a serious pandemic because it would amount to 'a proportionate means of achieving a legitimate aim', under s19 (1) of the Equalities Act – namely fulfilling the requirement to use limited NHS resources to their best effect.[27]

While this assessment may well be right in relation to the legitimacy of the aim of using resources to their best effect – something we have seen courts reluctant to interfere with in the context of judicial review and Human Rights Act challenges to resource allocation – the proportionality element of the test may be less straightforward to satisfy. In particular there are a number of circumstances which might mean that the approach adopted here – or a similar approach adopted in future - is not a proportionate one. First, is where the assumptions on which the policy, or its implementation by clinicians, are based are unwarranted and themselves discriminatory. This was undoubtedly the case in relation to the original frailty scoring approach adopted by NICE, but there is also scope for assumptions about quality of life related to age or disability to inform assessment of capacity to benefit by individual clinicians in applying their own judgement. Evidence of age discrimination in clinical decision making – where chronological age may be used as a basis to deny treatment based on potentially unwarranted assumptions about the lifestyle and preferences of patients – was discussed in Chapter 2. The second circumstance, by contrast, is where there is potential for individual clinical assessment of patients to be made but it is not, as was the case for some in respect of DNACPR notices. Applying blanket criteria which may disadvantage individual patients because of protected characteristics such as age or disability is unlikely to be proportionate where individual, holistic assessment is instead a possibility. Finally, a measure is unlikely to be proportionate where the disadvantage caused by a policy or

[27] British Medical Association (n 18).

practice outweighs the benefits of the legitimate aim it is aiming to achieve. The next sections will consider these issues in turn.

Prioritization through capacity to benefit

How individual clinicians make decisions about capacity to benefit is not well understood. In particular, it is unclear what understanding(s) of 'benefit' are used – a narrow, physiological, understanding of the effects of a particular treatment or a broader conception of benefit involving value judgements as to the quality of life an intervention may produce. In relation to policy-based rationing, as seen in Chapter 2, Quality Adjusted Life Years offer a methodology to determine how much benefit will be produced by an intervention, and while not without difficulties from a discrimination and equality perspective, the decision-making process is at least (relatively) transparent. The factors relevant to decisions on capacity to benefit by individual clinicians about individual patients are, inevitably, more difficult to identify. This matters because, where decisions involve judgements about quality of life, there is scope for assumptions about what makes life worth living – including assumptions which may be discriminatory on the basis of age or disability – to decide access to life saving treatment. From an equality perspective, and particularly where clinicians are being asked to 'rank' candidates for admission or ongoing treatment in ICU by their capacity to benefit, it is crucial to understand whether and where there is room for this assessment to incorporate value judgements about the quality of life to which the proposed course of treatment will be likely to give rise and from whose perspective this should be judged.

Difficulties in drawing a distinction between 'purely clinical' aspects of decision making on the one hand and value based judgements about quality of life before and after treatment on the other, are well illustrated in the case law on end of life decision making in intensive care. Problems have arisen, in particular, on the question of whether and when continued treatment of very seriously ill patients becomes 'futile'.[28] Ordinarily, a decision about what treatment to provide to seriously ill or dying (or indeed any) patients involves two stages. First the doctor, exercising his or her professional clinical judgement, decides what treatment options are clinically indicated and offers these to the patient. If a clinician believes a course of treatment is not clinically indicated, they are under no obligation to provide it, although the patient should normally have access to a second opinion.[29] Second, the

[28] C. Auckland (2021) 'A Façade of Futility', *Law Quarterly Review* 137: 451–476; S. Michalowski and W. Martin (2022) 'DNACPR Decisions: Aligning Law, Guidance and Practice', *Medical Law Review* 30(3): 434–456; Newdick and Danbury (n 2).

[29] *Tracey v Cambridge University Hospitals NHS Trust* [2014] EWCA Civ 822.

patient may then consent or refuse consent to the treatments under offer or, in the event a patient lacks mental capacity, a decision be made as to whether or not a proposed course of treatment is also in the best interests of the patient under the Mental Capacity Act.[30]

The best interests test involves a much wider range of considerations than does the question of whether a treatment option is clinically indicated. As Lady Hale explained in *Aintree*:

> [T]he purpose of the best interests test is to consider matters from the patient's point of view. That is not to say that his wishes must prevail, any more than those of a fully capable patient must prevail. We cannot always have what we want. … But in so far as it is possible to ascertain the patient's wishes and feelings, his beliefs and values or the things which were important to him, it is those which should be taken into account because they are a component in making the choice which is right for him as an individual human being.[31]

In determining best interests, the Mental Capacity Act Code of Practice suggests that:

> [T]here will be a limited number of cases where treatment is futile, overly burdensome to the patient or where there is no prospect of recovery. In circumstances such as these, it may be that an assessment of best interests leads to the conclusion that it would be in the best interests of the patient to withdraw or withhold life-sustaining treatment, even if this may result in the person's death.[32]

In assessing best interests in this context, courts have struggled to provide clear guidance to clinicians as to whether the futility of a treatment should be assessed in a narrow sense and only in relation to its immediate physiological effects, or whether a broader approach should be taken by considering whether the outcome of the treatment would have any value to the patient themselves. *Aintree* is a good example. The case concerned a patient, David James, who was 68 and in intensive care for seven months. He had suffered multiple organ failure, cardiac arrest, stroke and a series of serious infections and was dying. Neurological deterioration meant that he lacked mental

---

30 *R (on the application of Burke) v General Medical Council* [2005] Lloyds Rep Med 403 at 50.

31 *Aintree University Hospitals NHS Foundation Trust v James* [2013] EWCA Civ 65; [2013] at 45.

32 Department of Constitutional Affairs (2007) *Mental Capacity Act 2005 Code of Practice*, 5.31, available at: https://www.gov.uk/government/publications/mental-capacity-act-code-of-practice (accessed December 2024).

capacity but he had some level of consciousness which enabled him to respond with pleasure to company, in particular the company of his family. All of the clinicians responsible for his treatment were of the view that further treatment would be futile and applied to the court for a declaration that it would be lawful to withhold it in the event of further deterioration. The Court of Appeal had granted the declaration on the basis that treatment would be futile unless it could offer 'real prospect of curing or at least palliating the life threatening disease or illness from which the patient was suffering'.[33] This understanding of futility adopts a narrow, medical, approach to the question. By contrast, the Supreme Court, in agreement with the judgment of the High Court at first instance, determined that this approach to futility was 'setting the goal too high' because 'a treatment may bring some benefit to the patient even though it has no effect on the underlying disease or disability'.[34] Rather, Lady Hale argued, 'resuming a quality of life which the patient would regard as worthwhile is more readily applicable, particularly in the case of a patient with permanent disabilities'.[35] This approach clearly goes beyond a narrow assessment of the likely therapeutic benefit and focuses instead on the question of whether the quality of life, post-treatment, will have some value to the patient.

Auckland has argued that there is a real need for greater transparency in the way these decisions are made by the courts:

> Deciding whether or not a person derives a benefit from life-sustaining treatment … inevitably involves value judgements about their perceived quality of life. By conflating these with questions about the efficacy of treatments under the broad umbrella of 'futility', these value judgements are being obscured, a problem exacerbated by a propensity for judges to move between talking about the treatment being futile and the patient's life being futile. While some value judgements may be unavoidable in cases such as these, it is crucially important that … this assessment is made honestly and openly, and is capable of scrutiny and challenge. It should not be concealed behind statistics on therapeutic success.[36]

Auckland's concerns about the lack of transparency arising from the conflation between 'clinical judgement' – which appears, at first glance, to be objective and value neutral – and value judgements about quality of life, are equally important where clinicians are responsible for allocating resources

[33] *Aintree University Hospitals NHS Foundation Trust v James* (n 31) at 34.
[34] Ibid at 43.
[35] Ibid at 44.
[36] Auckland (n 28) p 451.

on the basis of their judgement about whether a patient has capacity to benefit, and whether that benefit is likely to be greater or lesser than that of another patient. Unlike best interests decisions, the factors relevant to clinical decision making are not set out in a legal framework (although clinicians must act in accordance with their common law duty of care in making them) and there is no corresponding direction from the court as to how judgements about capacity to benefit are to be made. If rationing by 'capacity to benefit' is to be justified as a fair means of using limited resources to maximize health in the population then it is vitally important for those implementing the policy to have a clear and consistent understanding of what factors are relevant to making an assessment and which factors are not, and for this to be transparent. Without this, there is a risk that apparently neutral and objective decision making will in fact hide ageist or ableist assumptions (even if well intentioned) about the values and preferences of patients, unfairly creating or compounding disadvantage in access to care.

Policy and lack of individual assessment

Where a policy decision is made as to which patients have capacity to benefit and which do not, or establish criteria which will serve as a proxy for 'capacity to benefit', a different set of problems may arise. This approach is more transparent (although there is of course room for clinical judgement in the application of criteria set out in such policy). But policies which use broad criteria to categorize patients are likely to lack predictive accuracy, such that they will sometimes mean those (often older, or disabled) patients who would benefit equally or more than others are excluded from care. These difficulties were seen in relation to both the NICE frailty scale for admission to intensive care, and to the broad approach to the inclusion of DNACPR notices on the notes of patients in care homes (although the latter never amounted to official NHS policy). Policies such as this may amount to age or disability discrimination, where they cannot be justified as a proportionate means of achieving a legitimate aim (in this case likely to be the need to distribute scarce resources to those most likely to benefit from them).

We saw in Chapters 2 and 3 (and again when thinking about screening policies in Chapter 5) that an assessment of proportionality in circumstances such as this is likely to include at least three considerations. The first is the accuracy of the criteria used – where evidence does not well support the use of criteria as proxies for capacity to benefit, then they are less likely to be an appropriate and necessary means of achieving the aims in question. Had a court been called on to review the original NICE policy for COVID-19 triage, with its instructions on the use of the CFS, it is certainly possible it would have found the policy to be in breach of the Equality

Act because, in the case of patients with certain disabilities, the CFS was a very inaccurate predictor of their ability to benefit from critical care for COVID-19. A second consideration relevant to whether a policy approach is proportionate is whether or not individual clinical assessment, which may serve as a less discriminatory alternative, is appropriate or feasible. There may be circumstances where individual assessment is simply not possible for reasons of time or resources. But where it is, a policy not to do so may well be disproportionate. Certainly in relation to critical care admission during the pandemic, NICE subsequently amended its guidance to reflect this, noting that the CFS should be 'used only as part of "a holistic assessment"'.[37]

In relation to DNACPR notices in particular it is worth also noting that Article 8 of the European Convention on Human Rights (ECHR) will require individual consultation in most circumstances, meaning a blanket policy is unlikely ever to be lawful. In *Tracey*, the claimant had had a DNACPR notice added to her notes without any consultation with either her or her family (when she lacked capacity). The Court of Appeal held that:

> The fact that the clinician considers that CPR will not work means that the patient cannot require him to provide it. It does not, however, mean that the patient is not entitled to know that the clinical decision has been taken. Secondly, if the patient is not told that the clinician has made a DNACPR decision, he will be deprived of the opportunity of seeking a second opinion.[38]

Finally, where eligibility for treatment is determined by policy criteria rather than individual assessment of capacity to benefit, the possibility of making an exception where an individual patient is able to demonstrate that the relevant criteria are an inaccurate measure of their capacity to benefit, may make it more likely that the policy is proportionate. This is discussed in detail in Chapter 3.

There is, therefore, scope for potentially unlawful discrimination in either approach – individual assessment of capacity to benefit by clinicians and policy based determination of capacity to benefit by the application of set criteria. In circumstances like the COVID-19 pandemic, and where a 'capacity to benefit' approach to rationing scarce resources is taken, it might be impossible to avoid disadvantage caused to older patients or those whose disabilities make them particularly susceptible to the disease and less likely to recover even with treatment. However, in order to minimize this disadvantage, there is a need to strike the right balance between clear and

[37] NICE (n 21).

[38] *Tracey v Cambridge University Hospitals NHS Trust* (n 29) at 55.

consistent understanding of what capacity to benefit means, while leaving room for as holistic assessment of each patient as is possible given the context – including pressure on time and resources in an emergency – in which the decision must be taken.

Justifying age discrimination

Even if these difficulties can be adequately addressed, there is a need to consider whether the inevitable disadvantage caused to older patients (and those with certain disabilities) by using capacity to benefit as the basis on which to allocate resources, can be justified. Advocates of utilitarianism argue that – even in ordinary times and especially in the setting of a public health emergency – disadvantage caused to age and disability is likely to be a price worth paying for the benefit gained by the population as a whole. This approach is not to disregard the harms caused by discrimination (direct or indirect) because under utilitarian calculus these will be weighed in the balance alongside the benefits to determine the utility generated by any particular rationing approach. Within the legal framework it is the proportionality assessment that affords scope for this form of weighing and balancing. Savalescu et al, for example, argued that 'there are no egalitarians in a pandemic … very large numbers of lives are at stake. Equality, even for those opposed to utilitarianism, is only one value amongst others. Discrimination may be proportionate if the stakes are high enough and alternative measures are not available'.[39]

In relation to age discrimination (although not to other forms of discrimination) an alternative approach to justifying disadvantage exists which has been used, in other contexts, by courts and is worth considering here. It is not (as in the case of the utilitarian argument) that disadvantage caused by discrimination is outweighed by the greater good, but rather an argument that no inequality is caused where a policy treats a particular age group less favourably than another or an age group is disadvantaged by it. There are two variants of this argument. The first, the 'complete life view' of equality, suggests that there is nothing wrong with rationing resources by age, or in a way that disadvantages a particular age group, because, while it may result in unequal treatment or impact *today*, it does not create inequality over the course of our complete lives. No unfairness is created by age discrimination because – when judged over a lifetime – the same opportunities and constraints will have been available equally to everyone. If I am to be denied access to an intensive care bed because I am old, so that a younger patient can have it, it may feel unfair today but it will not

[39] Savulescu et al (n 17) p 620.

give rise to inequality, judged across my lifetime if I have benefited, at a younger age, from policies that advantage the young at the expense of the old. This approach suggests that we *may* discriminate on grounds of age – use chronological age to organize and ration access to various benefits, for example – because no inequality is thereby created.

A second, related, argument, known as the 'fair innings' argument, says we *should*, sometimes, discriminate on grounds of age in order to avoid inequality or to achieve substantive equality between the generations. This is because the older generations have acquired some advantage over the younger, as a result of having lived or worked for longer. Treating old and young equally today may preserve this advantage to the older generation at the expense of the younger and may serve to permanently exclude younger generations from the opportunities enjoyed by those who have gone before them. There are several versions of the fair innings argument,[40] but, typically, its advocates argue that where resources (such as health care funding or intensive care beds) are scarce, priority in the distribution of those resources *should* be given to the younger generations who have not yet had something – a long time alive – over the older generations who have. It is, in essence, an argument for a form of positive discrimination. The substantive inequality it aims to correct is not – as is usually the case in relation to sex or race discrimination – one rooted largely in historical discrimination against or persecution of a particular group, but one that is necessarily generated by the passage of time.[41] Thus, while the complete life view arguments for restricting access to health care are generally equally applicable to restrictions on health care at any age (justifying lower and upper age limits for screening programmes or IVF, for example), fair innings arguments apply to restrictions on health care for older patients who have already lived a 'fair innings', however that is defined, for the benefit of those who have not yet done so.

There are a number of well-known objections to both of these approaches. First is that, even if no distributive inequality is created over a lifetime – I am denied a ventilator today because I am old but was able to access one earlier in my life because I was young – at least some uses of age to ration access to resources may still be harmful for other reasons. Cupit, for example, has argued that:

[40] See Tsuchiya who identifies at least four versions of the fair innings account: the original fair innings account; the extended fair innings account; the relative fair innings account; and the biographical account. in A. Tsuchiya (2000) 'QALYs and Ageism: Philosophical Theories and Age Weighting', *Health Economics* 9: 57–68.

[41] And, in some cases, by changing circumstances which mean the younger generation is unable to access the same opportunities as the older generation once enjoyed – for example, barriers to entry to the job market for young people.

> [I]f we want to know whether such practices as denying expensive medical care to the very aged … are unjust, then … we have to ask not (or not simply) what distribution of benefits (over, or within, a life) such practices will tend to generate, but what, if anything, such practices will *express*.[42]

Policies which suggest that older people are less valued by society, for example, may be harmful even in the absence of distributive inequalities. In the context of a proportionality balancing, such harms may of course be outweighed by the needs of others, particularly in the midst of a health emergency; but there is an argument that they should at least be counted. This certainly chimes with accounts of substantive equality such as Fredman's, according to which a range of harms and disadvantages, rather than just distributive inequalities, must be addressed.[43]

A second objection is to note that it is simply wrong to assume that an older patient has either had the opportunity to take advantage of earlier benefits to compensate for not having them now; or that they have had a 'fair innings' in any sense beyond years lived. Circumstances (including medical and legal advances or the absence of a global pandemic) may mean that I have not been able to benefit from a positive distribution of resources in my favour at an earlier stage of my life in a way that compensates for lack of access to resources now. And while I may have lived a long life I may not have lived most or many of those years in good health, making it difficult to conceive of my innings as a fair one. This is a problem recognized by Norman Daniels, otherwise an advocate for a version of the fair innings argument, who notes that in reality the worst off among the elderly are very often those who have been worst off at every stage of their lives. An intersectional approach may be particularly important here. While those of the same age have lived the same number of years, there will be considerable differences between them in experience of health (and other benefits) which, as seen in Chapter 1, are likely to correlate both to socio-economic status and membership of some other protected groups.

The refusal of life saving care purely on the basis of chronological age (or other protected characteristic) is not something that has ever been tested in the courts so it is not possible to say with certainty how the courts would have responded to such a policy in the pandemic. It is worth noting that arguments about intergenerational fairness and equality – and reference to the complete life view and fair innings arguments – have featured in

[42] G. Cupit (1998) 'Justice, Age and Veneration', *Ethics* 108(4): 702–718, emphasis in original.

[43] S. Fredman (2016) 'Substantive Equality Revisited', *International Journal of Constitutional Law* 14: 712–738.

legal decisions involving direct age discrimination in other contexts and in particular in relation to employment. In *Seldon*, discussed in earlier chapters, a claim concerning a challenge to compulsory retirement from a legal partnership at the age of 65, Lady Hale used the complete life approach to explain why age was 'different' to other characteristics protected by the Equality Act and why direct age discrimination could therefore be justified in circumstances in which discrimination on other grounds could not:

> [A]ge is not 'binary' in nature (man or woman, black or white, gay or straight) but a continuum which changes over time … this means that younger people will eventually benefit from a provision which favours older employees, such as an incremental pay scale; but older employees will already have benefitted from a provision which favours younger people, such as a mandatory retirement age.[44]

There is also evidence of the fair innings argument in jurisprudence on age discrimination in employment – the argument that age discrimination may be *necessary* to create equality – because, for example, without it older workers will have more than their fair share of employment opportunities at the expense of younger workers. While the evidence on which such claims are founded is contested,[45] the argument still carries significant weight with the judiciary. Neither the Court of Justice of the European Union nor the UK courts have had any trouble accepting as legitimate aims those that promote 'intergenerational fairness'.[46] In *Seldon*, for example, the defendant partnership had argued that the use of mandatory retirement was justified, among other things, by the legitimate aim of ensuring that associates were given the opportunity of partnership after a reasonable period. This was readily accepted by the Supreme Court as being the type of legitimate aim identified by the Court of Justice of the European Union. Indeed, Lady

44 *Seldon v Clarkson, Wright and Jakes (a Partnership)* [2012] UKSC 16 at 4. See also the Opinion of Advocate General Kokott in *Association Belges des Consommateurs Test-Achats ASBL v Conseil des Ministres* (C-236/09) delivered on 30 September 2010 (at para 50 and footnote 37) where she makes a similar point in relation to age related insurance premiums.

45 See, for example, Department for Business, Innovation and Skills (2011) *Phasing Out the Default Retirement Age: Government Response to Consultation*, available at: https://assets.publishing.service.gov.uk/media/5a78b3a240f0b62b22cbc19e/11-536-phasing-out-default-retirement-age-government-response.pdf (accessed February 2025) which concluded that the abolition of the default retirement age would not have negative impact on younger workers.

46 See, for example, *Rosenbladt v Oellerking GmbH* [2011] CMLR 1011; *Fuchs and another v Land Hessen* [2011] 3 CMLR 1299; *Petersen v Berufungsausschuss für Zahnärzte für den Bezirk Westfalen-Lippe* [2010] 2 CMLR 830; *Seldon v Clarkson Wright and Jakes (a Partnership)* (n 44).

Hale noted that the aim of intergenerational fairness was 'comparatively uncontroversial'. These arguments may, of course, be treated differently in the context of a refusal of life saving care to a patient who may benefit from it, not least because a challenge may also arise under Articles 8 or 2 (right to life) of the ECHR, alone and in conjunction with Article 14. Certainly in relation to the suggestion that blanket DNACPR decisions were being made on the basis of age (and disability) the Equality and Human Rights Commission argued that '[t]he right to life is "non-derogable", which means it must be maintained even in times of emergency. Public authorities have positive obligations to protect life, including a duty to prevent avoidable deaths'.[47]

Religion and intensive care

Finally, this chapter briefly considers the relevance of the religious belief of the patient in end of life decision making. Intensive care clinicians, in making decisions about refusing or discontinuing treatment, will sometimes be faced by circumstances where relatives of a patient object to the cessation of treatment because they believe to end life (or confirm death) in these circumstances would be contrary to the religious belief of the patient. This, in turn, gives rise to questions about whether equality law – in this case most likely Article 9 of the ECHR which protects the right to freedom of thought, conscience and religion – requires that decisions take into account, or are determined by, religious belief.

Defining death

There is no statutory definition of death in the UK but the courts have held that legal death is established when there is an irreversible absence of brainstem function.[48] This approach is not without its critics.[49] In particular, different perspectives on what death means can be found among different faiths and a number of these reject the use of neurological criteria to establish death.[50] While courts have acknowledged this, however, it is clear that in the UK, satisfaction of the neurological test of brainstem death amounts to legal death and there is no legal room for conscientious or religious objection to this approach. This was clear in *Re A (A Child)*, a case which concerned a

[47] CQC (n 26) 5.

[48] *Airedale NHS Trust v Bland* [1993] A.C. 789.

[49] See, for example, discussion in J. Herring (2020) *Medical Law and Ethics*, Oxford: Oxford University Press, p 534.

[50] L.S.M. Johnson (2016) 'The Case for Reasonable Accommodation of Conscientious Objections to Declarations of Brain Death', *Bioethical Inquiry* 13: 105–115.

young child, diagnosed with brainstem death but remaining on ventilation, whose parents were of Muslim faith and unable to agree that this amounted to death.[51] The Court noted the need to be sensitive to different religious perspectives on this issue:

> The facts of this case are a reminder once again that in a multi-cultural society there has to be recognition that people, particularly those with strong religious beliefs, may differ with medical professionals as to when death occurs. In the Christian, Muslim and Jewish faiths the concept of the 'breath of life' has ancient and important resonance. It is hardly difficult to understand why the still breathing body is regarded as alive, even though 'breath' may be entirely delivered by machine.[52]

Nonetheless the Court upheld the legal test for death, concluding that 'whilst expressing profound respect for the father's views, the time has now come to permit the ventilator to be turned off and to allow Child A, who died on 10th February, dignity in death'.[53] It was recently made clear in the Court of Appeal that where neurological criteria are satisfied, a test of best interests ceases to be relevant.[54]

Different jurisdictions take different positions where this occurs. In New Jersey, for example, the New Jersey Declaration of Death Act 1991 includes a (rarely used) provision that where clinicians have reason to believe 'that the individual's personal religious beliefs would be violated by the declaration of death upon the basis of the neurological criteria, then the death of the individual shall be declared … solely on the basis of cardio-respiratory criteria'.[55] Similarly the State of New York provides that reasonable accommodation should be made of an individual's religious or moral objection to the criteria used to establish death.[56] Some argue that this more flexible approach should be adopted elsewhere.[57]

---

51 *Re A (A Child)* [2015] EWHC 443 (Fam).

52 Ibid at 24.

53 Ibid at 26.

54 *Re M (Declaration of Death of Child)* [2020] EWCA Civ 164.

55 New Jersey Declaration of Death Act 1991, 26: 6A-5; and see discussion in R. Son and S. Setta (2018) 'Frequency of Use of the Religious Exemption in New Jersey Cases of Determination of Brain Death', *BMC Medical Ethics* 19: 76–82.

56 New York Department of State – Division of Administrative Rules, State Compilation of Codes, Rules and Regulations of the State of New York, Title 10, CRR-NY 400.16 and see discussion in D. Gardiner and A. McGee (2020) 'Diagnosing Death' in C. Danbury, C. Newdick, A. Ruck Keene and C. Waldmann (eds) *Law and Ethics in Intensive Care (2nd Edition)*, Oxford: Oxford University Press, pp 137–159.

57 Gardiner and McGee (n 56).

There has been no challenge to the neurological definition of death under Article 9 ECHR. Indeed, it is not clear whether Article 9 would be engaged in circumstances where national law regards the patient as no longer living. And should the approach to death in UK law require legal justification, it is unclear whether resourcing would be, or would be claimed to be, a relevant factor. Certainly resourcing has not factored in the few cases on definition of death; but permitting religious and other perspectives to be accommodated may result in prolonged use of mechanical ventilation, meaning in turn that access for other patients may be delayed or restricted.

Choosing life or death

More common are cases where clinicians and courts need to determine whether or not to continue to treat patients who remain alive but where quality of life is judged to be absent or minimal, with no chance of improvement. We saw earlier that these decisions involve consideration of whether treatment is futile or is otherwise not in the best interests of the patient. In the same way that broader conceptions of futility may take into account quality of life related to age or disability, so too the religious perspective of the patient on end of life may be relevant here. Certainly the Courts have made clear that the religious views of the patient are relevant to the determination of best interests because they are often highly relevant to an assessment of the patient's 'wishes and feelings', which the Supreme Court in *Aintree* placed firmly at the centre of the analysis.[58]

An important case on this point is that of Tafida Raqeeb.[59] The case concerned a young child who was on life support following traumatic brain injury. Her clinical team in London believed that further treatment was futile and that, in consequence, life support should be withdrawn. Her parents wished life sustaining treatment to continue so that they could, at their own expense, transfer her for treatment at a hospital in Italy. They argued that continuing life support was in the best interests of Tafida because, among other reasons, it was compatible with their religious beliefs and, they believed, the nascent and future beliefs of Tafida. While they accepted that further treatment may be futile from a 'narrow medical perspective' they argued that for those sharing the belief system in which Tafida was growing up, life sustaining treatment conferred the benefit of 'protecting the sanctity of life'.[60]

In assessing Tafida's best interests the Court made clear that Article 9 was engaged, although noted that the rights of the child and parents under Article

[58] *Aintree University Hospitals NHS Foundation Trust v James* (n 31).

[59] *Raqeeb v Barts NHS Foundation Trust* [2020] 3 All E.R. 663.

[60] Ibid at 77.

9 could be circumscribed where they conflicted with the best interests of the child.[61] In relation to futility it noted that 'the benefits of life-sustaining treatment may extend beyond the merely medical' and held that:

> [T]he argument that a child who feels no pain and no or minimal awareness can derive no benefit from being kept alive is similarly fallacious in circumstances where … the foregoing assumption does not accord with many people's intuitive feelings about their lives, and particularly those people who have a strong religious faith.

As a result, the Court concluded that:

> [W]hilst not by itself sufficient to justify the continuation of life sustaining treatment on the basis of Art 9 or otherwise, a further benefit of continued life sustaining treatment is that it permits Tafida to remain alive in accordance with the tenets of the religion in which she was being raised and for which she had begun to demonstrate a basic affinity.[62]

Likewise, in *Fixsler*[63] it was clear that while the religious perspectives of the patient on end of life are a relevant factor to be taken into account in an assessment of best interests, they cannot alone be determinative. In *Fixler* the clinical team wished to discontinue active treatment for a two-year-old girl who had suffered catastrophic brain injury at birth and to move her to palliative care because they believed that she had no prospect of recovery and, further, that ongoing treatment caused her pain. The parents, who were ultra-orthodox Jews, disagreed because they disputed that their daughter experienced pain and because their (and therefore, they argued, their daughter's) religious belief was that life should be preserved and that no steps should be taken to hasten death. They argued that the best interests test must be framed within the Jewish belief system. The Court disagreed, confirming that while the belief system followed by the parents was *one* factor to be weighed in the balance when determining best interests, the best interests test could not be reduced to this single question. In any event, distinguishing the case from *Raqeeb* it also noted that there was, in this case, no evidence that the child had ever had knowledge of or shared the same religious values as her parents.

Religious belief is, therefore, one factor that must be considered during an assessment of best interests but one which may be outweighed by other

61 Ibid at 116 and 130.

62 Ibid at 172 and 173.

63 *Manchester University NHS Foundation Trust v Fixsler and ors* [2021] EWHC 1426.

considerations. This accords with the framework of Article 9 which permits interference with the right to manifest religious belief where this is justified. It is important to remember, also, that the best interests test is not intended to be determinative of the treatment a patient should receive – it *permits* clinicians to provide treatment in the absence of consent but does not require them to provide it against their clinical judgement. Nor can it require the state to fund a course of treatment. For, as Lady Hale had made clear in *Aintree*, a decision that treatment was in a patient's best interests did not mean they were entitled to it. In practice, however, once a court has ruled that a particular course of treatment would be in a patient's best interests, it may be difficult for clinicians to withdraw treatment, or to refuse to provide it. Best interests judgements, therefore – in fact if not in law – may impact on the availability of resources. Indeed, in *Aintree*, as Auckland notes, the Intensive Care Society and Faculty of Intensive Medicine, intervening, estimated that a requirement to provide three more days of life support for each patient that eventually dies in intensive care, would put such pressure on intensive care beds that it could delay admission for an additional 50,000 patients a year.[64]

Conclusion

Decisions in intensive care are no doubt among the most challenging doctors can make, from an ethical and legal, as well as clinical, perspective. While decisions about who to admit to intensive care in ordinary times are not intended to be made with reference to the availability of resources, it is apparent that this is not always the case. And in the COVID-19 pandemic, clinicians were expressly called on to – if necessary – prioritize patients on the basis of their capacity to benefit.

While a capacity to benefit approach to intensive care admission is often likely to disadvantage older patients, and those with certain disabilities, on the basis of reduced ability to tolerate and respond to relevant interventions, it has been argued that, from an equality perspective, it is particularly important not to reinforce this disadvantage by applying an assessment of capacity to benefit in discriminatory manner. There is a lack of transparency and understanding about – and legal regulation of – the way 'capacity to benefit' decisions are made. And while 'capacity to benefit' may appear to be an objective, clinical, test, there is scope for an assessment of capacity to incorporate value judgements about quality of life and patient preferences, in much the same was as has been found to be the case in relation to assessments of futility.

[64] Auckland (n 28).

Conclusion

In many ways, investigating the implications of equality law for the decisions health care commissioners must take about how to allocate scarce resources leaves us with as many questions as answers. This is because, among other things, the test for legal justification relevant to most of the examples of potential discrimination we have identified, as well as to positive action – whether or not the policy or decision in question amounts to a proportionate means of achieving a legitimate aim – will often involve the same difficult balancing of competing aims and interests that those engaged in thinking about health care rationing have grappled with from the start. The courts, as we have seen, have been reluctant to direct policy makers as to the substantive principles that should inform this balancing exercise precisely because these decisions are ones involving values on which there is no consensus and which, in the view of the courts, are therefore usually best left to democratically accountable decision makers. As a result, equality law cannot provide any definitive answer to the problem of how to weigh the needs of groups or individuals against the needs of wider populations nor how to choose, where a choice must be made, between different groups who are disadvantaged in relation to their health. It cannot give us a road map to deal with health inequalities. Nonetheless, it is possible to identify a number of important ways in which equality law informs and constrains the way the National Health Service must approach priority setting.

First, and perhaps most importantly, equality law, particularly in the form of the Public Sector Equality Duty (PSED), requires commissioners to pay attention to the potential for discrimination and inequality to arise as a result of their decisions or their failure to act. While the duty does not dictate the way policy makers should then respond, it does at least mean that they should take active steps to ensure that the potential disadvantage to protected groups is identified and properly considered, an obligation which has generally been reinforced by the courts. As a result, any such disadvantage should at least be in the scales in any balancing exercise, even if, in the end, it is outweighed by other considerations, or by the needs of others. The PSED also has potential to shine a light on health inequalities that may otherwise have been overlooked, although, as we saw in Chapter 1, the lack of any systematic approach to intersectional or socio-economic disadvantage may undermine its potential in this respect.

Second, health care professionals must justify their decisions where they disadvantage protected groups in a way that would otherwise amount to discrimination. It is not enough, in the words of the High Court in *Cambridge*, for policy makers to 'toll the bell of tight resources'.[1] While the balancing of competing interests is something on which courts are reluctant to interfere, they are sometimes willing to take a more robust approach to the questions of whether discriminatory measures are appropriate or necessary. This may include questioning whether or not the evidence on which the decisions are based is accurate and inclusive and whether or not a less discriminatory approach exists that would not compromise the aim of the policy decision. Most importantly, commissioners will normally struggle to legally justify their decisions where they have failed, in their exercise of the PSED, to pay due regard to disparate impact and the steps that could be taken to mitigate it.

Third, and related, policy makers and clinicians alike should be alert to the possibility that judgements about the clinical benefit or effectiveness of a treatment may involve unwarranted assumptions about how patients – including older or disabled patients – experience health related quality of life. In the case of treatment decisions by individual clinicians, these assumptions may be particularly hard to identify. Further research to understand more about when – and how – individual clinicians use protected characteristics in their decision making and how they assess capacity to benefit would be welcome, as would transparent debate and guidance about what conception of 'benefit' should be used when a commissioning strategy aims to prioritize access on the basis of capacity to benefit and/or cost-effectiveness.

Fourth, there is scope for policy makers to take positive action to prevent or redress disadvantage experienced by groups and individuals, related to their protected characteristics, where this is proportionate. In order to address inequalities, health care professionals may need to adopt strategies that are sensitive to the differences between, and disadvantages attaching to, those with different characteristics. Sometimes positive action may be required. As argued in Chapter 3, this may involve a broader perspective than is currently taken in relation to exceptionality or to 'different' treatment for individuals or groups, where disadvantage relating to personal characteristics is generally not taken into account. The equality law framework should certainly not act as a deterrent for positive measures. However, there remains considerable uncertainty about scope of both permitted and mandatory positive action, largely as a result of limited and sometimes inconsistent case law and the

[1] *R. v Cambridge Health Authority, ex parte B* [1995] 1 FLR 1055 (QBD) at paras 1064–5.

general reluctance of the judiciary to engage in intense scrutiny of the justification for these decisions. There also remain important questions as to the role of positive action in access to health care as a mechanism for addressing health related disadvantage and health inequalities. In particular, interesting questions arise about the scope of the disadvantage(s) to be weighed in the scales during an analysis of proportionality. Should the focus be on disadvantage caused by a particular rule? Or on existing disadvantage which is further compounded by lack of access to health care? And if the latter, need that disadvantage itself relate to disadvantage caused by prior discrimination – individual or structural – in access to health care or to the social determinants of health? There is certainly room for greater doctrinal and conceptual clarity here.

Finally, policy makers should be alert to the full range of harms that can be caused by measures that discriminate, directly or indirectly, against individuals or protected groups. Even where they are not intended to, for example, such measures can serve to communicate that some lives or some groups are less valued than others. Where this harm cannot be eliminated by better transparency and communication, it should at least be weighed in the balance. Fredman's four-dimensional framework for understanding substantive equality – outlined in the Introduction – may prove a useful tool here. This framework, it will be remembered, stresses the need to redress disadvantage; to address stigma, stereotyping, prejudice and violence; to enhance voice and participation; and to accommodate difference and achieve structural change. All four of these dimensions should feature in consideration of the way health care should be commissioned.

As a last point, it is also worth remembering that equality law may have something to learn from the difficulties posed by health care commissioning. Exploring the interaction between equality law and health care commissioning can direct our focus onto the ways in which the law currently succeeds or fails to offer an adequate framework for addressing some of the most pressing inequalities there are. In particular, and as we saw in Chapter 1, health, and health care, is a context where an intersectional understanding of inequality, and an understanding of the relationships between socio-economic disadvantage, discrimination on status grounds and the social determinants of poor health, are vital. If equality law is to serve to make real progress on health inequalities, and its potential is to be fully realized, it needs to evolve to find a way to ensure that these dimensions of inequality are addressed. Implementation of the socio-economic duty and the combined discrimination provision of the Equality Act may serve as first steps. But further research is also needed on the way in which the PSED is managed in a health care context and the challenges an expansion in the ways described would pose. How might data be produced and managed? And how might the duty serve to promote a more equality sensitive approach to the commissioning, funding and ethical approval of health care research? If steps are to be taken to address inequalities discovered as a result of the exercise of the PSED or otherwise, how might institutions be given more confidence in the boundaries of permitted positive action (and clarity on when it may be required?). In addition, further research would be useful to understand, given the limited case law to date, why equality law appears to be relatively underutilized in this context and whether that is something that should concern us.

COVID-19 proved a test for equality law in many of the contexts in which it operates, including health. As is evident from the brief overview of some of the examples in this book, it did not always live up to its role in preventing discrimination or in ensuring that the needs and disadvantages of different groups were taken into account. The unequal impact of COVID-19 reflects underlying structural inequalities which themselves persist in spite of the equality law framework. This reinforces the need both for robust enforcement of equality law in 'ordinary times' and for considering how the law may be made more resilient so as to ensure that, as far as possible, even in a future emergency, disadvantage to protected groups is not further compounded by a lack of care and attention.

Index